Making Musical Instruments

Making Musical Instruments
STRINGS AND KEYBOARD

Edited by
CHARLES FORD
with a Foreword by
ANTHONY BAINES

Pantheon Books
New York

All rights reserved under International and Pan-American
Copyright Conventions. Published in the United States by
Pantheon Books, a division of Random House, Inc., New York.
Originally published in Great Britain by
Faber & Faber, Ltd., London.

Library of Congress Cataloging in Publication Data
    Main entry under title:

Making musical instruments.

    Bibliography: p. 179.
    Includes index.
    1. Musical instruments—Construction. I. Ford,
Charles
ML460.M33   781.9′1   77-88774
ISBN 0-394-49210-2
ISBN 0-394-73561-7 pbk.

Manufactured in the United States of America

First American Edition

Contents

Foreword by Anthony Baines p. 11
Editor's Preface by Charles Ford p. 13

1 *The Viol*
DIETRICH KESSLER
p. 15

2 *The Lute*
IAN HARWOOD
p. 37

3 *The Violin*
including the Baroque Violin
ADAM PAUL
p. 69

4 *The Classical Guitar*
JOSÉ ROMANILLOS
p. 101

5 *The Harpsichord*
MICHAEL JOHNSON
p. 131

6 *Restoration and Conservation of Historical Musical Instruments*
FRIEDEMANN HELLWIG
p. 155

About the Contributors p. 177
Bibliographies p. 179
Index p. 189

Illustrations

Plates

BETWEEN PAGES 176 AND 177

I Baroque seven-string bass viol by Dietrich Kessler after Richard Meares

II Inside view of the large octave bass lute by Michielle Harton, Padua 1602

III Eight-course lute by Charles Ford after Harton

IV Viola by Adam Paul

V Cross-sections of a modern and a Baroque violin, illustrating the differing construction details

VI Guitar by José Romanillos based on a design by Hermann Hauser sen.

VII Front and reverse sides of the head

VIII Harpsichord by Michael Johnson after Taskin

IX The harpsichord and its keyboard before assembly

X Plan view of a harpsichord by Giovanni Battista Giusti, Lucca 1681

XI A radiograph of the instrument showing details of the interior

XII Technical drawing of the harpsichord by G. B. Giusti. Details taken from radiographs, the instrument was not opened

XIII Two details of a harpsichord soundboard, one showing where bars from a recent restoration have been removed and the other where the glue marks left by the original barring have been made visible by the fluorescence from ultra-violet radiation

Line drawings

1 *The Viol*

1 A simple gas-heated bending iron	16	6 Soundpost-setter	17
2 Purfling tool and cutter assembly	16	7 Mould for a viol, with cramping blocks and cramping jig	20
3 Wooden cramp used for assembling belly and back to ribs	17	8 Plan and cross-section of a viol	21
4 Thicknessing callipers	17	9 Belly thicknessing, two different methods	28
5 Peghole reamer and peg cutter	17		

2 *The Lute*

1 Geometrical construction for a lute outline	39	2 True shape of the rib and its derivation	40

Illustrations

3 Construction of the solid former   42
4 Construction of the mould   42
5 Neck–body joint   43
6 Capping strip or end-clasp   47
7 Pegbox design for a seven-course lute   49
8 Pegbox-to-neck joints: simple butt joint, and rebate joint   50
9 Marking out the soundboard   52
10 Rose pattern, a basic geometric design   53
11 Soundboard-to-rib assembly   55
12 Fingerboard and soundboard overlap   57
13 A typical bridge design, c. 1600   58
14 Tying double and single frets for lutes and viols   65

3 The Violin

1 The violin design   70
2 Cross-section detail   72
3 Form or mould and cramping jig   74
4 Thicknessing the back and belly   80
5 Back and belly outlines   82
6 Bass-bar design and placement   84
7 Cross-section of neck-to-body assembly; plan of the back button; and the neck-body mortise plan   90
8 (a) Modern violin cross-sections and details   94
(b) Baroque violin cross-sections and details   95

4 The Classical Guitar

1 Soundboard and barring layout   104
2 Cramping jig for fan struts and transverse bars   106
3 Plan and cross-section of neck, heel, and foot   108
4 Back and bar positions   110
5 Neck and soundboard-to-baseboard holding device   113
6 Neck–head splice-joint   116
7 Plan and cross-section of the head   118
8 Cross-section of the assembled body   122
9 Cross-section of bridge and saddle   123
10 Plan and side elevation of the bridge   124
11 Cramping device for gluing and holding the rosette   128

5 The Harpsichord

1 Laminated bentside former, constructed from three or more boards   134
2 Keyboard- and action-design for a French double-manual harpsichord   136
3 A simple circle cutter   142
4 Eye-twisting tool   145
5 Cross-section of arcade cutter bit   147
6 Plan, cross-section and end elevation of a key lever   148
7 Tool for punching plectra holes   149
8 Four-foot and eight-foot jacks   151

6 Restoration & Conservation

1 Cross-section of a tree showing how cut lumber is likely to be affected by shrinkage according to its position within the tree's annual growth rings   157
2 Typical cross-section of a woodwind instrument showing how the tube may be cracked as a result of moisture from playing   158

Foreword

ANTHONY BAINES

I feel it an immense honour to be given the opportunity of introducing this most necessary book. There will probably always be some room among people who take an interest in instruments for those, like myself, who are purely executants and historians. But times have changed, and we all now recognize the supreme importance of those others who are, in addition to these two things, instrument makers also. To one who has witnessed it over recent years, this widening of attitudes appears as an astonishing revolution. One looks back across the long years through which, in the field of revival of ancient instruments, the Dolmetsch family operated in this country virtually as lone wolves. For us, they began it all. Then, after the last war, new artist-craftsmen appeared on the scene, led by two distinguished contributors to the present volume, Dietrich Kessler and, later, Ian Harwood. Yet it still took a few more years for the great 'psychological barrier' to be generally removed: namely that the skills of actually making a successful instrument do not, after all, necessarily have to be handed down from father to son, from foreman to apprentice, as trained artisans after the ways of the last century – men who were somewhat patronized in a jovial manner by the better-paid musicians, celebrated or rank-and-file, who appeared before the public.

True, there were always men like Heron-Allen – how many hundreds of amateur fiddle-makers must have profited from his book[1] – but they were exceptions to what was generally expected. Today, and one records the fact with genuine excitement, people who feel the urge come upon them, often young people with no more previous training than perhaps a little woodwork at school, simply plunge in, quickly to produce some passable work and confident of eventually producing very good work and announcing a waiting list. How few would have contemplated – one could say, dared – even to embark on the first stage fifty years ago?

Best it is, of course, when the novice maker, perhaps one who wishes to go beyond 'kits', has the advantage of guidance by a craftsman already experienced, successful and enterprising (meaning in particular by the last, having a thoughtful interest in history). Failing this guidance, published manuals are needed, and within these covers there are a whole series of them, each by an acknowledged expert in his field – whereby the chapters will prove no less valuable to makers who have already had some experience. No one need doubt the worth of following instructions in print. In our workshop here a young friend who had barely touched a lathe before has just completed a beautiful set of small-pipes in boxwood, working wholly from Cocks and Bryan.[2] All who open this book will no doubt immediately think of similar examples of personal enterprise, probably led by himself or herself, but has it *always* been possible to back the enterprise with a comparable set of expert instructions? I know that this cannot have been so. So now please find your chapter and read on.

A.B.   *Oxford, 1978*

---

1. E. Heron-Allen, *Violin-making as it was and is*, London, 1884, etc.
2. W. A. Cocks & J. F. Bryan, *The Northumberland Bagpipes*, Newcastle upon Tyne, 1967.

Editor's Preface

CHARLES FORD

Making musical instruments is a most satisfying art and, as a reaction to our mechanical age perhaps, many people are eager to learn once more the old skills which gave handmade instruments their special value. This book is intended to guide and encourage those who want to make their own instruments; professional as well as non-professional makers will find much useful information here, for when experts talk or write on their subject even the learned may learn something new. The final chapter in this book, on the conservation of musical instruments, should also be of great interest to makers and restorers alike, for the value of existing historical instruments and their careful preservation and restoration is now fully appreciated. Our attitude towards the making of new instruments or reproductions of historic instruments, and the methods of construction, must be flexible, for an instrument's personality is surely determined largely by the maker's own style and methods of construction. The contributors to this symposium describe how they themselves make musical instruments, and for this they have assumed that the reader already has a basic knowledge of woodworking and of the use and handling of tools, which is a subject in itself. Those who are encouraged to make one of the instruments described here will benefit enormously from the experience and, by closely following the experts' advice, will learn a great deal; and producing the first instrument usually results in a life-long involvement!

The instruments featured in our book, viol, lute, violin, guitar, and harpsichord, have been chosen because they seem to represent the most popular string and keyboard instruments. Neither wind nor percussion instruments have been included as it was felt that the very different construction principles and techniques, and the vastness of those subjects, would fill another book. String and keyboard instruments can be made with surprisingly few tools and, with ingenuity, one can do without many of the 'special' tools used by professional makers. Well-seasoned timbers, so essential to the instrument maker, such as spruce, ebony, rose-wood, and so on, are becoming increasingly difficult to find; however, there are various sources and some of these can be found advertised in the pages of magazines concerned with music and musical instruments. Many museums now have available scale drawings of the instruments in their collections and these, and the study of the instruments themselves, provide unique information for those who are concerned with making historically accurate instruments.

It remains for me to thank my colleagues who have contributed these chapters and who have co-operated over the long period of this book's preparation. For generous help given throughout this period, my sincere thanks to Dr Anthony Baines, Miss Phyllis Benjamin, Professor Robert Donington, Mr David Godden, Mr Friedemann Hellwig, Miss Judith Osborne, Mrs Diana Poulton, Mr José Romanillos, Mr Howard Schott, Mr John Thomson, Mrs Keith Witt, and Dr Berthold Wolpe. For the design of the book, my thanks to Shirley and Michael Tucker.
C.F.   *London, 1978*

Making Musical Instruments

I

The Viol

DIETRICH KESSLER

1. *Introduction*

It is very nearly thirty years since I started making my first viol; it was a vastly different looking – and sounding – instrument from the ones being made now, some hundred-and-sixty viols later. With every one of these I have tried to achieve as good a result as possible, both tonally and from a workmanship point of view, but because one's own taste and ideals change, the latest viols are bound to be different from the earlier ones. This process of experimenting and – hopefully – improving is something that is bound to go on. The most that can be claimed for this chapter, therefore, is that it is a faithful record of how I feel viols should be made at the moment.

I have never been of the opinion that, simply because an instrument is old, it is bound to be good; there were good and bad makers, then as now. Over the years I have adopted more and more of the ideas of seventeenth-century English makers, but this approach had to be selective, as I have never been interested in making copies for museums, only real instruments for musicians. In selecting certain features as worth copying and rejecting others, I have tried to learn from both their successes and their failures. Future generations of players will have to decide if I have made the right decisions.

This chapter describes how the bass viol illustrated here was made. I have assumed that any reader who intends to make a viol has had some previous experience, if not in instrument-making, then at least in fine woodwork. For those who would like more detailed guidance of a practical nature, the book by E. Heron-Allen, *Violin-making as it was and is* (London, 1885), should provide most of the answers. For more information on design and proportions of viols, their sizes and tunings and a lot of other background material, Nicholas Bessaraboff's book, *Ancient European Musical Instruments* (Boston, 1941), cannot be too highly recommended. Many of the processes described in this chapter sound complicated and difficult, but I hope no potential maker is put off by this; I, for one, find making a viol much easier than writing about it.

2. *Tools and Materials*

There are only a few special tools required for making a viol over and above the ones a cabinet-maker uses. I am only going to list the most important of these; anybody seriously interested in making viols will soon find out which others can be helpful and save time.

One of the most obvious is a bending iron, which is basically a piece of metal tubing, approximately 4 cm in diameter and some 15 cm long which is heated through the centre by a gas flame, and which can be made easily. More elaborate ones are available – usually from Germany – in which the heating is done by electricity and the temperature is controlled by thermostats.

A set of three or four small violin-maker's planes is important. It is very difficult to make an arching, or to thickness a belly without them, and once one has got used to handling them, any number of other jobs can be done with them more quickly than by conventional methods.

Purfling tools exist in various designs, although the idea behind them is always the same. The gaps between the two cutters and between the cutters and the guide must be fully adjustable. The type illustrated is superior to other types if one wants to inlay purfling ornaments: the cutter assembly can be removed from the rest and used without the handle and guide.

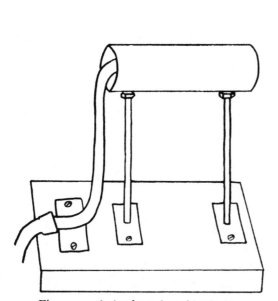

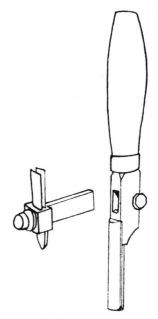

Fig. 1.1   *A simple gas-heated bending iron*   Fig. 1.2   *Purfling tool and cutter assembly*

For gluing backs and bellies most instrument-makers use cramps similar to the one illustrated. This (Fig. 3) is made entirely from wood but sometimes spindle and thread are of metal, and, depending on the size of the discs and of the viol, between thirty and forty cramps are needed to go round a bass viol. To apply the pressure evenly they are best placed close together without any gaps in between.

About the most important tool for a maker is his knife. It is usual to buy the blade and make the wooden handle to fit your hand. The three most useful blade widths are 6, 15 and 20 mm. The latter two are for all purposes, whereas the narrow blade is for cutting soundholes and bridges.

Apart from a big cabinet-maker's scraper (approximately 15 × 7 cm) it is a good idea to have one or two smaller ones made from spring steel 0.4 to 0.5 mm thick. These should be so shaped that concave surfaces can be scraped, such as the inside of a belly for example. These thin scrapers should be ground from one side at 45° all round, and honed until perfectly sharp, when with the help of a scraper steel the edge should be pushed over towards the flat side to form the burr.

16

For accurate thicknessing of bellies and a host of other jobs, it is essential to have good callipers, preferably with a clock-dial. Some of these dials are calibrated in units of 1/20 mm, which is rather unnecessary; most makers would be quite happy if all their work was accurate to 1/10 mm.

When fitting up the finished viol, we need a peghole reamer and a peg cutter which match as far as the angle of the taper is concerned. The peg cutter is similar to a large pencil sharpener and will give the pegs a taper identical to the reamer. For setting the soundpost a cello soundpost-setter should be acquired.

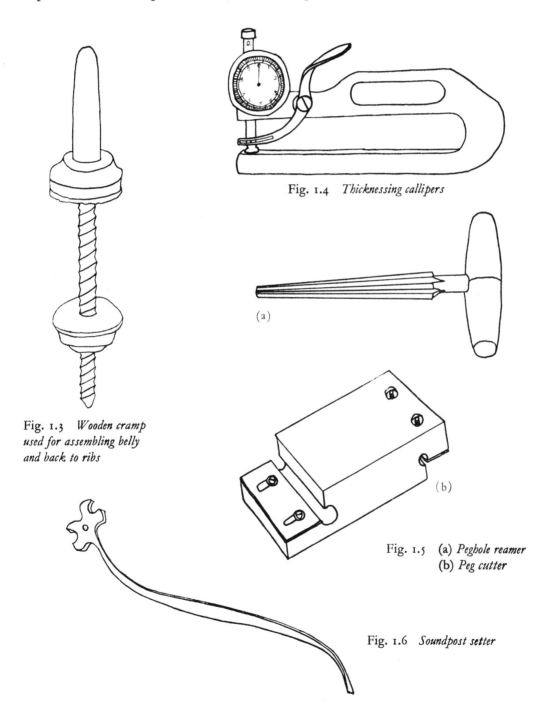

Fig. 1.4   *Thicknessing callipers*

(a)

Fig. 1.3   *Wooden cramp used for assembling belly and back to ribs*

(b)

Fig. 1.5   (a) *Peghole reamer*
(b) *Peg cutter*

Fig. 1.6   *Soundpost setter*

Most of the materials are the same as are used in violin-making:

Sycamore (known in America as a type of maple) is the most widely used hardwood for back, ribs, head, neck, and bridge of a viol. The figured variety is especially attractive, but is tonally no better than plain sycamore. All sorts of other timbers have been used by early viol-makers for these parts, such as pear, plum, cherry, or even walnut. Sometimes two woods of contrasting colour, arranged in stripes are used on backs and ribs. Most sycamore for instrument-making is imported from Germany, France, and Switzerland, although some British and American timber is perfectly suitable. It costs only a fraction of the price charged by tonewood dealers if bought directly from a sawmill.

Spruce is the best wood for the belly, the bars on the back, bass-bar, and soundpost. It is also used frequently for blocks and linings. Unlike sycamore, good-quality spruce has to be imported from Europe as the best trees grow fairly high in the mountain regions, where the growing season is short and the winters are severe. Various types of pines and firs have also been used, especially in England, for these purposes, but the results have seldom been very satisfactory in comparison with spruce.

Willow, Poplar and Lime are useful for blocks and linings, the last perhaps least so because of its greater specific weight. All three can be worked easily, bend and glue well and show little tendency to split.

Ebony, because of its extreme hardness, is very good for pegs, nuts, and tailpins. It has also been used to veneer the top of fingerboards and tailpieces, either by itself or in conjunction with other woods in elaborate marquetry work.

Rosewood. The Brazilian variety, Rio, is the hardest and most expensive of these; it is really excellent for pegs. Bombay or Indian rosewood is too soft for this purpose, but perfectly all right for fingerboards and tailpieces.

Boxwood. Another hardwood which was extensively used for making pegs for all sorts of stringed instruments. One of its problems is that it is difficult to stain, except with nitric acid.

Purfling. The best purfling is no doubt made from two fillets of ebony with a strip of sycamore in the centre. When they are glued together they become very rigid and cannot be bent round narrow curves. If used by a beginner round the edge of an instrument this can be a great advantage: the chances are that the finished work will still look respectable, even if the trench was badly cut, as the purfling cannot follow all its deviations. It is very difficult however to use this purfling for ornaments with curves; it would have to be used in three single strips unless one made a mould for every curve of the ornament and glued them together in those shapes. For this reason the use of fibre purfling can be recommended. This demands much greater skill in cutting the trench but facilitates the inlaying, which will be described later on.

Glue. Last, but not least, a few words should be said on this subject. In spite of the many products of modern research in this field, I would still recommend an old-fashioned skin glue as has been used for hundreds of years in instrument-making. What appears to be its main drawback, namely that it can be dissolved in hot water, is, in my opinion, its advantage: anybody who has had to remove a belly or a fingerboard which had been glued with an epoxy resin glue will, I believe, agree with me. Another of its good characteristics is that it gives the maker or repairer time to align the pieces to be glued before it starts to set. Imagine trying to glue a crack perfectly flush with an impact adhesive! Furthermore, with a hot-water glue, when used correctly, the layer of glue between two well-fitting pieces of wood is so thin that it cannot be detected by eye.

Skin glue can be purchased in either pearls or small chips, but it is important to get it as light a colour as possible. It should be soaked in cold water (at least twice as much water as glue) for a few hours, in which time the glue will have swelled up considerably. The container with the soaked glue should then be placed in boiling water, until it has all melted, when it can be thinned further if necessary with hot water. For best results the glue should always be used hot and freely running, never the consistency of treacle.

3. *The Mould*

Making the ribs for a viol presents something of a problem. For a violin or a cello these can easily be built up either on a board or on the back itself, as the surface levels are on the same plane and the ribs meet the back in all places at right angles; therefore, the need to spend a lot of time and energy on making a mould can in these cases be avoided. Not so with a viol: not only does the back (at the top of the body) slope towards the belly, thus reducing the height of the ribs, but the latter also flare out from the back towards the belly, making the belly somewhat larger than the back. Because of all this the top block of a viol has a complex shape which it is very difficult to achieve accurately without the help of a mould. My advice to anyone wanting to make a viol is to make a mould first, although it is a tedious and time-consuming job; the final result will be so much better and fully justify the extra effort.

Before the mould can be started, however, a model for the bass viol has to be chosen. Keep looking at and comparing as many good instruments as possible, both old and new, and bear in mind also who is going to play what on your viol, before deciding which size to make. If the bass is going to be used mainly for consort playing one would probably choose a slightly larger model with only six strings, but for playing divisions (and for small people) a division viol, which is considerably smaller than our illustrated instrument, would be best.[1] The viol illustrated here is based on an instrument by Richard Meares of London, which dates from the end of the seventeenth century, and which has been fitted with seven strings (something which I believe no earlier English maker ever did). It was intended primarily for solo work including the playing of French music by Marais and Couperin among others, but because of the fairly small hand of the player the size of the instrument had to be kept down.

Once the model has been chosen, templates have to be made for one half of the outline of the mould, as well as for one soundhole, head, and neck. I consider 1 mm plywood the best material for this purpose as it is easily worked, can be bent and does not warp or shrink. For the mould itself, blockboard is very convenient: it is much lighter and cheaper than plywood and yet nearly as stable.

Make up a block as thick as the total height of the ribs, but in two halves (see Fig. 7) which are held together by screws. The mould and cramping blocks should now be drawn

1. The construction methods used in making a viol of the Renaissance period are very similar to those described here. Readers who wish to build a Renaissance viol, using this chapter as a guide, are referred to Ian Harwood's pioneering article, 'An Introduction to Renaissance Viols', *Early Music*, Vol. 2, No. 4, October 1974. [Ed.]

on, and the whole sawn out carefully (with bandsaw or bowsaw), after which the two halves of each cramping block are glued together. Into the cut-outs (marked by shaded areas in Fig. 7) fit the top, bottom, and corner blocks in such a manner, that the grain of these runs from front to back of the instrument and away from the mould.[1] The slanting plane at the top of the back is made next and on it we draw the outline which the back is to take, up to the beginning of the neck. Both ribs will slope progressively from the start of this plane, finishing closer together than they do on the belly-side of the top block.

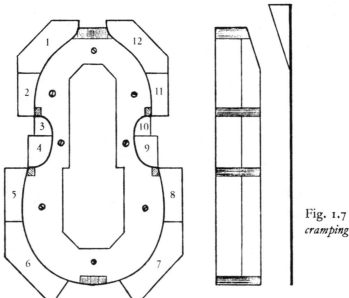

Fig. 1.7   *Mould for a viol with cramping blocks and cramping jig*

The lower and centre bouts, as well as the lower part of the upper bouts including the bottom and corner blocks, are now rasped and filed perfectly square to the front surface of the mould. The top block with its adjoining areas is also shaped in accordance with the markings on the front and back of the mould. The sides of the mould must be perfectly straight between back and front in every place when checked with a ruler. All the cramping blocks should now be filed and checked for fit against the mould; blocks 1 and 12, in particular, will need considerable reshaping to make them fit tightly against top block and mould. Finally, a cramping jig has to be made, which will facilitate the gluing on of belly and back. Draw the outline of the belly on a piece of hardboard or 4-mm plywood, allow an extra 5 mm all round and 5 cm at the neck end, and saw it out. A wooden wedge has to be constructed which fits perfectly against the sloping plane of the back when the mould is placed on this jig. Glue this wedge to the hardboard and all the preparations are now completed.

4. *The Ribs*

If the wood for the viol has been bought from a tonewood dealer, the ribs are usually in three strips which have the same length as the back. The most convenient way to arrange them is to use one strip on each side for the bottom and centre ribs, and the

1. A similar method may be usefully referred to in Chapter 3, p. 76. [Ed.]

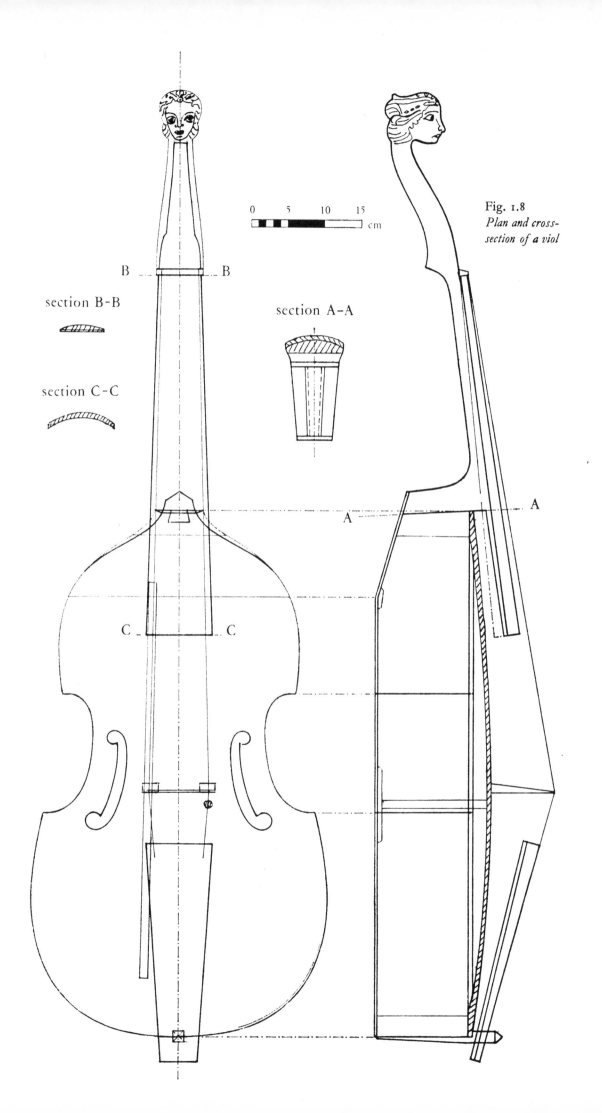

section B-B

section C-C

section A-A

0 5 10 15
cm

Fig. 1.8
Plan and cross-section of a viol

third for the two top ribs. Mark them so that the curl slants the same way on each rib, and the more heavily figured edge of the rib will be next to the back. The outside of the ribs should now be made perfectly smooth with a small plane (if necessary), cabinet scraper, and coarse (No. 100) sandpaper on a block, after which the rib sections are turned over and planed from the inside to the correct thickness of 1.6 mm. Cut them to length, but allow 2–3 cm extra for safety and convenience. The linings ought to be prepared next, so that they can be bent at the same time as the ribs. Tonally it makes little difference how wide they are, but in order to save weight, they should not exceed 15 mm in width and 2.8 mm in thickness.

For best results in bending, the iron should be as hot as possible, but not hot enough to burn the wood. If a drop of water is dropped on to the iron, it should sizzle off immediately. To protect the rib against scorching, a piece of brown paper can be placed between it and the bending iron, which will show if there is too much heat, before the rib itself is damaged. The ribs for the centre bouts have to be bent first: thoroughly wet one of them with water on both sides and place it on the hot iron applying a moderate amount of pressure. As the water on the rib is turned into steam, which enters the wood, the latter will soften and start to bend. Check frequently against the mould to see that the correct curves are achieved, and finish the bending by drying the rib thoroughly on the hot iron. If the rib is not absolutely dry, it will start to straighten out again. Test the fit by placing the rib on the mould and cramping it in place with the two cramping blocks and cramps. (It may be necessary to place one or two offcuts from the ribs as packing between the two cramping blocks to force the rib hard against the corner blocks.) If this test is satisfactory, glue the corner blocks to the ribs. First apply dry soap or candle wax liberally to the side of the mould, especially near the blocks; this will prevent any surplus glue which has been squeezed out of the joint from gluing the ribs to the mould permanently. Then brush the glue carefully on the corner blocks, place the rib, and cramp it as before, making sure that it overlaps the mould all round.

When both centre ribs have been glued and are dry, plane them level with the top and bottom of the mould, and cut their length so that they overlap the corner blocks by the amount of their own thickness, i.e. 1.6 mm. This overlap is now bevelled with a sharp chisel to form part of the mitre joint of the ribs at the corners. Top and bottom ribs can now be bent and fitted against the centre rib by bevelling them correctly; check with cramping blocks, and glue to corners and blocks. When all the ribs are on the mould and planed flush with the mould's surface plane, they should be worked over once more, starting, if necessary with a file, and finishing with fine (No. 240) sandpaper on a block, to smooth out all uneven and rough places.

At this stage it is best to join the back and plane it to its correct thickness, as described on p. 23. The mould with the ribs can then be placed on to the back. Line up the centre of the mould with the centre joint and trace the outline on the back, tilting the mould in order to do so from the start of the slope to the top of the top block. Now remove the screws from the mould and carefully lever the lower part from the rest. The linings should be cut to length so that they fit tightly between the blocks and the curve of each bout. Apply glue and cramp them with clothes pegs and carefully wipe away all surplus glue. Because of the slope the linings of the top bouts have to be made from two pieces joined at an angle so that they follow the ribs exactly. They should now be bevelled with a knife and finished with sandpaper. The blocks and corners should at this stage also be given their final shape as far down as possible before touching the upper half of the mould. Finally, the linings are planed flush with the ribs and the blocks and corners are sized with glue to ensure better adhesion when the back is finally fitted.

5. *The Back*

It is unusual to find a piece of sycamore or maple wide enough for a back in one piece; in most cases two pieces are joined together but some makers used three or even more for each back.

For a two-piece back it is necessary to have a piece of wood a little wider and approximately 10 cm longer than our template, and about 12 mm thick throughout, so that when sawn down the middle we have two halves, which at this stage should be no less than 4 mm in thickness. On a quarter-cut plank of sycamore the grain is always closest and the figure most pronounced near the outside of the tree. For this reason we arrange the two halves of the back so that this outside forms the centre joint which, of course, has to run as near parallel with the grain as possible. As the figure or curl is seldom exactly at right angles, we have the choice of using it sloping up or down on each side of the joint.

For joining, the quickest way is to plane both edges at the same time with a long, sharp, shooting plane. For joining the belly, we cramp the two pieces in the vice; the back, however, because it is much thinner, is best dealt with flat on the bench. Place the two halves on top of each other on a board 1–2 cm thick; hold them down firmly with the left hand, while moving the plane, which has been turned on its side, with the right hand. When the planed surface is quite straight, check the joint by placing the halves side by side, as though opening a book, and applying slight pressure. If they do not meet perfectly along the entire length, the planing has to be continued until they do. The gluing is most conveniently done on a board of nearly the same width as the whole back. Warm both halves of the back slightly and apply glue. Place them flat on the board (with paper underneath to prevent sticking) and rub them together vigorously to expel surplus glue. Cramp with three crack clamps which have been straightened out, and at the same time batten down the back to the flat board to stop it from curling up under the pressure of the cramps. When thoroughly dry, the back can be finished on the outside and finally thicknessed from inside to approximately 3.3 mm all over, again with plane, scraper and sandpaper. Draw the outline of the mould on it, not forgetting to allow 4–5 cm for the button at the top, and finally saw out the back.

If it is decided to have a purfling ornament in the centre of the back, this is the time to do it: trace one line of the chosen ornament on to the back with carbon paper and then cut along it, about 1.5 mm deep with a sharp knife. Having done this round the whole of the ornament, the second line should first be marked and then cut, absolutely parallel with the first one at the correct distance, which is of course the same as the width as the purfling used. (If a purfling tool of the type shown in Fig. 4 is available, use its cutter assembly for marking the second line: set one cutter a little further out than the other, and by running it in the first cut, the second cut will be marked.) With a very narrow chisel, the wood between the two cuts can now be chipped out to form the trench for the purfling, but take care not to chip away any corners. If that should happen, keep the tiny piece of wood safely until the purfling is being glued in, and glue it back then. This will show up far less on the finished instrument than if you used some filler to fill the hole. If the ornament is a geometrical design of straight lines, there will be no difficulty in fitting the pieces of purfling into the trenches, making mitre joints at the corners, and alternately stopping and carrying through at the other crossing-points to achieve a weaving effect. When all the pieces have been fitted into the grooves, glue them by taking out one at a time, filling the trench with glue and tapping the piece back in again with a small hammer. This operation has to be done as quickly as possible as the hot glue causes the wood to swell up with the effect that the groove becomes too narrow to accept the purfling, if too much time is taken.

If, however, the ornament is one with curves, the purfling has to be eased carefully into the groove so that none of the three strands break. With tight curves each piece has to be bent over a hot metal rod until it fits the groove. (Dipping the metal rod into boiling water makes it hot enough for this purpose and eliminates the danger of badly burnt fingers.) If some of the curves are so tight that even with bending the purfling one cannot get it round without breaking, it has to be cut with a razor blade through the middle of the white centre strip along its length. The two pieces can then be bent much more easily to the correct shape. In this manner it should be possible to cope with all types of purfling ornaments. One word of warning: having just glued the ornament, all surplus glue should of course be washed away, but use as little hot water as possible to minimize the risk of ungluing the centre joint. If the back should start to bulge, cramp it flat with a block of wood on to a board, but with a thick wad of absorbent paper (newspaper) between ornament and block. Leave to dry for at least twenty-four hours, then cut the purfling down to the level of the back with a gouge, and finish off with sandpaper on a block.

To bend the top of the back to the required angle, start by making a saw-cut with a fine tenon saw along the line of the break, going at least two-thirds of the way through the back from the inside. This cut must then be made even deeper with a knife, but keep checking, by holding the back against a strong light, that you are not cutting right through in any place. The saw-cut is then opened up with a chisel to make it into a v-shape. Run a little hot water into this cut with a table knife, and warm up the outside of the back against an electric fire. By holding the back at the top and bottom, and applying firm pressure, you should be able to bend it slowly along the saw-cut without breaking it. Place it on the cramping jig with the wedge, cramp it in place and let the back dry thoroughly.

The transverse bars for the back should now be prepared. In English viols of the sixteenth and seventeenth centuries we find in most cases only one bar, often up to 10 cm wide, in the area where the soundpost stands. The break or back-angle just described is usually covered on the inside with a strip of linen or parchment.[1] Apart from narrow strips of cross-grained wood glued over the joints, there are usually no other reinforcements in the back at all. In old continental viols the soundpost bar is in many cases much narrower, but often there are between two and four additional bars to help the back keep its shape. These bars are the same as those used in guitar and lute construction.

I usually fit two bars in my viol backs, one in the soundpost area, and the other one, much narrower, right over the break, to give it extra strength. Draw the position of both

1. This reinforcement tape may be applied by the same method as that described in Chapter 2, p. 46. [Ed.]

bars on the back, and arrange the soundpost bar so that the soundpost will stand in the centre of it. Good-quality quarter-sawn spruce should be used for this purpose. As all viol backs have a tendency to become concave, I try to counter this by planing the bars slightly convex, in effect pushing the centre of the back out with the bars. In addition to this rounding, the break bar obviously has to be planed to the correct angle as well; both bars can now be cut to their proper length. When eventually the back is glued to the ribs, the ends of the bars should follow parallel with the linings and corner blocks, but there should be a gap of roughly 1.5 mm between them.

At this point we should consider the fact that wood is hygroscopic; that is, it constantly absorbs and gives off moisture, depending on whether its surroundings are damper or dryer. The damper the wood becomes the more it swells up, and when it dries out it shrinks again. Over the width of a bass viol back this swelling and shrinking can amount to more than 3 mm, even in well-seasoned timber. It needs very little imagination to see that one is courting disaster if one makes a viol in a dampish workshop, and then keeps the finished instrument in a dry, centrally-heated music room: if one is lucky, the back and belly will merely come unglued from the ribs and will not fit any more as the ribs will appear to be too large. If one is unlucky, however, the centre joints will open up or worse still cracks will appear in both back and belly. The obvious way to avoid this problem is to shrink back and belly before gluing them to the ribs by more than they are likely to shrink in ordinary conditions. If the finished viol is then kept in a damp place, the back and belly will be pushing against the ribs as they swell up, and become rounder (unless they come unglued from the ribs), but at least, there is no danger that cracks could develop. Even if the instrument is kept in a very dry place, it is unlikely that the plates will shrink to a smaller size than they were immediately before being glued to the ribs. In practice, before we glue the bars, we have to warm both sides of the back in front of an electric fire (in U.S.A. a space heater), taking the greatest care to do this evenly and slowly so that no extra stresses are set up which might cause the centre joint to open up. While the back is still warm, the bars should be glued on quickly. This drying out will have to be repeated just before the back is glued to the ribs, and for the front, when it in turn is ready to be glued to the rest of the body.

When we are actually gluing the bars to the back, we must be sure that the back is bent to the rounded bar, and not the other way round. This is best achieved by placing a thick and solid block of wood on top of the bar which, with the back, is then placed on our cramping jig. Not only will this block distribute the pressure of the cramps evenly, but, as it is totally inflexible, the back and the cramping jig have to bend to meet the convex bar. After thorough drying, both bars are planed flat to their final thickness, which will be slightly greater in the centre of the instrument than near the ribs, due to their roundness. As the pressure of the strings which is transmitted through the soundpost, will be pushing against the soundpost bar, we must leave the latter sufficiently resilient to counteract this force; on the other hand, if left too solid, the sound and response of the viol will be impaired. It has been found that if the bar is left approximately 5.5 mm thick in the centre a happy balance is achieved. At this thickness it is just possible to bend the back and bar a little by hand. The break-bar can be planed somewhat thinner than the other one, after which both should be finished with fine sandpaper. Finally, a bevel about 15 mm wide should be cut at both ends of each bar, down to within 2 mm of the back. It is a good precaution to give some additional strength to the centre (or any other) joint by gluing a 12 mm-wide and 1.5 mm-thick strip of wood over it along its entire length. Make sure, however, that the grain of this strip, which can be of spruce, willow, or even sycamore, runs at right angles with the joint for maximum effectiveness. To finish it off, round it with a chisel and finish with sandpaper.

When the back and the ribs have been checked all over yet again (make sure, for instance, that the ends of all the bars and linings are not coming loose), we are ready to glue them together. The back should be warmed, as described earlier, and placed with the mould and the ribs on to the cramping jig. Align the ribs and back carefully so that the centre joint is exactly in line with the middle of the viol and check that the ribs and back fit together all round with very little pressure. It might be found necessary to adjust the angle of the break, which is most easily done by planing the ribs slightly, until everything corresponds. Use the wooden cramps to hold ribs and back in place on the jig.

The viol is now ready for gluing. Remove the cramps from one centre bout, including the two corner blocks; then, after dipping a table-knife in glue, ease the back and ribs apart and apply the glue to the gluing surfaces. Wipe any surplus away with a dry rag and cramp together again. Move on to the next bout, and so on, until the whole back is glued. It is worth remembering that it is very unwise to get the ribs wet at all in the course of washing away glue: they would lose some of their rigidity, and would almost certainly buckle under the pressure of the cramps. It is far better, in this instance, to wipe away the worst with a dry rag and to let the rest dry. This can later be dissolved again with hot water, if it is done reasonably quickly, without impairing the strength of the joint, but do remove the cramps first.

6. *The Belly*

As with the back, it is usual nowadays to use two pieces for the belly with a joint in the centre, although the English viol maker Barak Norman (d. 1746), for instance, almost always used three pieces. Again, as with the back, it is advisable that the two halves should have been one thick board before they were separated, so that when opened and joined (outside to outside), they form a symmetrical picture with the wide grain in the wings, getting narrower towards the centre joint. It is well worth choosing as good a piece of wood as possible for the belly as, in my opinion, this is just about the most important factor contributing to the quality of the viol's sound. The grain should be straight and of medium width, and each hard grain-line should be as fine as possible.

The actual jointing is done again with a very sharp shooting plane; the softer the wood, the sharper the tools have to be to get a really smooth cut. Plane both halves together and check them frequently until they fit perfectly with only the slightest hand-pressure. Although it is possible to glue this joint by rubbing the two halves together and leaving them to dry without cramps, I would still recommend the use of two sash cramps, if available, for more consistently good results. However, they have to be used correctly. Most bellies for bowed instruments are wedge-shaped, and if the flat side is placed on the bars of the cramps, it is almost certain that the top of the joint will open up, due to uneven pressure. If on the other hand the belly is reversed so that only the point of it touches the cramps, and the flat side is away from them, a good joint should be achieved – always provided, of course, that the joint was true in the first place!

It goes without saying that all the cramping should be tried and rehearsed before glue is applied, so that all difficulties can be ironed out. This applies not only to the gluing of this centre joint, but to all gluing operations. Once the glue is applied one has to move very quickly, otherwise it will start to get cold and the surfaces we want to join will slide about, making accurate work impossible.

When the joint has dried thoroughly, plane the underside of the belly flat with the long plane, and finish with coarse sandpaper (No. 100) on a block, across the grain. The mould with the ribs is now placed on it, so that the outline can be drawn, and the belly sawn out. Do not saw too closely to the pencil line, but allow at least 3 mm all round as a safety margin for shrinkage.

The archings on all old English viols are quite different from the ones on instruments of the violin family. On viols there is no groove at all round the edge, in which the purfling is placed. Lengthwise, that is between top and bottom blocks, the arching is absolutely convex, which makes it tremendously strong. At right angles to the centre joint on the other hand, it is very round in the middle and dips towards each side in a quite pronounced concave curve, which makes it very flexible. It is interesting to speculate why old English makers always used this type of arching on viols, when they were perfectly aware of the existence of the violin type of arching. With Barak Norman we become particularly conscious of this, as there are a great many of his viols, as well as his violins and cellos, still in existence: I cannot remember having seen a single instrument on which he used the 'wrong' type. Perhaps the kind of sound and response expected from a viol by seventeenth-century musicians could only be attained if this sort of viol-arching was used.

The shaping of the arching is started with a gouge, about 2–3 cm wide and with a very shallow curve. The first aim is to carve away all surplus wood round the circumference, and form a uniformly thick edge of about 4.5 mm; but all the time an image of the arching wanted should be in one's mind, so that the correct shape can gradually emerge. After most of the shaping has been done with the gouge, the small arching planes are used for the finer work of smoothing out the gouge marks, and giving the curves their final shape. Be sure to plane always in the correct direction with the grain, so that the wood is cut smoothly and not torn. On the convex surfaces a plane with a flat sole and cutter is best as it leaves fewer ridges and no grooves, but it cannot of course be used where the arching dips and is concave. For this work it is important to have the correct lighting conditions: the light should be coming from one direction only, and if possible from an angle of about 45°. Top light is no use at all. If only top light is available in the workshop, leave the arching and do it at night with the help of a table lamp. In this kind of directional lighting it is possible to detect even the smallest unwanted hollows or protuberances.

To finish the arching, a scraper is the best tool, and one needs a considerable amount of skill to do the arching well; the object is to eliminate all the ridges left by the plane, and even out all lumps and hollows, but not to produce a plastic-like smoothness. If a belly which has been finished with a scraper only is examined carefully, it will be seen to have a ribbed appearance – almost like corduroy cloth – the hard grain lines forming the valleys. When eventually the varnish is applied, it will accumulate to a greater extent in these valleys, and so help to show up the grain much better, and give more character to the belly.

If you have difficulty finishing the belly with scrapers only, take a sandpaper block (approximately 5 × 12 × 3 cm) round the bottom of it to fit the dips in the arching, and sandpaper the arching crosswise with medium coarse sandpaper (No. 150) until the curves stand up to a close examination in strong directional light. Obviously all the sandpaper scratches have now to be removed again, which is done with a very sharp scraper working in the direction of the grain. As this time round no corrections have to be done to the arching it should prove much easier to give the belly this scraper finish.

Having finished the arching in this manner, the purfling ornament on the belly should now be tackled, if it is desired to have one. Remember, however, that working in spruce is much more difficult than in sycamore. To start with it splits much more readily, and fine points break off very easily; furthermore, as the dark grain lines are much harder than the rest, it is very difficult to cut a true curve without any wobbles. It might be advisable, therefore, to try out a part of the ornament on a spare piece of spruce so that the finished belly is not in jeopardy.

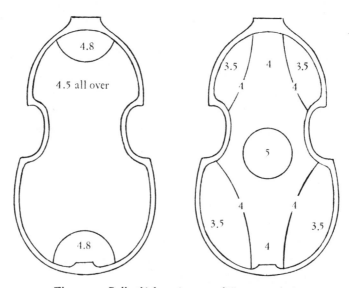

Fig. 1.9   *Belly thicknessing, two different methods*

The hollowing out and thicknessing comes next. If it is intended to make several viols of the same size and model, it will be worth while making a mould into which the belly can be laid while it is being hollowed out with a gouge. (It is of course perfectly possible to improvise some padding which will protect the arching during this process.) As much surplus wood as possible should be removed with the gouge, after which the arching planes are used to work the front to nearly the final thickness. About two-tenths of a millimetre should be allowed for scraping and sanding. It is impossible to give more than a rough guide to the actual thicknesses of the belly: this depends on many factors, including the size and stringing of the viol, the resilience of the wood, whether it is cut exactly on the quarter, and also what sort of system for thicknessing is adopted. There are nearly as many theories on this subject as there are instrument makers, but two of the most common are: (1) to work the whole belly to an even thickness, leaving it only slightly thicker round the top and bottom blocks, and (2) to have the thickest part in the centre under the bridge, getting thinner towards the edges. Either system can give good results if the actual thicknesses chosen are reasonably correct for the given circumstances.

If too much wood is left in the belly it will be stiff and inflexible, and the finished instrument will lack a quick response. On the other hand, if it is too thin, it will sink very soon on the bass-bar side under the pressure of the strings and, although initially the viol will speak readily and sound quite well, there will soon be a loss of sound, which is often accompanied by a general instability. Experience has shown that viols are less likely to have wolf notes if the area immediately below the soundholes is left fairly thick and rigid. An experienced maker will gently flex the belly with his hands, and thin it out until he gets the required flexibility. He will also tap it with his knuckles, until the tap tone is as low as he can get it without making it too flabby. From all the foregoing it can be seen that the thicknesses given in Fig. 9 are only a suggestion which will have to be reviewed by the maker each time a belly is thicknessed.

There is little to be said about the soundholes: when they have been drawn in the right place, they should be sawn out with a fretsaw, and cut with a narrow-bladed knife. The soundholes as well as the purfling really show up the competence of the maker, and should for this reason be given particular attention. It is not easy to cut them accurately and achieve a good line as well as a smooth finish with only a knife, but it is well worth trying. If necessary, some fine, half-round files can be used to finish with, but a knife-cut finish always looks better. Following old English tradition we now cut a bevel all round each soundhole on the inside to make the thickness of the front appear to be only 1.5–2 mm thick when viewed from the outside. This is of no significance tonally, but makes the instrument look lighter and more delicate.

The bass-bar is a strip of spruce, approximately 52 cm long (depending on the body length of the viol), 12 mm thick and initially about 3 cm high. The grain should be standing so that the top and the gluing face are quarter-cut. The bass-bar is positioned under the left bridge foot (under the bass strings), and runs at a slight incline to the centre joint. To mark its place, we draw the feet of the bridge on the inside of the belly, position the bar 1 mm inside the bridge foot and swivel it in relation to the centre joint by half its thickness. In practical terms: as we are working on the inside of the belly, the bass-bar will of course be on the right-hand side of the centre joint. Its length should be four-fifths of the vibrating length of the front and, assuming that we want to use a bridge which measures 10 cm from the outside of one foot to the outside of the other, the outside of the bar should be 4.9 cm from the centre joint on the bridge line. To arrive at the correct incline, add a quarter of the bar's thickness, i.e. 3 mm, to the 4.9 cm; this gives us the distance of the bar from the centre joint at its lower end. The measurement for the top end is 4.9 cm minus 3 mm. These three points connected by a straight line indicate the position of the outside edge of the bass-bar.

The fitting is done with a sharp knife, although some makers prefer to use chisel, planes, rasps or files for this job. Place the bar in its correct position on the belly, observe where it touches and trim that portion of the bar away. Repeat this procedure until it touches the belly along its entire length, but check also that it is absolutely upright. It is advisable to fit the bass-bar in such a manner that the belly is pushed slightly outwards and thus tensioned, which will help to counteract the pressure of the strings to some extent. To achieve this, both ends should be cut further so that when the bar is laid in position on the belly only the central third touches; from there the gap between bar and belly increases gradually towards both top and bottom ends, until it reaches 2 mm.

When the bass-bar fits perfectly with only slight hand pressure, it is prudent to rehearse the cramping of it before the glue is applied. Use one cramp on each end, and 4 or 5 others in between, but protect the outside of the belly from damage with a strip of cardboard. In any case, only very light pressure should be exerted with each cramp: if the fitting has been done carefully, this will be sufficient to hold bar and belly together; if not, no amount of pressure will ensure a good joint, and the most likely result will be damage to the arching. For gluing, warm both belly and bar slightly, apply glue generously to the bar only, place it in position and cramp lightly, but do not wash squeezed-out glue, as this often causes distortions in the arching. It is much better to remove as much of this excess glue as possible with a chisel or rag, and clean it thoroughly with a damp rag only after it has dried, and with only one cramp very lightly in place on each end.

The final shaping of the bass-bar is very much a matter of taste, and every maker will do it differently. We usually leave the bar around 25 mm high under the bridge and approximately 5 mm at each end. The actual curve is round in the centre under the bridge, and dips towards the ends, so that the bar gets progressively shallower – in fact it is not unlike the cross-section of the arching of the belly. Finally, the top is rounded over, and the ends are bevelled down to the belly, a bevel of about 12 mm in length.

The time for assembling the body has now come. Take out the second half of the mould, and glue in the top linings immediately. When dry, these should be bevelled as were the back linings, and the blocks and corners should be given their final shape. If there is any glue still visible anywhere on the inside, now is the time to remove it. The end-grain of the blocks and corners should be sized with glue, and the whole of the inside finished with fine (No. 240) sandpaper. Do not forget to glue in your label; it is so much easier to do it at this stage, rather than juggle it in through the soundhole later on. The procedure for gluing the belly is very much the same as for gluing the back: shrink and warm it first, align and cramp it to the ribs (with cramping jig against the back), and finally glue it section by section. Again, surplus glue should not be washed while all the cramps are still in place, for fear of buckling the ribs.

Now that the whole body is assembled, back and belly are cut and filed flush with the ribs, and the ribs are once more sanded with medium sandpaper (No. 150) on a block. Check that the curves of the outline are without blemish; minor corrections can and should be made even at this late stage. The button is also shaped now; it can be made round or with corners as in Plate 1, but whichever shape is adopted, make sure that it emerges naturally out of the curves of the top bouts.

Almost all old English viols have a double row of purfling round the edge of both back and belly. On the continent, more often than not, only one line of purfling was used, and sometimes the back was left completely plain. Although I am convinced that one line of purfling has a beneficial effect on the sound of the viol, it cannot be concluded that double purfling is twice as beneficial. I am inclined to think that the second line of purfling was used for ornamental purposes only. As on our instrument the purfling nearest to the edge is marked, let in, and glued first, a decision between single or double can be put off until this has been completed.

Adjust the blades of the cutter to the width of the purfling, and ensure that both blades protrude a similar amount. Assemble the tool and set the gap between edge and purfling and mark the double lines on the belly and back. This may be found to be rather difficult at first as firm pressure is required against the edge but very little is required downwards, and the tool has to be handled so that the marks run exactly parallel to the edge. The scratches should be very light only; they are meant as a guide for the knife and not to replace it. The rest of the procedure is the same as that described in Section 5. If fibre purfling has been chosen, make sure that the knife or gouge used for cutting it flush is very sharp. With this type of purfling there is a tendency to spread and squash the two black lines to some extent; later, when the viol is being varnished, they often stand up again, creating a very undesirable effect.

When all the purfling has been scraped down and finished (with scraper only on the belly and scraper and sandpaper block on the back), clean up the rest of the viol body with fine sandpaper (No. 240), making sure that no file or finger marks are left. Finally, the edges have to be rounded: file a bevel about 2 mm wide at 45° all round the back and belly. The two ridges which this creates are now bevelled in turn, and only after this is sandpaper used sparingly just to remove the file marks. Only in this way can an even and aesthetic rounding of the edges be achieved.

7. *The Head and Neck*

A decision has to be taken now on whether to make an open scroll or a carved head. In either case it is advisable to make an accurate template first, transfer this to a suitable piece of sycamore and saw it out. (The quarter-cut should be on the side of neck and pegbox and the slab on back and front). The pegbox is marked out on the outside next, after which the carving of the scroll or head should be done, before the pegbox is finally hollowed out.[1] For the wedge of the fingerboard take the measurements from the drawing (Fig. 8), and plane it to near the final dimensions. Again, like the neck, the wood has to be cut so that the top surface of it is slab-cut. When planing round the playing surface of the fingerboard, check that it is slightly concave along its length, approximately 2 mm overall, but in such a way that the biggest dip is in the third nearest to the nut, flattening out towards the wide end. This is to ensure that the string will not buzz against the fingerboard or frets when it is pressed down at any point. Again a choice has to be made, this time about the style of the fingerboard and tailpiece. On some old English viols, these were decorated with intricate marquetry work; others were simply veneered with ebony, and in some cases these had an ornamental ivory line round the edge. Another possibility is to inlay ornamental patterns with purfling or to leave both fingerboard and tailpiece altogether plain. It makes good sense to make the tailpiece at the same time as the fingerboard: they will match much better, and this also saves time later on.

The method of securing the neck to the body varies with different makers: some simply glue it to the top block, without any further reinforcement. In my experience, this kind of joint always sooner or later gives way, because adhesion to end-grain is never very good, and also because of the tremendous leverage: even a small knock on the head can easily dislodge the neck from the body. For these reasons I add 12 mm to the length of the neck, and use this to make a tapered dovetail, which is fitted into the top block in such a manner that the neck holds firmly, when it is correctly placed, even before it is glued. The angle to which the heel of the neck is to be sawn, can be taken from the drawing (Fig. 8), or, with the help of bevel, rulers and fingerboard wedge, from the viol

1. The method for marking out and drilling peg holes is similar to those described in Chapter 3, p. 89. [Ed.]

itself. Plane this end-grain surface and scribe all round the 12 mm allowed for the tapered dovetail, after which the latter is drawn and cut, and the end-grain is sized with glue. (The amount of taper on the dovetail, over its whole length of around 10 cm, is only about 8 mm.) This dovetail is now drawn on to the body of the viol and chiselled out, but not yet to its final measurements: it is prudent to have enough wood in hand to be able to correct any slight errors in height and direction of the neck-setting which may have crept in. This setting has to be checked at frequent intervals: cramp the fingerboard wedge on the neck and insert the latter into the body as far down as the mortice will allow; then place on the fingerboard a ruler which extends as far as the bridge, measure its height over the belly at this point, compare it with the distance the neck still has to go down into the body, and work out if any corrections are necessary. For checking the direction, measure from each of the viol's top corners to the end of the fingerboard, and also from the end of the fingerboard vertically down to the belly on both treble and bass side. Enlarge the mortice for the dovetail gradually, incorporating all necessary corrections, until the neck is set correctly in every respect. It should now hold quite firmly in the body, be straight, and fit well against the top ribs and the button. Mark on the fingerboard where and how far it has to be cut, and hollow the underside of the lower end, to make it lighter in both weight and appearance. On the neck the dovetail should be cut off from the top down as far as the rib level, after which the fingerboard can be glued to the neck. When the nut has been fitted and glued lightly, the heel of the neck is shaped with gouges and small planes, and the neck itself rounded and reduced to the correct thickness. In shaping the neck, we should try to achieve a minimum of weight with sufficient strength and, most important of all, a shape which is comfortable for the player's hand.

When gluing the neck to the body, we have to ensure that it is pressed against the button as well as against the ribs. To achieve the latter, cramping the viol between bench stops is most convenient, having of course first protected the bottom of the instrument and the heel of the neck with cramping blocks. The vertical pressure is exerted with a large G-cramp, which pushes the neck down on to the button, which in turn is supported by the cramping jig with the wedge. Watch carefully that the force of the G-cramp on the neck does not push the back away from the top block, and also that the height of the neck-setting is still right after this gluing and cramping. This height can often be affected quite considerably by moving the G-cramp marginally backward or forward on the fingerboard. Let the glue dry thoroughly before finishing the heel of the neck, and make quite sure that it is flush with the ribs and button, and that there are no steps or dents in any of the lines and curves.

The tailpin or hook-bar should now be prepared: use a piece of hardwood (rosewood or ebony preferably, although Barak Norman sometimes used sycamore, which he then painted black!); leave it about 17 cm long and plane it to 15 mm square. The end which fits into the body is tapered from two sides down to 9 mm at the bottom, and only the part overlapping the belly stays parallel. The hole for this tailpin should now be cut into the tailpiece; it should be cut at the correct angle, and placed with sufficient wood behind it to withstand the tension of all the strings. Let the tailpin into the body (about 8 mm deep) so that it fits rather tightly, cut the notch for the tailpiece, and finish the top in a decorative way. After a thorough and final check of the whole instrument, everything is now ready for varnishing.

8. *Varnishing*

This is probably the most controversial aspect of instrument-making, and dozens of publications have appeared over many years, always claiming to be the ultimate solution to this problem. This is neither the place, nor is there enough space here to get involved in long discussions about the advantages of one method over another. I have to confine myself to a few remarks, which I hope will be of practical use, and for the rest indicate only the existence of various possibilities.

The 'varnishing' of an instrument is really divided into three separate stages, of which applying varnish is the last. Before that we have to consider the questions of colouring and priming.

It is generally agreed that the colour of an instrument depends not only on the shade of the varnish used, but also on the shade of the wood underneath it, which shines through. An instrument which has had the chance to turn golden brown naturally while hanging in the sun will look much better than one whose colour has been varnished directly on to the white wood. Unfortunately, very few people have the time to hang up an instrument for two or three years before varnishing, and therefore various methods have been used to simulate or speed up this natural process. Treating the instrument with acids or baking the wood should be rejected, as in both instances the structure of the wood is damaged. Staining with chemicals like potassium bichromate or potassium permanganate will not damage the wood, but will give it a dead and stained appearance, which should be rejected for aesthetic reasons. A far less controversial way of colouring an instrument is to give it a coat of thin watercolour, saffron dissolved in water, or even tea. However, care should be taken that this wash is applied evenly and thinly. If the soft grain of the belly, which inevitably absorbs more of the liquid, is allowed to get darker than the hard grain lines, a rather unpleasant negative colouring effect is the result.

The next step must be to fill the pores of the wood with some sort of priming, otherwise the coloured varnish will be soaked up unevenly, and ruin the look of the instrument for ever. One obvious way to prevent this is to use colourless varnish as a filler, applying one coat after another until no more is absorbed. It can be argued, however, that this affects the acoustic characteristics of the wood in an undesirable way, and that it is much better to keep the varnish on top of the wood only. To achieve this, old makers in Mittenwald – the Kloz family amongst others – primed their instruments with a coat of diluted animal glue, on top of which they applied their varnish. (Instead of glue, ordinary gelatine can be used with equal success.) The greatest drawback to this method is that all the varnish will come off the instrument if damp penetrates through to the priming and softens it. Other substances which can and have been used are linseed oil (boiled), tempera (mixture of egg and oil of turpentine), propolis (resinous substance found in beehives, dissolved in alcohol), and gamboge (yellow resin, dissolved in alcohol). This last acts as both a colouring agent and filler, but is rather difficult to apply evenly. One complicating factor is that not all varnishes adhere to all these primings equally well. It might be found that the varnish, once it is thoroughly dry, can be chipped off its base quite easily. Curiously enough, linseed oil used in conjunction with most varnishes, offends very little in this respect. All the same, it is advisable to experiment thoroughly before applying anything to your viol.

Only now do we come to the varnishing itself. I imagine that most readers of this chapter will use a commercially available varnish, but, even so, a decision has to be taken on whether this should be a spirit or oil varnish. It is often assumed – quite erroneously – that a spirit varnish is always hard, brittle and chippy, whereas an oil varnish is soft, supple and flexible and, in short, has all the attributes we are looking for. Depending on the combination of resins and gums used, it is quite possible to make a spirit varnish which is soft and an oil varnish which is hard and chippy.[1]

It is advisable to apply at least one coat of colourless varnish to the primed instrument before proceeding with colour. Coat after coat has to be applied, until the desired shade is obtained. Applying spirit varnish evenly, especially on a large instrument, is quite difficult, as it dries very quickly; for this reason, use it very thinly, but apply many more coats, and step up the intensity of colour only very little between each coat. One of the problems with oil varnish is that it often takes more than a week for each coat to dry, and, assuming a total of 10 to 12 coats, three months can easily pass before the viol is varnished. (Some oil varnishes dry much quicker if exposed to ultra-violet rays; tubes emitting ultra-violet are available in various lengths.)

It should be unnecessary to mention that one needs a warm, dry and quite dust-free room for varnishing with either kind of varnish. Never should one coat be applied unless the previous one is absolutely dry. It is also useful to rub each coat down, but only very lightly, with a very fine silicon carbide paper (No. 320). This will remove any specks of dust or hairs from the varnish brush. When the desired depth of colour has been achieved, two or three coats of colourless varnish should be applied so that the viol can be rubbed down without cutting through the colour. Finally, if a disaster should happen, and it is decided to strip all the varnish off and start again, do use one of the many paint or varnish strippers available. They do not damage the wood or raise the grain, but remove all traces of varnish and are much quicker and cleaner than methylated spirits and scrapers.

9. *Fitting up*

The object of rubbing the varnish down should not necessarily be to obtain a mirror-like surface, but to remove some of the excessive gloss, as well as dust and brush marks. As even very fine sandpaper or steel wool would leave unacceptable scratches on the varnish, either pumice or tripoli powder should be used in conjunction with oil or water. Put these abrasives in a small bag made from an old and worn cotton sheet; only the finest particles will shake through the pores of the bag, leaving behind the lumps which might cause scratches. If a higher gloss than can be achieved with pumice or tripoli is desired, vienna chalk used in the same way, should provide the answer.

Rubbing down a carved head or carved ornaments, presents another problem. If done in the usual way with a piece of cotton dipped in oil, and with the abrasive powder sprinkled on the varnish, it is practically impossible to avoid rubbing the varnish right through to the wood on the high spots, and not touching it in the lower areas. If however one uses instead of the rag a paintbrush, the bristles of which have been cut off to a length of only 1 cm, this difficulty never arises.

1. For a detailed analysis of varnishes and their many recipes, see Joseph Michelman, *Violin Varnish*, Cincinnati, 1956. [Ed.]

The Viol

It is the usual practice nowadays not to varnish the neck with the rest of the viol. Apart from the convenience of being able to hold the instrument during varnishing, a harder-wearing varnish for that part is a definite advantage. Clean the unvarnished part of the neck with scrapers and sandpaper, and colour-stain it to the shade of the instrument or, better still, colour by rubbing some artists' powder colour into the wood. To finish, cover it with several coats of a tough spirit varnish, such as a clear shellac.

The soundholes will also need some attention now: there are usually quite thick and uneven accumulations of varnish, which have to be cut away carefully with a knife, right down to the wood. These cleaned surfaces should now be varnished with a spirit varnish, either the same colour as the rest of the body, or a contrasting dark brown or black. Remove all varnish from places which are meant to remain bare, i.e. the top of the fingerboard, the nut and tailpin, and polish them up using very fine sandpaper and oil, or pumice and oil.

All that remains to be done now is to fit the pegs, soundpost, bridge and frets. Great care should be taken to do this work as accurately as possible, as the final success or failure of the viol depends to a large extent on how it has been fitted up. When fitting the pegs, clean all traces of varnish, pumice powder etc., out of the peg holes with the peg reamer, and enlarge them until the diameter of the smaller hole is about 7.5 mm for each peg. Done in this way, the longest peg will be the thickest, and the others will be progressively thinner. This is not a critical measurement, but one which experience has shown will produce a peg of convenient thickness: thin enough to enable easy tuning, and yet not so thin that it will break. Once the holes are the right size, the pegs should be shaped with a peg cutter, which works on the same principle as a pencil sharpener, and is of course adjusted to the same taper as the peg reamer. Reduce the thickness of the shanks until the collars of the pegs are only approximately 18 mm from the outside of the pegbox. By now, the pegs should fit at both ends, but for best results, fractionally more tightly at the thick end, which will prevent whipping, and make tuning quicker and more secure. Cut off the thin ends so that, when slightly rounded, they are flush with the pegbox, and drill the hole for the string 1 cm from the inside face of the pegbox at the thicker end. The shanks can be finished now with very fine sandpaper and oil, and the pegs should finally be well lubricated with a good peg paste.

The soundpost should be made from best-quality spruce, and should be 10–11 mm thick, which is slightly thinner than a cello soundpost would be. It should stand behind the right bridge foot and just inside it, be absolutely upright and tight enough not to fall down, even if the viol is moved before the strings and bridge are fitted. On the other hand it should not be so tight that the belly is forced up to any noticeable extent, but it must fit perfectly both at its top and bottom end. To achieve all this needs a considerable amount of skill and certainly time and patience. A cello soundpost-setter is still the best tool to place and manoeuvre the post, and a dentist's large mirror to check the fit. A final adjustment of the post is, of course, only possible when the instrument is fitted up and playable. Moving it towards the centre joint will usually improve the bass strings (normally at the expense of the trebles) and the response can be altered by placing it nearer or further from the bridge. It is very easy, however, to damage either the C hole with the soundpost-setter or the inside of the belly with the post if it is moved without the string tension having been reduced first. For these reasons alone it is recommended that moving the post should not become a frequent occurrence. After a final adjustment give the instrument (and the player) a chance to settle down and get played in.

The bridge for the viol is made from unfigured sycamore, which is cut in such a manner that the medullary rays are most pronounced on the side which faces the tailpiece. The design and arrangement of the cut-outs is of great importance, as it affects the sound of the instrument, and although the bridge has to bear the pressure of six or seven strings, it should not be left too solid or it will hinder the vibrations. It is also important that the feet are fitted very accurately to the belly, and experience has shown that lasting success is more likely if the bridge has feet like a cello bridge, rather than the solid ones illustrated by Christopher Simpson in his book *The Division Viol*.[1] As the belly of the viol will go up and down with the humidity of the surrounding air, the solid feet will not be able to cope with this movement. It is usually the inside edges which start digging into the belly, damaging first the varnish and then the wood itself. If no bridge blank is available, fit the feet first, then shape the top and arrange your bridge design within these limits. Saw the cut-outs with a fretsaw and finish them with the narrow-bladed knife last used for the soundholes. The curve at the top of the bridge should be concentric with the curve of the fingerboard, but arranged in such a way that the top string will lie closer to the fingerboard than the lowest string. Finally, leaving the back of the bridge (the side facing the tailpiece) quite flat, shape the front towards it, until the top edge has a uniform thickness of just under 3 mm. Place the string notches on the curve of the bridge and fingerboard nut, round them over and finish with fine sandpaper.

The viol is now ready to be strung and tuned for the first time, but until the strings have ceased stretching take care that the bridge is not being pulled forward. For the seven frets on the neck either gut (cheap violin A strings are about the right thickness) or nylon can be used, the latter having the advantage of being much more durable and less likely to become loose later on. Use the special fret knot for double frets as described in Chapter 2, p. 65, and tune them by ear, using octaves and fifths, not forgetting that the tuning has to be tempered. This is as far as the maker can go; the rest is in the hands of the player.

1. London 1659, 2nd ed. as *The Division-Viol*, London 1665–7.

2

The Lute

IAN HARWOOD

1. *Introduction*

The lute was highly esteemed in Europe from the later Middle Ages until the end of the eighteenth century, during which time it underwent many radical alterations. These developments have been outlined elsewhere[1] and will not be retraced here. The present chapter will be concerned only with the making of one of the several kinds of lute in use around the year 1600, namely, a seven-course tenor instrument.

The strings of the lute were in pairs, known as 'courses', though the highest was often single. There were many sizes, tuned to different pitches but always keeping the same intervals between the six main courses. During the sixteenth century a seventh course was added in the bass, and a typical 'tenor' lute was tuned D G c f a d' g'. It is such a lute as this, suitable for the majority of music up to about 1610 (and a good deal written later), that will be described here.

The first step should be the preparation of a full-size working drawing of the instrument, in the course of which many things will become clear that at first seem obscure. Although it is perfectly possible to draw a lute outline freehand, it seems very likely that some early makers derived their designs by geometrical construction.[2] A simplified method is given here for those who wish to follow their example; others may wish to base their instruments on particular early specimens, using drawings now available.

There is nothing sacred about the system described here; it is only one of a number of possibilities, but it at least has the merit of simplicity and should produce an aesthetically pleasing shape. Other criteria may be used to produce a different outline.

2. *The Design*

Certain proportions will be useful in the preparation of the design, some of which were mentioned as early as 1450 by Arnault of Zwolle in a collection of notes about instruments. Others are average values derived from observation and measurements of existing old lutes. Those that affect the body outline are as follows: (1) the joint between the body and neck comes at the eighth fret, which divides the string length in the proportion 5:8;

---

1. See Friedemann Hellwig, 'Lute Construction in the Renaissance and the Baroque', *Galpin Society Journal*, XXVII, 1974, 21–30; Ian Harwood, *A Brief History of the Lute*, Lute Society, 1975.

2. A first suggestion on this subject is given in David Edwards, 'A geometrical construction for a lute profile', *Lute Society Journal*, Vol. XV, 1973, p. 48; see also Abbott & Segerman, 'The geometric description & analysis of instrument shapes', FoMRHI, Comm. 5, Jan., 1976.

(2) the bridge is positioned at one-sixth of the distance from the bottom of the body to the joint with the neck; (3) the maximum width of the body is two-thirds of the body length. Other proportions will be discussed in the course of marking out the soundboard.

The body proportions can easily be expressed numerically if the string length is taken as the starting point. This is itself fixed within quite narrow limits by considering the material of the strings and the pitch to which they are tuned. The oft-repeated instruction of the early tutors to tune the top string until it is just about to break may raise a smile today, but it is in fact the crucial factor. The breaking pitch of a string of a given material is determined by its length; for a gut string tuned to g′ the absolute maximum is about 60 cm. This measurement will be used as the basis of the present design, which results in the dimensions given below:

A	Open string length (bridge to nut)		60.0 cm
B	Neck joint from bridge (8th fret)	$(A \times \frac{5}{8})$	37.5 cm
C	Total body length	$(B \times \frac{6}{5})$	45.0 cm
D	Maximum body width	$(C \times \frac{2}{3})$	30.0 cm

Another important criterion is the width of the neck, which in turn depends on the number of courses and the spacing between the strings. To some extent this may be tailored to suit the player's hands, but a useful average spacing at the nut will be 4.5 mm between courses and 3 mm between the strings of each pair. At the bridge the spacing should be rather greater, say 10 mm between courses and 4.5 mm between strings. These measurements are all given between string centres, and the single first string is treated as though it were the nearest of a pair to the second course. As an added refinement the spacing may be slightly closer for the top three courses and slightly wider for the basses, especially if gut strings are to be used throughout.

The distance between the outer strings may now be calculated at nut and bridge. For a seven-course lute we shall need at the nut 6×4.5 mm between courses and 6×3 mm for each pair, making 45 mm. At the bridge the distance will be 6×10 mm plus 6×4.5 mm, which comes to 87 mm.

An outline of the body plan may now be constructed by geometry. It must be emphasized that this will not give an exact replica of any particular early lute, though the resulting shape is quite typical. The method is described step by step, with reference to Fig. 1.

1. Draw centre line (*cl*) and mark open string length A B.
2. Mark position of 8th fret C ($\frac{5}{8}$ A B).
3. Draw perpendiculars to *cl* through A, B, C.
4. Mark position of end of body D ($\frac{1}{5}$ A C).
5. Mark positions of outer strings at A (bridge) and B (nut); draw outer strings E F and G H, cutting the perpendicular through C at J, K.
6. Draw two lines L M, N O, parallel to *cl*, of arbitrary length, to mark maximum body width.
7. Draw two lines P Q, R S, parallel to *cl* at distance C D above line L M and below line N O.
8. Centre C, radius C D, draw arc through D to give end of body.
9. Centres J, K, radius C D, draw arcs to cut lines P Q, R S, at T, U.
10. Centres T, U, radius C D, draw arcs through J, K, to give body sides.
11. Mark point V on *cl*, one-third of maximum body width from D.
12. Centre C, radius C V, draw arc through V.

13. Centres T, U, radius CV, draw arcs cutting previous arc at W, X.

14. Centres W, X, radius DV, draw arcs to join body end and side arcs.

The body outline is then given by the envelope JDK. The outer edges of the fingerboard will be parallel to the outside strings, at a distance of 5 mm each side. The figure shows the body and neck outlines slightly bolder than the construction lines.

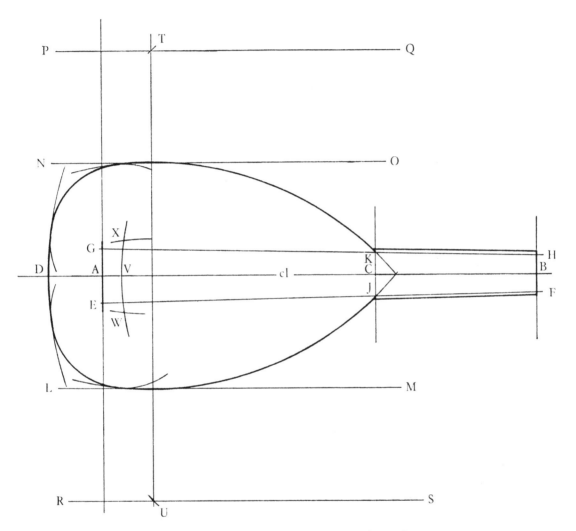

Fig. 2.1 *Geometrical construction for a lute outline*

In the sixteenth century smaller sizes of lutes were sometimes of semi-circular cross-section (end elevation), which simplifies construction as the side elevation is the same as half the plan, and all the ribs of the body are identical. The number of ribs varied, with nine, eleven or thirteen being very common. For the present purposes we will consider a nine-rib body, though the same principles apply whatever the number. Having completed the body outline we can now derive the true shape of the ribs, as shown in Fig. 2.

Suppose ABC is the side elevation. The end elevation will be the semi-circle DEF, divided into nine equal rib segments, of which GHI is the central one. The true length of

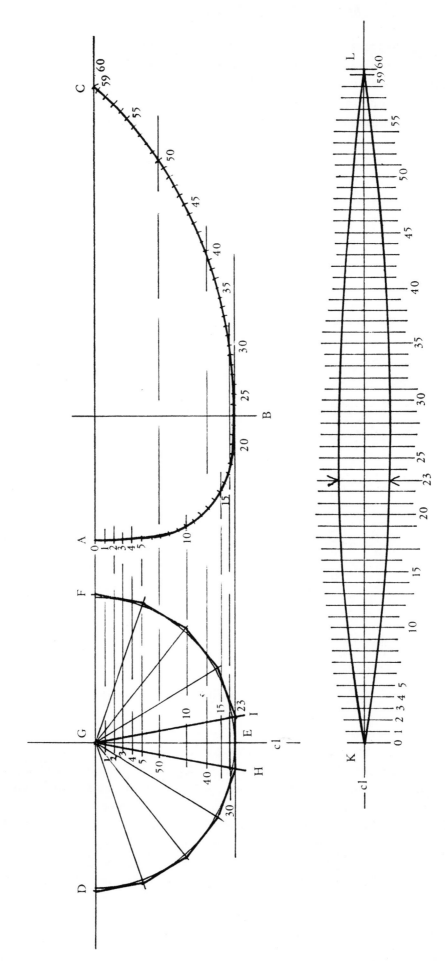

Fig. 2.2   *True shape of the rib and its derivation*

each rib will be the same as that of the curve A B C. Divide up this curve into a number of small equal steps, numbering them as shown. The smaller these steps, the greater the eventual accuracy of the rib-shape, but 1-cm divisions will give a reasonable result. It is unlikely that the last step will fall exactly at the end of the curve; if not, simply mark an extra smaller portion as shown at 59 and 60. Now draw a centre line for the true rib shape K L and step off an equal number of the same steps, marking them 0 to 59 and adding the final smaller step to 60. The straight line K L is now the same length as the curve A B C. Draw short vertical lines through each numbered point.

Now mark off the vertical distance below the base line A C of each numbered segment on the side elevation, and transfer this to the vertical *d* G E on the end elevation. The width of the segment G H I at each point will be the width of the rib at the corresponding number. These distances can be measured off with dividers from the *d* of the end elevation and marked on the vertical lines on the rib plan. Thus, if B is the deepest part of the body outline, which happens to be at point 23 in this case, the width of the rib at the point will be H I. This is indicated by the arrow-heads on the rib outline at point 23. For clarity at this small scale, only numbers 1–5 and certain others are shown in the figure; proportional dividers will give the rib widths directly.

A smooth curve drawn through all the resulting points will give the true shape of the rib. It should of course be symmetrical, and your accuracy may be checked by comparing the two halves! Trace the outline on to a piece of 1-mm plywood (or, failing that, cardboard) and cut out carefully, to make the master rib template.

3. The Rib-Former

The main problem in constructing a lute is the building up of the body, and its solution depends on the accuracy with which the separate ribs can be shaped and bent, so as to fit together snugly on the mould.

Since the ribs are at an angle to each other, their edges must not be perpendicular to their surface, but must be bevelled to ensure a close fit. Because the rib is bent to a curve, this bevel is not constant, but must vary throughout its length. This can be achieved by bending the rib to the correct curve over a former of the correct wedge shape, against which the edges are trimmed. The former may be made by several methods, either built-up or solid, provided it is accurate. The following is one way to produce a solid former.

The drawings all show the *outside* of the finished instrument. In making the former and the mould allowance must be made for the thickness of the ribs, by drawing outlines for the *inside* of the body. Otherwise the lute will be slightly larger than intended.

Take a piece of softwood slightly larger than the body length and depth of the lute, of thickness slightly more than the maximum width of the rib. For maximum stability this may be built up from two pieces laminated together and bonded with PVA glue. Plane one long edge and both faces straight, flat and at right angles to each other. Carefully trace the outline of the *inside* of the rib on to each face, aligning them together carefully. Cut out this curve and trim to the line, checking frequently with a square. Mark a centre line all round (this will be the joint in a laminated piece) (Fig. 3a). Now place the rib template on the curved edge, making sure that the two points come exactly to the centre line. Secure the template with adhesive tape, and draw its outline with a sharp hard pencil to transfer the rib shape to the curve (Fig. 3b). Saw and plane the two faces down to make a wedge, like the segment of an orange. Both surfaces must be flat, meeting in a sharp edge along the centre line of the straight side (Fig. 3c). The final outline should coincide with the pencilled shape from the template. If it does not, there is no cause for alarm; provided the maximum width of the former is correct and its faces are flat and at the correct angle, it may well be more accurate than the rib template.

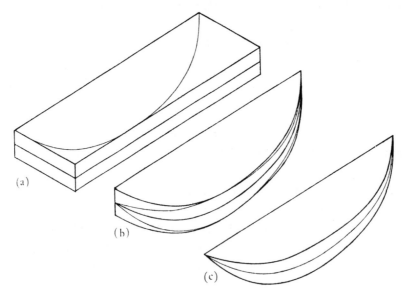

Fig. 2.3 *Construction of the solid former*

4. *The Mould*

The body of the lute may be assembled over a mould which can be either solid or built up. The more accurately the ribs are shaped and bent, the less the need for a mould; indeed, it is perfectly possible to make a lute with no mould at all.

Fig. 4 shows the construction of a simple framework-mould, the parts for which are obtained from side and end elevations, given at Fig. 2. As in the case of the rib-former, due allowance must be made for the thickness of the ribs. The base is a straight strip, the width of which (10 cm) is the same as that of the neck block, which will be attached to the mould as described later. The inside end-strip will be fastened to the other end of the mould, which is curved to the body shape. The cross-member, with nine rib facets, is set

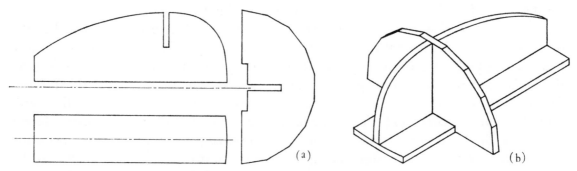

Fig. 2.4 *Construction of the mould*

into the spine with a halved joint as shown. The mould may be made from 12-mm plywood, and secured with countersunk screws. A block attached to the bottom (not shown on the drawing) will enable it to be held in the vice.

5. *The Body*

Traditionally, the lute body has a block only at the neck end; the ribs being fastened at the bottom to a thin strip of surplus rib-wood, about 3 mm thick, which should overlap the mould baseboard by 2 or 3 cm at each side and should be 2.5 cm or so wide. This should be prepared and bent to follow the curve of the end of the body. A small electric fire (in U.S.A. a space heater) is all that is required for all the bending necessary in making a lute.[1] Hold the wood close to the metal guard in front of the element, at the same time flexing it between the fingers in the intended direction. When the wood reaches a certain temperature, the fibres soften and it will take on a permanent 'set'. Proceed slowly until the end-strip follows the curve of the lower end of the mould. Secure initially with two drawing-pins to the mould.

The neck block will be basically semicircular in section and must follow the mould outline. The upper surface of the block, to which the soundboard will be glued, extends 2 cm into the body from the neck joint. Because the neck is less than a semi-circle in section, the joint will be at an angle in side elevation, as shown in Fig. 5. The block must be made longer than necessary, and the excess trimmed off when the neck is to be fitted. Make cardboard templates to help with shaping this block, which must be carved from a pine or spruce block. Make the block slightly oversize, square it up and attach to the mould by its bracket and screws. Mark the centre line. Remove it from the mould for marking out and shaping.

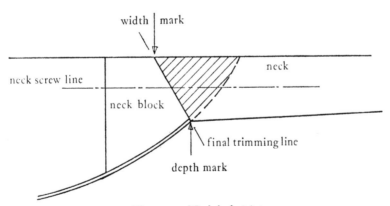

Fig. 2.5 *Neck-body joint*

It is easier to shape this block if it does not continue right to the point, as shown. The semi-circles are marked on each end and steps are marked for the facets where the ribs will fit. The outline is marked on the top face and the sides. Excess wood is then cut away with a saw and carving begins. Hold the block between the two ends and aim first at a conical shape just touching the required curve, using the template to reach the final shape and starting the flat facets (remember to use the template at right angles to

1. The bending iron mentioned in Chapter 1, p. 16, can be used here and for the construction of the other stringed instruments described in this book. [Ed.]

each facet in turn). Mount the finished neck block on the mould by means of an over-lapping bracket, screwed to both block and mould baseboard, checking that it is accurately aligned and positioned. Mark a vertical centre line on each end, and drill a hole right through the block 12 mm from the top face for the screw that will fix the neck in place.

6. *The Ribs*

Mark the rib-shapes on the wood and cut them out, leaving fairly generous excess all round. If the ribs are to be cut from separate narrow strips, they can be done in batches, taping four or so together before sawing. They can be cut with coping or bow-saw, or a band-saw which will probably cut all the ribs at once. If wider guitar ribs are used, three lute ribs may be cut separately from each piece. The most economical way is to overlap them, though of course the figure will not then match exactly.

The ribs must now be planed to their final thickness. In doing this operation, deal with the eventual outside surface first. This is because it is much easier to get a good finish on figured wood when planing a thicker piece than when it is very thin, and consequently less rigid. A block-plane with adjustable mouth, set very close, will be best for this, and the plane iron must be kept razor-sharp. It may be necessary to re-sharpen the plane three or four times per side, which usually surprises people very much! The old adage 'Time spent sharpening is never time wasted' was never more true! Care must be taken not to tilt the plane over at the edges, or the ribs will be thinner there than in the middle. For this reason some makers prefer to plane the ribs before they are cut to shape.

It is not possible to be dogmatic about the final thickness of the ribs, which depends on the stiffness of the wood. They should be flexible but not flimsy; springy but not flabby. Somewhere between 1.5 and 2 mm will generally be right, and evenness of thickness is important to avoid kinks while bending. In case of accidents a 'spare rib' should also be prepared at this stage. Even if all goes well it will still be required, for use as the capping strip or end-clasp.

When the thicknessing is complete, lay all the ribs face up on the bench and look at the figure. A pattern may well suggest itself which will dictate the order in which the ribs should be assembled. Arrange them in this sequence and turn them over. If the ribs have been cut from a single block, you will of course keep them in their natural sequence. Number the inside faces: o for the centre rib; +1, +2, +3, +4 on one side and −1, −2, −3, −4 on the other. Rib o is now ready for bending.

7. *Bending*

Proceed as described for the end strip, beginning where the bend is greatest, which will be somewhere about a third of the length from the bottom point. Work first towards the point, checking the curve against the wooden former. Try to avoid bending too sharply; this risks a breakage, especially with highly figured wood, and is also very difficult to eliminate once introduced. If the wood is very dry indeed, it may be reluctant to bend (but this can also be because it is too thick). If this is so the rib may be dampened on each side with a wet rag, which should help the wood to 'give' to the right curve. This may also be necessary if too much heat is applied by being too timid in bending, for this will dry the wood out before it is bent. A trial run with offcuts will show the best way.

8. *Trimming*

Once Rib 0 is bent accurately to shape, it must be secured to the wooden former for trimming and chamfering. For this purpose an 'impact' adhesive may be used, to give a firm but easily-removable join. Put three spots of adhesive on the former, at each end and near the middle, and three corresponding spots on the rib. When these have become tacky, press the rib to the former, making sure there is even overlap all round.

With the block-plane set a little less fine than for thicknessing the ribs, take off the excess until no more than 1 mm remains all round. Now take a flat board (chipboard is ideal) about twice the length of the former and a little wider. Cut a strip of medium grade glasspaper about 4 or 5 cm wide and secure it to the board with two drawing-pins at the upper corners. Place the former with slightly oversize rib on the board, and rub the edge of the rib to and fro throughout its length. Inspect from time to time and continue until the edge is exactly flush with the former. It is essential to keep the former flat on the board during this process. Repeat for the other side. Take care not to sand away the face of the former! In practice it is quite easy to feel when the rib is finished, as the friction changes the moment the whole surface of the former comes in contact with the glasspaper.

Now remove the rib from the former, inserting a thin blade such as a palette-knife if necessary. Clean off the adhesive from rib and former with a suitable solvent such as carbon tetrachloride (CCl_4) or white spirit. Do not leave it on the latter, as it will cake and prevent subsequent ribs from fitting correctly.

9. *Fitting the First Rib*

Fit the rib to the mould, placing the point carefully on the centre line marked on the end-strip. Check that the curve follows the central spine; that the width is the same as the flat on the cross-member and that it fits the facet on the neck block. Mark the position of the point on the end strip, apply woodworking adhesive[1] to this area and to the central facet of the neck block. Place the rib exactly in position again, and hold the points in position with two drawing-pins. Some workers prefer to use masking tape for this purpose; transparent tape has the advantage of showing the state of affairs underneath. If the tape shows any sign of tearing the grain of the wood when removed, it can be released without pulling by damping the back with a damp rag. This will leave the rubbery adhesive on the surface, which may be rolled away with the fingertips. The tape is ready for release when it assumes a milky appearance with the damp. (The point will eventually be covered by the end-clasp, so drawing-pin marks do not matter, but at the other end a strip of tape should be stuck on first before pinning to avoid marking the wood. The pins should of course be beyond the edge of the rib, using the broad head to provide pressure.) If the rib is correctly bent excessive pressure will not be needed.

The correct positioning of the centre rib is of the utmost importance, as any errors will accumulate as the rest of the body is built up. Clean off any excess adhesive before it sets hard, to save time and trouble later.

1. The advantages of using animal or Scotch glue for musical instrument making are pointed out in Chapter 1, p. 18, but care must be taken to size end-grain in particular to ensure efficient adhesion. [Ed.]

10. *The Remaining Ribs*

While Rib 0 is drying, Ribs +1 and −1 should be bent and trimmed in exactly the same way. Hold the mould on its side in the vice. Remove the drawing-pins and tape from Rib 0, and clean off any excess glue. Offer up Rib +1, which should fit snugly beside 0 all the way along. If not, trim very carefully with the block-plane set very fine and held upside-down in the vice. The shaped rib may be drawn across the plane so as to remove a small shaving around any high spots. Mark the outside edge on the end strip, and apply adhesive to this area. Also apply glue to about 5 cm of the edge of Rib 0 where +1 will fit. Position +1 carefully in place and hold with a drawing-pin near the point. Draw it tightly against 0 with adhesive tape and secure to 0. Now proceed along the length towards the neck-block, in steps of 5 cm or so, gluing and pulling up with tape. When approaching the neck, apply glue to the +1 facet as well. Secure as before with tape, adding drawing-pins if necessary. Allow this joint to set, and then proceed with Rib −1 in exactly the same manner. Before the adhesive has set off too far, clean off the excess with a damp rag; it is easy to remove at this stage but very difficult later. The tape may spread the adhesive over the surface of the rib, which may be hard to see. Take care to remove this, or light patches will result when varnishing.

Continue to build up the body from the centre outwards, until all the ribs are attached. When the outside ribs +4 and −4, are reached, leave the outer edges unplaned, to allow a little overlap for trimming later. The two original drawing-pins holding the end strip in position must of course be removed in order to fit these ribs.

When the last glue is dry the remaining drawing-pins are removed and the shell can be released from the mould by unscrewing the neck-block. At this stage it is rather fragile and must be handled with care. Hold it up to the light and check the joins from inside. No gaps should be seen, but if there are some, apply a little adhesive on the inside and work into the join until it squeezes through to the outside. Pull the offending joint together with tape.

Now stick strips of parchment or linen tape about 1 cm wide along each join. This is best done with rather thin hot Scotch glue, applied to the joint with a stiff brush. The tape is laid on and rubbed down with the finger until the glue completely impregnates the fibres. Once this has dried the body will be very much stronger.

Any slight unevenness between ribs can now be smoothed out. A curved cabinet scraper is ideal here for the expert but a sanding block with fine Garnet paper may be more convenient for the amateur.

11. *The Capping Strip*

The body is finished by attaching the end-clasp or capping strip, which is made from the spare rib, or if you have cracked one, from part of that. This was one of the few places where the old makers allowed themselves some decoration. Some suggestions are given in Fig. 6.

Position the centre line in the correct place; bend the capping strip in the same way as the ribs, to fit the body curve; cramp with small G-cramps in the centre where the inner strip is also located and with clothes-pegs further from the centre. Allow the edge to overlap a little, as shown in the figure by the dotted lines. Make sure that the two ends will be the same after trimming, which is done with a plane when the glue has set.

The edge of the body must now be trimmed flat, to take the soundboard without distortion. A plywood shape may be cut out to fit just *inside* the body profile, and secured to the neck-block and end strip by overhanging brackets. The body edges are then trimmed flush with the plywood. Final adjustments may be made with the shell upside-down on a flat board with glasspaper attached, just as the ribs were chamfered. The plywood shaper helps prevent distortion while the rest of the instrument is being made.

The next stage is to shape the upper end of the body ready for fitting the neck. From the drawing, measure the exact width of the neck at the joint with the body, and mark this same width across the neck-block and ribs.

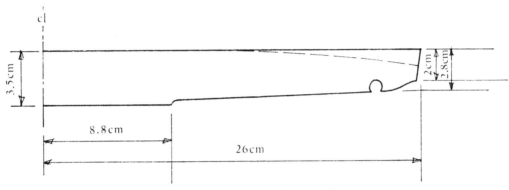

Fig. 2.6 *Capping strip or end-clasp*

The neck-joint will not be vertical in side elevation, because the neck is not semi-circular in section like the body. The suggested depth of the neck at the body end is 2.5 cm; this distance must be marked on the centre rib and will be nearer to the end than the line across the block. The unwanted portion of the body must now be removed with a fine back-saw, proceeding with caution and finishing with the adjustable block-plane set very fine. This operation is easier if the body is replaced on the mould and the block secured with its screws. The mould can then be held in the vice to keep the whole assembly steady. The end surface must be quite flat when finished to the marks; progress may be checked with a straight-edge. On no account go beyond the marks or the neck will have to be made oversize to compensate. The joint is given at Fig. 5, which shows the positions of the width and depth marks, with the shaded portion to be trimmed off.

12. *The Neck*

This is usually made from a quartered piece of beech, sycamore, or other dimensionally stable hardwood. From our original dimensions, we know that the total length from body-joint (eighth fret) to nut is 22.5 cm. To this must be added 0.5 cm for the nut itself, making 23 cm. The pegbox, which butts on to the end of the neck, is 1.8 cm thick, so the neck itself must be 21.2 cm long. It tapers in both width and depth. The width must match that of the body at one end and the pegbox at the other. In depth the suggested taper is from 2.5 cm at the body end to 2 cm at the pegbox. It is best, however, to start with a rectangular block, cut generously oversize to allow for possible alignment

47

errors. Plane up one face (the top) and one edge. Both the ends will eventually be angled, for joining to body and pegbox. Mark a line at one end across the planed face, for the neck-block position. Measure 21.2 cm from this line and mark across for the pegbox end. Measure the angle of the neck-block with the adjustable bevel and mark this on the planed edge. Reset the bevel to 80° for the angle of the pegbox, and mark this also on the edge. Mark a vertical centre line on the body-end, and drill a pilot hole 12 mm from the face for the fastening screw which is inserted through the front block into the neck. This hole must be deep enough for the screw to penetrate when the neck is assembled. Now cut the body-angle across the neck, and finish smooth with the block-plane. Check that it is the same as the neck-block on the body with the adjustable bevel. Now screw on the neck-block (but do not glue!) to the body. Check for alignment. The top surface of the neck should line up exactly with the block, but owing to the angle it may well pull forward a little. This does not greatly matter, as it can be planed down later. With a long rule or a straight-edge, line up the centre line at the bottom of the body on the capping strip with the centre line of the neck-block, and mark the continuation of this along the neck. All other dimensions must be marked from this. Mark also the edges of the body. With a really sharp scriber, mark the curve of the body on the end of the neck, keeping really close to the body.

Now remove the neck once more, and mark the plan outline on the top surface, using the new centre line as a datum. Cut the pegbox end at the required angle and plane flat. Mark a curve for the top of the neck on this end. This should be done with a template; and must be symmetrical. Now cut the taper c f and plane this under-surface flat. Although it will eventually be curved, it will be much easier to work if the surface is flat and the thickness correct to start with. Finally, plane the curve, checking against the body as work nears completion; there should be no steps or gaps at the joint.

13. *The Pegbox*

This is built up of five basic pieces: two end blocks and two sides, with a flat backing piece (which should be about rib-thickness). The length will depend on the number of string courses and consequent number of pegs. Allow 2 cm for the end block; 1.25 cm between block and first hole centre; 1.25 cm between centres. Pegboxes normally taper in plan view, but the earlier the lute the less the taper. A small taper in side elevation is also common; suggested dimensions are given in Fig. 7.

The side pieces should be cut and planed to the correct cross-section but left over-long. Make the tapered end blocks with a small plane. Mark the inside edges of end blocks on the side pieces, but do not mark the peghole centres yet. Scratch the blocks and side pieces where they will be glued. Apply woodworking adhesive and hold them together with adhesive tape. Some, though not all, pva adhesives show signs of 'creeping' under tension and may allow the pegbox sides to move after a period of time; other synthetic resin adhesives do not do this and so are probably better for this purpose. Ordinary clamps may also be used, but tape is advisable first, as otherwise the taper may cause the assembly to slip when clamped. Now glue on the back, trimming up finally when the glue is dry. Draw lines on a level with the inside edges of the end blocks and mark down the sides. Mark a centre line along each side (*not* a marking gauge, which will show!) and mark the peghole centres. Prick these with a scriber or centre-punch ready for drilling. Alignment of the pegholes straight across may present problems owing to the taper of the pegbox. There are various possible solutions, depending on the equipment available. In any case, it is best to start with a small pilot hole, say 2 mm or 3 mm in diameter. If you have access to a lathe, place the drill in the headstock and a pointed centre in the tailstock. The pegbox can then be aligned between the corresponding holes. Drill each side separately, using the holes in the first side as centres for the second side.

If you have a vertical stand for an electric drill, make a drilling jig, simply a piece of wood of the same taper as the pegbox, and again drill each side separately.

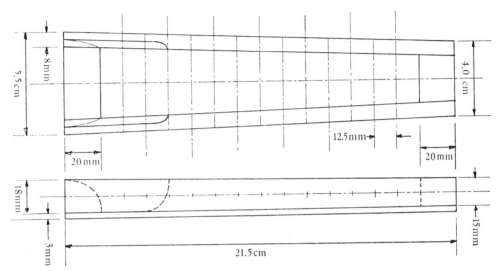

Fig. 2.7   *Pegbox design for a seven-course lute*

With a hand drill, it is best to mark the hole centres on the inside of the pegbox as well as the outside. This makes marking out somewhat tedious, but is well worth doing. Hold the pegbox in a vice with the *cl* horizontal, and drill vertical holes, checking in two mutually perpendicular directions from time to time. Having the centres marked on the inside helps greatly by giving a target to aim at with the drill.

It is possible that there may have been a little wander even with a lathe or drilling jig. This is one reason why a small pilot hole is drilled first. The other is that it is almost impossible to avoid the wood chipping out when the drill first breaks through. If the sides are drilled separately and a small size is used for a start, any such damage will be on the inside and will anyway be removed when the holes are opened up with the reamer.

Progressively larger drills are used until the size of the small end of the peg reamer is reached. The holes are then finished by hand using the taper reamer (see p. 62).

14. *Joining Pegbox and Neck*

This is simplicity itself, using a straightforward butt joint and modern glues (but remember the cautionary remarks about PVA adhesives). Hold the neck vertically in a vice (cushioning with a piece of rag to avoid marks). Check that both the surfaces to be joined are flat and clean. Apply adhesive to the top of the neck; place the pegbox in position and hold in place with adhesive tape. The weight of the pegbox will provide sufficient clamping pressure. Disbelievers may use dowels or screws, but in more than a hundred lutes I have only had a couple of pegboxes come off, and when another *had* to be removed for modifications, the wood of the pegbox block split rather than the joint! An alternative neck-pegbox joint is shown at Fig. 8.

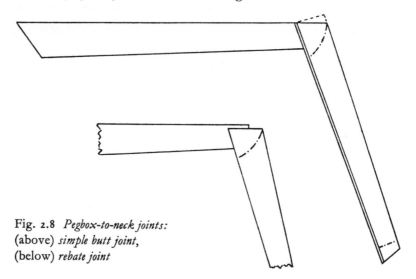

Fig. 2.8 *Pegbox-to-neck joints:*
(above) *simple butt joint,*
(below) *rebate joint*

15. *The Soundboard*

Lutes usually have a soundboard jointed down the centre, as it would be difficult to obtain sufficiently even grain in a single piece of pine of sufficient width. The top will be purchased in the form of two matched pieces, of which the two outer edges where the grain is finest must be joined. For this purpose a long jointing plane is ideal, but with care and perseverance it can be done with a shorter one. Besides keeping quite straight, the plane must not rock at all from side to side, which is difficult to avoid with a thin piece of wood in the ordinary way. Use the plane on its side, together with a shooting board. The two halves are planed together, the plane being pushed along on its side, taking off a very fine shaving. It is worth checking that the sole of the plane is really flat with a straight-edge, as great skill is required to get a good joint with a curved plane!

As soon as the saw marks are removed, check the joint by holding the pieces together against the light. The chances are it will either show a gap in the centre or at one or both ends.

Proceed with caution to take down the high spots. A single stroke of the plane may be sufficient in the final stages.

Once no light is to be seen along the join, the soundboard halves can be glued together. This again is best done on a flat board. First lay down a wide strip of adhesive tape on this board, to avoid its becoming covered in glue. Take one soundboard half and apply PVA glue along the surface to be joined. Place this piece on the board with the join on the tape and immediately bring the other half into contact with it. Slide the two to and fro a few times to get rid of excess glue and air and to make sure they are in close contact throughout their length, making what is called a 'rubbed joint'. Attach strips of adhesive tape to the upper half, pressing down firmly. Then stretch the tape towards you and attach it to the lower half, smoothing it vigorously to avoid it coming away. Do this first in the centre, then towards each end. You now have the two halves 'hinged' with tape on one side. Lift the whole soundboard and turn it over, taking care not to let the 'hinge' open. Now proceed as before with the other surface.

Once both sides are firmly taped, the two halves will not come apart, and the assembly can be inspected for gaps. Further strips of tape can be attached if required, but if the jointing was properly done they should not be needed. Put the soundboard aside to dry.

There is still not enough information about the finer details of the thicknesses of old lute soundboards. Until many more have been measured it is not possible to be too specific, but there is often a tendency to be thicker around the bridge, thinner at the rose area and thicker towards the neck-block. For a lute of the size we are considering a mean thickness of perhaps 1.3 mm would be about right, perhaps increasing to 1.5 mm around bridge area and towards the neck-block, and perhaps thinning to about 1 mm around the rose area. These figures, which are necessarily vague, apply to pine sound-boards. Cedar needs to be rather thicker to give an equivalent result; perhaps up to 1½ times the suggested measurements.

The long jointer plane is useful again for planing down the soundboard, but once more, it is perfectly possible with a smaller one though slightly more laborious. As with the ribs, it is a good idea to prepare the outside surface while the wood is relatively thick and there is time to remedy any troubles. Because of the way the board is joined, one half will plane better in one direction and the other the opposite way. For this reason, be specially careful when working near the centre line. If the wood is particularly trouble-some, change over to the adjustable blockplane, set very fine in both cut and mouth, for the final stages.

A thicknessing gauge may be used, but is not essential. Aim for about 1.3 mm all round the edge, and a bit more at the top and bottom, then take down a shade around the rose. Later, when you come to make the first cut-out for the soundhole, you can check the thickness here and if necessary take a little more off. As a rule the quality of the timber will dictate the minimum thickness and a fine 'tight' piece of spruce can be considerably thinner than timber of lesser quality; however, experience will be the best guide.

16. *Marking out the Soundboard*

Fig. 9 represents the *underside* of the soundboard, whose shape has already been obtained, with its *cl* D A C, where A is the bridge position and C that of the eighth fret. Because the edges of the fingerboard are 5 mm outside the outer strings, the actual position of the body/neck-joint will be just inside the point C, as shown. Mark the inner edge of the neck-block, 2 cm from this line, shown as *c*.

Mark the mid point *d* of the line DA; draw a circle centre A radius A*d*.

Mark the position of the first main bar 1 on *cl*.

Mark the mid point *a* of the line D1; *a*1 is the distance between main bars.

Starting at point 1, step off bar positions 2, 3, 4, 5 on *cl*.

Divide the distance 5*c* into three equal parts and mark bar positions 6, 7 on *cl*.

Draw lines perpendicular to *cl* to represent the bars. The centre of the soundhole or rose is at bar position 4; its diameter is one-third of the body-width at that point.

Draw a circle to show the rose diameter.

The small bars around the bridge are positioned as follows:

Draw perpendiculars to *cl* at *d*, *a*, A.

Draw a tangent to the circle centre A through the point *b*, where the circle cuts the bridge line. This tangent is parallel to the *cl*, cutting the perpendicular through *d* at *e*. The bass-bar will run from *e* through *d*, perpendicular to *cl*, curving away to meet the edge of the soundboard at *f*, level with the bridge line.

Draw a line through the points 1, *b*, to meet the edge at *g*. The line *gb* is the first treble bar.

Draw a line from 1 to the point *h*, where the perpendicular through *a* meets the edge. Mark *k*, where this line meets the bridge line, *hk* is the second treble bar.

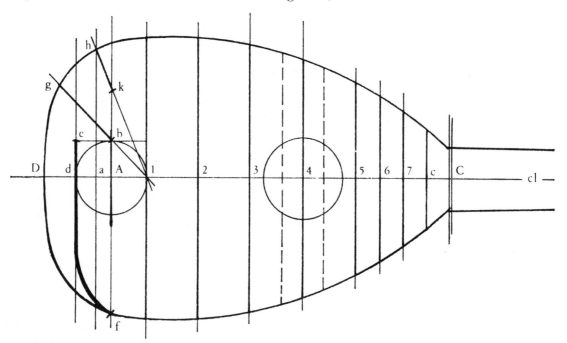

Fig. 2.9   *Marking out the soundboard*

17. *The Rose*

A lute soundhole is never an empty circular cut-out like that of a modern guitar; indeed, it is one of the few places where the early makers allowed themselves scope for decoration. The 'rose' is an intricate pattern pierced in the wood of the soundboard, carved in low relief, and often surrounded by an ornamental border. Its function is not only visual, however, for it affects the stiffness of the soundboard and thus the way in which it vibrates. This in turn influences the tone quality of the whole instrument.

Broadly speaking, lute rose designs fall into two categories: the 'geometrical' and the 'freehand'. Both types are symmetrical, with the pattern repeated in each quadrant of the circle. Rather surprisingly, surviving lutes show relatively few distinct rose types, which has led to the supposition that the makers may have bought ready-carved soundboards. Some experts have disputed this, pointing out that makers would require many different sizes to suit various models of lute. Be that as it may, the modern luthier must design and cut his own rose.

Fortunately, good photographs of lute roses are shown in books on musical instruments, which may be adapted and scaled as required. Many of the geometrical type are based on the interaction of two six-pointed stars, sometimes with the resulting openings intertwined with patterns of foliage. As a guide, a basic geometrical pattern is given at Fig. 10, which may either be used as it is, or modified as the maker desires. It is given at full size for the lute design previously described; other sizes of instrument will of course need different rose dimensions.

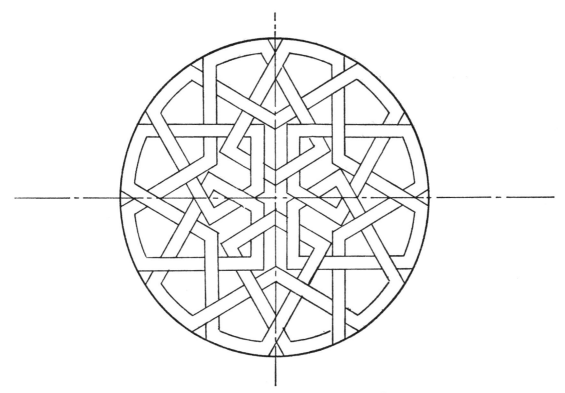

Fig. 2.10 *Rose pattern, a basic geometric design*

The paper pattern may be cut out and glued on the underside of the soundboard with its centre at the bar 4 position and its axis along the centre line. Placing the soundboard on a flat hard board, the rose may be cut out with a sharp knife such as a scalpel, using a steel rule to guide the point along the straight lines. Some workers find this troublesome and may prefer to use a very fine fretsaw or jewellers' piercing-saw. This involves drilling a small hole in each opening through which to insert the blade. Whichever method is used, extreme care is necessary to avoid chipping out any portion of the pattern, in order to achieve a clean and exact result.

The soundboard may now be turned over to cut the relief giving the 'over-and-under' effect shown on the drawing. An added refinement is to cut one or two v-shaped channels along each part, which requires further skill and patience. If desired a circular border may be added, using a sharpened pair of dividers or a special tool such as a guitar soundhole-cutter. These borders often have criss-cross chip-carving decoration; all of which can be best understood by looking at an early or good reproduction instrument.

18. *Barring*

The next step is to prepare and attach the bars in the positions marked. The main bars can all be the same thickness, about 4 or 5 mm, but the depths vary. Bar 3 is the deepest bar, at about 2.5 cm. Bar 5 is about the same or slightly less; 6 and 7 are about 2 cm deep; next in depth come Nos. 1 and 2 at 1.5 cm or so and finally No. 4 at about 1 cm. To support the rose two further bars are equally spaced the same height as bar 4 but only 2 or 3 mm thick. These are glued across the horizontal lines of the pattern, where they show least. Their approximate positions are shown by the dotted lines in Fig. 9.

On old lutes the grain nearly always runs across the bars, not up and down as on a modern violin bass-bar. It seems most likely that they were cut off the edges of the sound-board before it was planed, and this is still a good source of wood for lute barring. The upright grain would have structural advantages, it is true, as the risk of splitting would be minimized.

Cut the bars and plane to the correct depths, leaving a generous length. The edge must be quite straight and flat where it is to be glued to the soundboard. The opposite edge is lightly chamfered after gluing.

The problem of good adhesion to the soundboard can be overcome by a combination of weights and G-cramps.[1]

Proceed with pairs of bars of equal height, starting with the shallowest, which are those across the rose. Begin with bar 4 itself plus one of the others, then weight the third one with 4 again. Proceed with bars 1 and 2; bars 6 and 7; and finally 3 and 5. The weight and blocks keep the centre in contact with the soundboard, and the cramps attend to the edges. Some makers blacken the parts of the bars across the rose so that they will not obtrude into the pattern.

As extra strengthening and stiffening of the soundboard under the rose, early lutes almost invariably have a number of very small bars, 1.5 to 2 mm square, glued across and extending 15 to 20 mm beyond the circumference. These are held in position by scorching the ends with a hot iron to melt and then harden the glue. Once both ends are secure the rest will dry naturally. This method is employed when using animal or Scotch glue; if a different adhesive is used some other cramping method must be devised.

When all the bars are firmly glued, the ends must be trimmed, as shown in Fig. 11. Cut the curve first with a sharp trimming knife or scalpel, and then trim to the line with a fine back-saw. The angle of the end piece should correspond with the uppermost ribs, to which they will be glued. Continue to trim the ends little by little with the knife until they are just inside the line of the body drawn on the soundboard. Keep trying the body, until it just slides into place over the ends of the bars without forcing. Check for kinks in the outline, and make sure that each end of every bar is firmly in contact with the rib. If by any chance you have cut one too short, build it up again with a scrap of wood until it is exactly right. Nothing looks worse than a lute with a wobbly outline! In the last stages, when all appears to be well, draw round the body again and check the new line on the soundboard with the old one. This will show any irregularities very clearly.

---

1. See also method described in Ch. 4, p. 125, and Fig. 4.2. [Ed.]

19. *Alignment and Assembly*

When the outline and fit are satisfactory, the soundboard may be cut out, leaving about 2 mm outside the line round the whole body except at the neck. At this point the sound-board traditionally overlaps the neck, to a distance of about 2 cm beyond the actual body/neck-joint. Mark this on the soundboard and cut exactly to the line. Now check the whole instrument for alignment. Screw the neck tightly in place on the body; then put the soundboard on and secure with adhesive tape. Make sure the neck centre line coincides with the soundboard join, and mark the soundboard end across the neck. To ensure that the bars are in close contact with the sides, mark their position lightly in pencil on the ribs. Cut a number of small blocks about 10 mm square by 3 mm or so, and tape these over the bar end positions, as shown in Fig. 11.

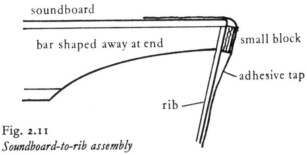

Fig. 2.11
Soundboard-to-rib assembly

Check first that the soundboard is flat, lengthwise and across. If the bars are too long, pushing the sides of the body out, there will be a dip in the centre; if they are too short there will be a hump. Check also that there is no twist in the soundboard, and if necessary correct by trimming the high spot on the rib. Once this is flat, the neck align-ment too can be checked. The centre line on the neck and the soundboard centre join should form a continuous straight line when viewed from above. From the side, there should be a gap equal to the soundboard thickness between straight-edge and neck surface. The neck should tilt neither back nor forward.

If the neck position is not correct, the instrument must be disassembled, the end of the neck trimmed, and reassembled. Do *not* trim the body, as this will make the surface too large for the neck. A very fine trim with the block-plane will be sufficient, taking more from the curved side to move the neck back and from the flat top to move up. Finish with a stroke or two right across and make sure the surface is quite flat.

When the neck angle is correct, the joint may be glued. Remove the screw, wipe each surface with a rag dipped in carbon tetrachloride to remove any trace of oil or grease, apply PVA glue or synthetic resin glue to one surface and screw up. Wipe off the excess that squeezes out with a damp rag and check alignment once more. If it is wrong, take it apart at once and try again. Leave to dry thoroughly.

The soundboard should be attached with old-fashioned hot animal glue, preparation of which is described in Chapter 1, p. 18f. Apply this with a glue brush or a stick of scrap wood to the ends of all the bars. The end-grain will soak up the glue, so do not stint! Leave these to dry hard.

The next operation is to attach the soundboard to the body. The glue can be thinner than is usual for general joinery. There is a considerable length of thin edge to join, and it would not be possible to keep the glue hot all the way throughout the operation. The principle, therefore, is to apply the glue to both body and soundboard, letting it cool and solidify slightly. The surfaces are then brought together and held lightly in place with adhesive tape. Heat is applied, melting the glue once more so that it flows together. While still melted, the surfaces are cramped together. The whole process is analogous to soldering, but the heat is applied by a normal domestic iron, together with a damp rag to avoid scorching the wood and to provide more moisture for the glue.

Begin at the neck overlap, where the centre line can be aligned and the soundboard brought exactly to the line drawn across the neck. Attach the soundboard to the instrument with a few pieces of tape. The joint can be cramped here, using a flat piece of wood over the soundboard top and protecting the surfaces with foam-plastic or cardboard. Have a trial run first!

Set the domestic iron to the middle of its heat-range, fold the damp rag into a flat pad about three layers thick and lay this on the overlap, not forgetting the neck-block inside the body. Place the iron flat on the cloth, and hold there for three or four seconds. This should be sufficient to send the steam and heat into the soundboard and to melt the glue. Cramp together, making sure that the soundboard does not slide on the hot glue. Check the alignment of centre line, centre joint and neck line. Leave to set, unless you have a helper. The whole thing becomes very unwieldy with a heavy cramp in place, and it is a pity to drop it all on the floor at this stage!

Remove the cramp when the glue is dry and check once more that all is well. The alignment of the whole instrument should still be correct. Now work downwards from the neck end little by little on each side alternately, working symmetrically. This will help to avoid distortion. Allow the damp rag to overhang the edge, which will help to melt the glue really thoroughly, and take special care at the ends of the bars, which must be firmly stuck to the ribs to avoid rattles and buzzing in playing. Fasten the soundboard to the body with tape, working first at the bar positions and using little blocks as previously mentioned. There is no need for blocks between the bars, as they may tend to push the sides in. Use 10-mm tape, and put strips really close to each other to give even pressure. Work gradually round the body and check that the *cl* on the end still matches the soundboard join. A millimetre or so either way will not matter, but aim to be as precise as possible. Take special care that the top is well down on to the three thicknesses at the bottom (rib fastener, rib points and capping strip), for the tension of the strings on the bridge will tend to lift it at this point. When all this is done, check once more that the joint is really tightly down all round, and leave to dry thoroughly.

Removing all the tape when the glue is hard can be tricky, as the grain of the softwood soundboard, and sometimes even of the maple, can easily be pulled up. The solution is to use a damp rag to release the tape, as described earlier.

The soundboard edge is now trimmed carefully to the sides with a trimming knife, plane, and fine sanding block. Smooth off the edge to avoid it digging in too much to the arm and thighs when playing! Finally, clean off any remaining glue with a warm damp rag.

20. *The Fingerboard*

In Renaissance lutes the fingerboard is usually flat, and must be made from a hard wood to withstand the wear from the left-hand fingers. Ebony or rosewood are both very satisfactory, and the contrast of colour with the pale soundboard is most attractive. Some old instruments have light-coloured fingerboards of boxwood or maple, and sometimes pearwood is used to match the bridge. Traditionally, the fingerboard overlapped the soundboard on to the neck-block, finishing in two fine 'points', as shown in Fig. 12. These points often extend as far as the bottom of the neck-block, but this is not good practice as cracks nearly always start from them and run down towards the rose.

Cut and plane a piece of the chosen timber, leaving all dimensions oversize, including the thickness. Place it in position and draw the edges of the neck lines with a fine pencil. Extend these lines to the length of point required. Draw a line across, to mark the soundboard extension and draw two lines from the lower end parallel to the edges. Mark the curve of the points[1] themselves and cut out to the lines.

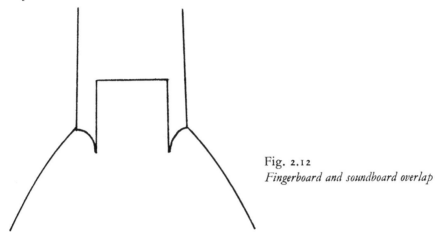

Fig. 2.12
Fingerboard and soundboard overlap

Position the points exactly on the soundboard overlap, and draw round with a sharp hard pencil. Cut the shape of the points out of the soundboard as deep as the block with a scalpel and ensure that the points fit exactly. Apply PVA glue to the neck surface, insert points and attach the fingerboard. Do not put the glue on the fingerboard itself as this will dampen one side and cause it to curve. Secure the fingerboard with adhesive tape at the edges, in a similar way to the soundboard assembly method. Clamp with G-cramps and a piece of wood faced with foam-plastic or cork; protect the back of the neck similarly.

21. *The Bridge*

The traditional lute bridge is quite different from that of the modern guitar, for there is no 'saddle' over which the string passes to form the termination of the vibrating portion. Instead, the bridge is much smaller and lighter, and a loop of the string itself forms the end of the free length.

The 'action', or string height, of the lute, should be as low as possible, provided the string does not buzz on the frets when stopped. The amplitude of vibration of the thicker bass strings is greater than that of the thinner trebles, and the string height is correspondingly greater on the bass side. This means that the bridge, too, is lower at the treble side than at the bass. Sixteenth-century bridges always use a minimum of wood, and the width is also less at the treble end than at the bass. A full-size drawing of the bridge is

1. Although the two 'points' are made from the same piece of timber as the fingerboard, they are often cut and fitted separately, the advantages of which will be obvious as the work proceeds. [Ed.]

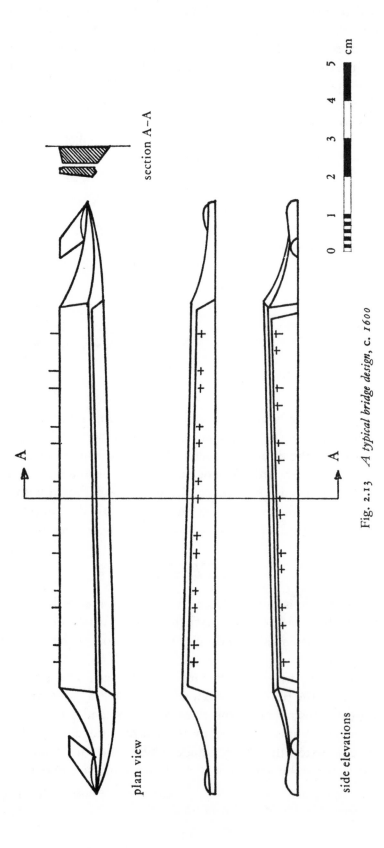

plan view

section A–A

side elevations

Fig. 2.13　A typical bridge design, c. 1600

given at Fig. 13, using the string spacings given earlier and allowing for a string height of 4 mm at the treble rising to 6 mm at the bass. Very hard woods such as box and rosewood should be avoided for bridges as their rigidity tends to make them lift up from the soundboard as it 'settles' over a period of time. Pearwood is very suitable, both for its working properties and flexibility, and is not so soft that the strings can pull through.

Drilling the 1.5 mm holes for the strings without wandering can be achieved by careful and accurate marking on both front and back *before* the bridge blank is tapered, pricking the centres. The holes are then drilled on a drill stand, to half the total depth from each side. They should then meet in the middle.

The heights for the holes are given as a guide, assuming that the alignment of the neck and soundboard is exact. In fact, any slight discrepancy in this respect will make an appreciable difference to the string height unless it is compensated at this stage. Once the bridge is fitted the possible string height adjustment is very limited indeed, and this is the reason why fitting the bridge should be left until after the instrument is assembled. It would be much easier to clamp the bridge in position on the soundboard earlier but there would then be no possibility of adjustment.

From a piece of scrap wood make a wedge tapering from about 3 mm to 10 mm. Mark the thickness in 0.5 mm steps. Place this on the soundboard at the bridge position and stretch a piece of cotton down the centre line from the nut position to the wedge. Check the height of the cotton above the fingerboard at the body/neck-join. This should not be more than about 3 or 4 mm. Move the wedge until this height is obtained and check the corresponding wedge height. This will be the height for the string-hole line in the centre of the bridge. The treble hole should be 1 mm lower than this and the bass 1 mm higher, giving a rise of 2 mm over the whole bridge.

This control over string height can only be used with discretion. If the neck is leaning back to such an extent a very high bridge is required, the bending moment applied to the soundboard by the strings will be excessive and will cause buckling and may pull the bridge off. A high bridge makes right-hand playing technique very difficult, too. If the neck is too far forward, even a very low bridge will not lower the action sufficiently, and can give the player the feeling of scratching the soundboard, which is most inhibiting.

The soundboards of old lutes were hardly ever varnished; neither were those of guitars until comparatively recently. If this precedent is to be followed, the bridge may now be glued to the soundboard; if not, the bridge should be set aside until after varnishing. No glue will attach a bridge to a contaminated soundboard, so the surface under the bridge position must be protected from contamination with varnish of whatever sort. The bridge is held exactly in position by hand, and its outline traced with a hard pencil, having first placed a strip of masking tape on to the soundboard beneath the bridge. Carefully cut round the line, being sure not to cut into the wood! Remove the tape from outside the line, leaving the shape of the bridge in place. The soundboard can then be smoothly varnished, covering the tape, as desired. When completely dry the tape can be peeled off, leaving clean wood on which to attach the bridge.

Most PVA glues are unsuitable for gluing the bridge because of the creeping tendency already mentioned. [See also Chapter 6, p. 168. Ed.] Animal glue is satisfactory, but it is necessary to work very fast before it cools and gels. Epoxy resins are fine, but in this case bridge and soundboard should be degreased with carbon tetrachloride (CCl_4) before joining. Some one-shot synthetic glues are also satisfactory.

One method of cramping the bridge during gluing is as follows: take two straight lengths of wood about 2 cm square, rather longer than the string length, say 65 cm. Lay a piece of scrap wood of about the same thickness as the bridge across the fingerboard at the nut end. The glued bridge is placed carefully in position, and the two lengths of timber placed along the neck to overlap the bridge. A small piece of wood is placed across these lengths at about the neck/body-joint, and a cramp is tightened between this and the neck, with the same protecting piece as was used for making that joint.

Check the bridge carefully to make sure that excess glue is being evenly squeezed out all round. Pressure on one end or the other can be increased by packing thin pieces of wood between the bridge and the length of timber. Leave cramped until the critical moment when the glue is set enough for the bridge to be firm but not so much that the excess cannot be removed. Clean up round the bridge with appropriate solvent.

22. *Finishing*

There are basically two ways of darkening wood during finishing: either by staining or by applying a coloured varnish. A combination of both may also be used. Certain precautions are necessary with both methods, which are not always understood, so a few words here may be helpful.

Spirit stain can be very effective, and in general is fairly easy to apply evenly. But it does penetrate the surface, and this can lead to problems with figured woods such as sycamore. The 'flame' in this wood is produced by a curly grain, and this gives the characteristic 'sheen', which varies according to the direction of the light. Unfortunately, stain penetrates to a different depth in some parts of the curl, thus 'killing' the rippling effect. This unfortunate result varies from one piece of timber to another, and is more pronounced with darker stains than with light. Any staining proposed should therefore be tested *on a piece of the same wood* before risking the lute itself. Also, the stain will penetrate more into a softwood soundboard,[1] which will turn out slightly darker than a hardwood body with a given shade applied. Proceed, therefore, with caution, and be quite sure of the effect before risking the instrument itself.

Coloured varnishes, too, have advantages and disadvantages. They are not so easy to apply evenly without streaks, and again the difficulties increase with darkness of colour. A coloured varnish should not be applied on bare wood, as it will soak in to a varying extent with changes in the grain, and can 'kill' the figure in sycamore or maple as effectively as can spirit stain. A clear sealer should be used first, giving enough coats to seal the surface. If the first coat is thinned considerably, it will penetrate the pores of the wood more effectively than if left thicker.

Once the surface of the wood is sealed, coloured varnish will no longer act as a stain and may be safely applied. The essential skill is to keep a 'wet edge', so that the brush-strokes flow evenly into each other without leaving a hard tacky line. For musical instruments, many commercial varnishes are too thick and will need to be appropriately diluted. Experience will show when a consistency is reached which flows freely and covers evenly.

A proper brush is essential if varnishing is to be carried out successfully, and these are not usually obtainable from the ordinary hardware shop. Firms who specialize in

1. See the remarks in Chapter 1, p. 33. [Ed.]

wood finishes should be able to supply flat 'lacquer' brushes, which can be obtained in a variety of widths, and artists' colourmen may also stock suitable squirrel-hair brushes. The essential point is to have fine soft hairs, and the ordinary household paint or varnish brush, of however good a quality, simply will not do.

Always work with the grain of the wood, whether it be along the soundboard or along the ribs of the back. Take special care at the edges of all surfaces, and at the angles of joints between one part and the next. The varnish will tend to collect in blobs at all 'inside' angles and to run away from the 'outside' ones. Do not be tempted to touch up a blemish after a coat of varnish has become tacky. The result will always be more unsightly than the original blemish and will be much more difficult to repair.

Work in as dust-free an atmosphere as possible. Avoid draughts, which stir up dust everywhere and cause uneven drying or even a milky 'bloom' on the surface. Any stray brush-hairs should be removed immediately. They can usually be lifted with a corner of the brush itself, and the area smoothed again as brushing continues.

Excellent results can be obtained with oil or spirit varnishes, with french polish, or even with modern polyurethane lacquer. An interesting possibility for soundboards is the use of an egg tempera emulsion with linseed oil and water. The type of finish has almost no effect on the tone quality of an instrument such as the lute, and in general old lutes have appreciably less varnish than contemporary viols and violins. Indeed, soundboards, as we have seen, often appear not to have been varnished at all. For the inexperienced, I would recommend a polyurethane finish, and will describe its application. The expert maker may well spurn such advice in favour of something more traditional.

First rub down the instrument with a fine paper: garnet or flour paper. It is most important to remove all traces of glue from the surface of every part. These, although they do not show much 'in the white', will spoil the appearance of the finished product. Close inspection all over is the only way, holding the lute up to reflect the light so that the slight sheen of a patch of glue can be seen. Points to watch are places where adhesive tape has been used: between ribs, along the soundboard edge, to secure the pegbox, etc., where glue may have squeezed out and spread under the tape.

After the first rub-down with fine paper, apply a very slightly damp rag over ribs, neck and pegbox. This will show up any glue-spots missed, and will slightly raise the grain. When the moisture has quite dried out, repeat the rubbing-down process. Wipe off all dust once more with a slightly damp rag.

Pour out a small quantity of *clear* polyurethane lacquer and dilute half-and-half with white spirit (or any other recommended solvent). Apply this all over the instrument, beginning (if required) with the soundboard, covering the adhesive-tape bridge shield. Next, cover the back of the instrument, working along the ribs and making sure there are neither overlaps nor gaps between ribs. Pay special attention to the edge of the capping strip, and make sure there are no runs at the neck-joint or on to the soundboard. Next, deal with the pegbox, which is a fiddly item, making sure there are no runs at the peg-holes. If necessary, clean them out with a twist of paper. Check for runs at all inside corners and at the joint with the neck. Now insert a tuning peg into one of the holes, and hold the instrument by it. Varnish the back of the neck, making sure, once again, that there are no runs. Leave the instrument to dry, hanging up by its single peg.

The thin first-sealing coat may well appear to have soaked in and dried almost at once, *particularly on the soundboard*. Nevertheless, it should be left for the recommended time between coats (polyurethane should not be left too *long* between successive applications, either, since if curing proceeds too far the later coat will not 'key' to the previous one, and may lift on rubbing down). After drying, the surface will probably feel slightly rough again, partly due to slight lifting of the grain and partly due to inevitable dust particles.

Before proceeding to a second coat of clear lacquer, examine the soundboard to see if it is adequately sealed. If it is desired to leave it with the appearance of untreated wood, it is advisable to stop now, but if the varnish has for any reason not completely covered the board a second coat may be necessary. For all the rest of the instrument, proceed exactly as before, once again finishing by lightly rubbing down with fine garnet or flour paper.

Varnishing proper can now begin with coloured lacquer. Some slight thinning may still be necessary, but this depends obviously on the original viscosity. The object now is to build up a certain depth of colour, and excessive thinning will slow down the process. On the other hand, if the varnish is too thick, it may be difficult to apply evenly without streaks. If there is any doubt, wipe off *at once* with a rag dipped in white spirit. This will remove the offending coat without affecting the previous clear sealing coats.

Opinions vary about rubbing down between coats at this stage. Personally, with polyurethane I only rub down if there is a particular reason; an undetected brush-hair, or a particularly large speck of dust, for example. Rubbing down will remove some of the thickness of varnish, and result in a lighter shade of colour. To rub down to exactly the same depth all over is almost impossible, and I prefer to proceed direct from coat to coat unless rubbing down is essential.

Four or five coloured coats should be sufficient, and these are followed by a couple of clear coats to finish. The instrument should then be left to dry thoroughly before the final rubbing down and polishing. This rubbing down, which should affect only the top coats of clear varnish, is done with the finest available 'wet-and-dry' paper, no coarser than grade 600, used wet, with very little pressure from the hand. The aim should be to obtain a uniform 'flat' surface, free from bumps or pits. The process should be done slowly and carefully, as even the finest paper will remove varnish from a sharp corner if applied in a harsh manner.

When the desired matt surface has been obtained, the final polish can be brought up by a liquid metal-polish or rubbing compound such as rottenstone. Any degree of shine can be secured from the initial matt to a mirror gloss, and this is entirely a matter of personal choice.

Those who wish to use more traditional methods are referred to the chapters on violin and viol.

23. *Pegs*

Until recently it was impossible to obtain ready-made lute pegs, and it was always necessary to make them oneself. Those who have access to a lathe may still continue to do so, but fortunately there are now specialist suppliers. The tension of the string is held by the fit of the tapered peg in an identically-tapered hole, and this again has been a problem. Violin makers have found by experience that a taper angle of 1 in 30 is very satisfactory, and various sorts of reamers are available for this purpose. The drawback is that lute pegs need to be much longer than fiddle pegs, and the large end would be far too thick if a violin reamer were used. Many lute makers therefore made use of an engineering taper-pin reamer, which uses a standard 'Morse' taper of 1 in 48, and can be obtained in a variety of diameters. These have two disadvantages: the angle is so slight that pegs very soon wear into the pegbox, and have to protrude rather far initially to last a reasonable length of time; also, the reamers, being intended for metal, have the cutting 'flutes' all round the shank which, when used in wood, can produce juddering and an unevenly shaped hole. Wood reamers should have half the circumference plain, and the other half fluted.

Fortunately, such reamers are now available in the 1-in-30 taper, with a much smaller starting diameter than the violin reamer. These are available in a number of sizes suitable for lutes, viols, citterns and virtually all stringed instruments.

The taper is, of course, the most important aspect of the peg from a functioning point of view, but the head must also be comfortable to use efficiently. There should never be any necessity for the clumsy 'bottle-opener' gadget provided with some instruments. Peg shapes are best studied in early paintings, as there are very few surviving instruments with their original ones. Two basic types which are often depicted are the 'heart-shape' and the 'crescent'. Both are sometimes seen with a small 'bobble' in the centre.

Pegs should be of a hard wood: box is a favourite for early instruments, plumwood, rosewood and ebony are often found later.[1] Beech or sycamore, stained black, are also very satisfactory.

When turning pegs it is essential to work from a master pattern for both the head and the taper; if each one is copied from the previous one there may be an astonishing variation between the first and the last! Personally, I prefer to work with the peg-head towards the headstock and the point towards the tail. Ordinary wood-turning tools can be used perfectly well, but if a metalwork lathe is available the cross-slide will come in very useful for the tapers. If not, it is best to turn the point, middle and top of the shank accurately to size, checking from the master with callipers, using the parting tool, and to 'fill in' the rest of the length with the gouge and straight chisel. If the tool-rest is set at the taper angle, the left-hand thumb can guide the tools and avoid any unevenness.

However accurately the taper is turned, it is advisable to finish it with a special shaper in the form of a giant pencil-sharpener. These, like reamers, can now be purchased, or one can be made from a block of scrap hardwood and an old plane iron or other piece of tool steel.

When fitting the finished pegs to the lute, proceed with caution and at first leave at least 15 mm of shank protruding from the pegbox. When all the pegs are inserted they can be made exactly even.[2]

24. *The Nut*

As this is the last item that 'gets in the way' of finishing the instrument, it is often given cavalier treatment by amateur makers. Nevertheless, on its correct shape and height a

1. See *The Burwell Lute Tutor*, Leeds, facs. 1974.
2. See also Chapter 1, p. 17.

great deal depends, and it should be treated with great respect. The strings of a lute have to bend round a considerable angle at the nut, and any tendency to bind in the slots can be very wasteful of strings and temper. Also a nut that is too high makes playing very difficult for the left hand.

It is essential for the strings to have a smooth passage over the nut, without any kinks or steps, and the nut must be hard enough for the strings not to dig in. After various experiments over many years I have found that the traditionally shaped ivory nut works as well as any of the more elaborate versions I have tried.

The groove need only be very shallow; enough to locate the string in its correct position and no more. Deep slots make added friction and cause binding. Make sure there is no step or kink where the groove runs out into the 'cushion' or curved portion. The grooves may be marked with a sharp knife and filed with a fine oval Swiss file. When all is satisfactory completed the entire surface, particularly the grooves, should be polished. Ivory polishes very well with a metal polish. A few pieces of scrap gut strings may be used to get the polish into the grooves themselves.

25. *Frets*

In common with other gut-strung instruments, bowed and plucked, the lute was fitted with movable gut frets, tied round the neck at semitone intervals. Metal frets were well known, and a very sophisticated method of inserting them was developed for wire-strung instruments such as the cittern, so there is no doubt that gut frets were a deliberate choice for gut-strung instruments. Modern players using nylon strings usually use nylon also for fretting, though nylon is harder to tie really tightly.

The various sets of instruction for fret placing from the Renaissance show that the modern system of equal semitones throughout was not in general use in earlier times. The easy assumption that the present system is obviously better has been questioned recently, and those interested should consult the literature. For everyday purposes, however, it is probably best to place the frets according to 'equal temperament' principles, and to make any subsequent adjustments by ear. It is easy to slide a gut fret slightly one way or the other.

An approximation to the correct positions for this is given by the 'rule of eighteen', well known to guitar makers, whereby each successive fret is placed one-eighteenth of the distance from the previous fret to the bridge. This is described in Chapter 4, p. 119. The eighth fret will be the last to be tied on the neck, as has been explained, but much lute music requires higher frets, particularly on the upper strings, and these four are generally made from thin strips of wood glued on to the soundboard from its centre line to just beyond the treble string.

Because of the very low string height of the lute, the thickness of frets was graded, with the thinnest nearest to the bridge. John Dowland's instructions, printed in his son Robert's *Varietie of Lute Lessons* (1610), are very clear: '. . . let the two first frets nearest the head of the instrument (being the greatest) be the size of your Contratenor, then the third and fourth frets must be of the size of your great Meanes: the fift and sixt frets of the size of your small Meanes: and all the rest sized with Trebles. These rules serve also for Viols, or any other kind of instrument whereon frets are tyed.'

Thus frets 1 and 2 are equal to the fourth course in thickness, 3 and 4 to the third,

5 and 6 to the second, and 7 and 8 to the first. It is certainly not correct to set the strings so high that a single gauge of fret throughout is satisfactory.

There are two kinds of tied frets, involving a single or double strand of gut. The double fret was apparently the earlier form, but both are explained below:

(i) *Double Frets* (Fig. 14a)

Pass a loop of gut over the fingerboard from bass to treble.

Bring the loop underneath the neck back towards the bass side.

Loop the longer end through the original loop, and pass the short end through the new loop.

Pull both ends tight, using pliers if necessary.

Push the fret up towards its final position, which will stretch the gut and help it to bed down.

Bring it back towards the nut and tighten again.

Tie a half-hitch with the two ends, and trim them to about 5 mm in length.

Singe the ends with a flame, as described on p. 66, and push the frets into position.

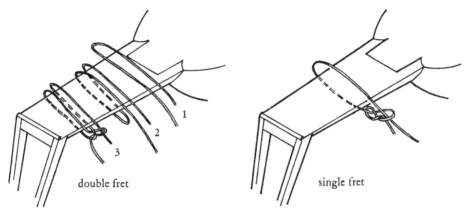

double fret   single fret

Fig. 2.14 *Tying double* (a) *and single* (b) *frets for lutes and viols*

(ii) *Single Frets* (Fig. 14b)

Pass a single length of gut over fingerboard from bass to treble.

Bring it underneath the neck back towards the bass side.

Pass the short end under the long end, then over it again.

Continue over itself, under, over and out beside the long end to make a figure-of-eight knot as shown.

Pull both ends tight with pliers, after which the short end may be left. Pull again on the long end to tighten the knot still further. Slide towards final position to stretch the fret; bring back towards the nut and tighten again.

Tie a half-hitch with the two ends, and trim to about 5 mm in length.

Singe the ends as before, and push into final position.

With both single and double frets, it is advisable to tie them nearer to the nut than their eventual position. As they are slid into their proper places they will then tighten still further. This effect depends, of course, on the taper of the neck and the stretching of the fret material. In general, nylon needs a distance of three or more frets to be fully tight, whereas gut needs only one or two. Particular care has to be exercised with the first fret, which besides being thick has least distance to travel. With double frets it is advisable to tighten and slide up several times to stretch the material *before* tying the final half-hitch. This is especially effective with gut.

Once the frets are finally in position, the ends may be trimmed with a pair of nail clippers, to within about 5 mm of the knot. The sharp ends so formed, which tend to catch in clothes, may be rounded by lightly singeing with a flame. This will cause gut to swell and nylon to melt into a blob. Nylon may tend to catch fire with a blue flame, but this is easily blown out! The resulting blob or fraying is quite smooth and also prevents any tendency for the fret-knot to come undone.

26. *Stringing*

The normal material for lute strings in Europe has always been gut, either plain or, from the second half of the seventeenth century, wire-wound. When the modern revival began, thin gut for the treble strings was hard to get and very unreliable, and some players used silk. For the bass strings, guitarists were using a stranded silk core with wire winding, and these were also adopted by lutenists. After the Second World War, mono-filament nylon strings were introduced for all kinds of plucked instruments, and they proved very successful for the guitar, though less so for other instruments such as the harp. Nylon can be produced very accurately to any given thickness, so that really true strings were available at a fraction of the cost of good gut strings. The effect of temperature and humidity on nylon is much less than on gut, so that tuning stability in changeable weather conditions was at last obtained. In a very short time nylon strings almost completely superseded gut for the guitar.

The quite sensational advantages of nylon strings tended to obscure the drawbacks. The physical and chemical properties of the two materials are quite different, resulting in a different 'feel', to the player and a different tone colour to the sound. Much more important, however, is the fact that nylon can be tuned much higher for a given string length without breaking. This had little effect in the case of the guitar, where the string length of a 'classical' Spanish instrument was well established.[1]

The situation with the lute, however, was and is quite different. Instruments survive in a bewildering variety of sizes, which were originally undoubtedly intended to be tuned to different pitches. The highest note to which the top string of these instruments was tuned was originally very closely fixed by the breaking pitch of gut strings. But with nylon the situation is quite different, and an instrument can be tuned a fourth or more higher than gut strings of the same length. There are thus many lutes being played today as tenor instruments (treble string at g') which must have been intended as bass lutes (top string at d'). This applies not only to old instruments, but to modern ones as well, where the demand for 'powerful' tone has persuaded makers to produce lutes of very large dimensions.

The use of nylon strings produces a change in sound on a given instrument even if the pitch is kept constant. By tuning a large lute to a pitch that would have been impossible with gut an even greater distortion is introduced, for the whole acoustic system is changed.

1. See Chapter 4, p. 117.

There is no point in using an old instrument, or in building a new one on 'authentic' principles, if we then totally alter the physical conditions of its use.

To sum up, nylon may well be used on lutes owing to its durability and stability, but these advantages should not blind us to the dangers outlined above. Exciting experimental work in the revival of authentic strings for Renaissance instruments is proceeding, and it is now possible to obtain satisfactory gut once again.[1]

1. Djilda Abbott and Ephraim Segerman, 'Strings in the 16th and 17th Centuries', *Galpin Society Journal*, XXVII, 1974, p. 48; Abbott and Segerman, 'Gut Strings', *Early Music*, Vol. IV, No. iv, p. 430.

3

The Violin

ADAM PAUL

1. *Introduction*

The system described in this chapter is the method I was taught while at the International School of Violin-making in Cremona. After leaving, I decided to make instruments using the original Stradivari system, which is accurate but at the same time allows a great deal of artistic freedom. My use of the Strad pattern is intended as a sound basis for the violin family; I do not try to imitate Stradivari but hope that my own character will emerge. I have carried out a number of repairs in the past which have been very helpful in learning to avoid repetition of faults, which, though they may remain hidden for some time, will eventually show up later in the life of the instrument. The Baroque instrument discussed on p. 98 was built specially for an exhibition to show the various differences between the Baroque and the modern violin. It proved an enormously interesting and valuable project.

2. *The Models*

When making a violin it is advisable to obtain a reliable model, or to copy an original instrument, as it takes experience to make one's own models. It is best to cut out the model in paper first but the final template can be made in either zinc, plastic, formica, plywood, or cardboard.

If you are building your first violin, I suggest that you use the drawings provided and make your templates by tracing these shapes on to thin plywood. Then cut these templates out very accurately with a fretsaw so that, when placed on the timber you wish to cut, and drawn round, they exactly reproduce the given drawings. If an original instrument is copied, it may be worn in various places so remember to correct this on your plan. Draw all your models first and check the measurements seeing that they are aesthetically correct; measure all curved surfaces accurately. When making a model for the body or for the soundhole, draw half the body and one soundhole only. The drawing can then be turned over and a symmetrical model will be obtained. It is important to incorporate the characteristics of the maker, such as the style of the scroll and the shape of the f-holes. Measurements must be extremely accurate. If a measurement is out by 1 mm, when the instrument is finished it may contain errors of up to 5 mm. When making a model of your own, remember to consider the player's requirements by giving adequate string spacing at the nut and bridge, for example, to facilitate the player's technique. In this respect you can do no better than to copy an original instrument for you can be sure

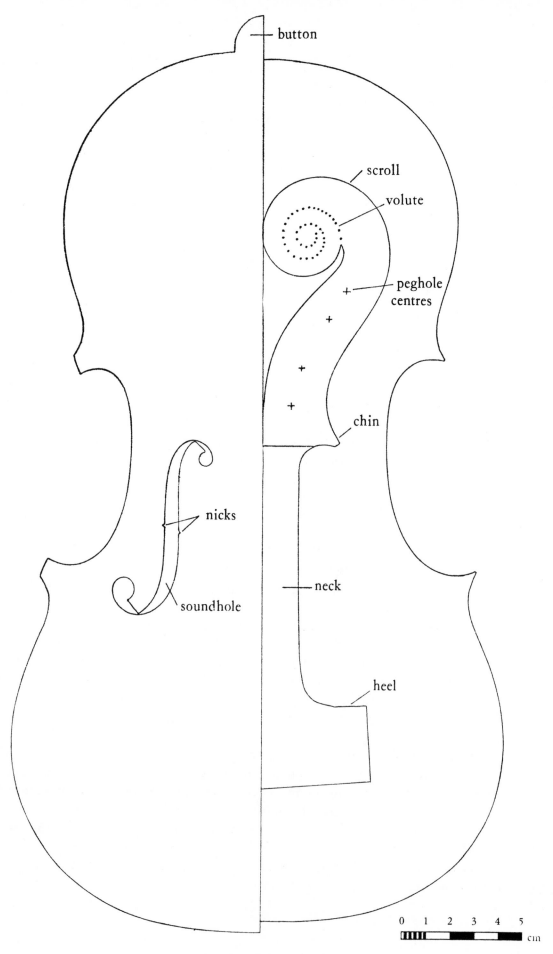

button

scroll

volute

peghole
centres

chin

nicks

soundhole

neck

heel

0 1 2 3 4 5
cm

Fig. 3.1   *The violin design*

that such details as neck thicknesses, string spacing and so on have been finally arrived at after years of experience with both violins and players.

To make the model for the outline of the violin, take a piece of paper larger and longer than the violin and fold it in half. Cut out a bottle shape, open up the paper and place it on an instrument rest and place the instrument on top. Adjust the paper so that the centre of the violin sits on the centre of the paper without folding the paper and draw round the outline. Remove the violin and, using dividers, ensure that the bouts are of the correct width, after which cut out the shape. The length of the body will be about 355 mm.

When making a model for the ribs, take the model from the outside of the violin (Fig. 1). Set your dividers at the distance from the outside edge to the inside edge of the ribs, leaving out the thickness of the ribs, and mark round the edge. Cut away with a knife and test with dividers.

A template can be made of the soundhole by using the drawing shown in Fig. 1. However, if you wish to copy the soundhole from an original instrument, then take a piece of paper and place this on the centre line of the violin with an equal amount of paper above and below the soundholes. Dip your finger in pencil-lead filings and rub over the paper on top of the soundholes and the model will appear. Often the edges of the soundholes are uneven or worn, so measure with dividers and correct your model before cutting out. Make sure you clearly mark the nicks in the f-holes. Draw a line at right angles to the centre joint at the soundhole nick for the diapason. The model must be graceful and elegant in relation to the whole instrument and should retain the characteristics of the maker, as previously mentioned.

To copy the scroll (Fig. 1) of an original instrument, take a rectangular piece of paper, the long edge being used as the surface of the neck. All measurements should be transferred to the paper using this edge as the base line. Mark on the paper at right angles to the neck surface where the top of the fingerboard will come. Having removed the pegs, then at the point where the volute comes cut out a circle of paper, allowing the volute to go through the circle to the depth of the pegbox cheeks. Keep the outer edge of the paper on the line of the surface edge of the neck and draw round the outside of the entire scroll. Cut out round the entire scroll and test with dividers, any worn places being corrected by eye. To copy the volute of the scroll is a matter of patient measuring with dividers (Fig. 1). When this has been drawn in, add the neck and heel shape, being sure to mark correctly the angle of the heel, viewed from the side. Finally, transfer all these to your template material, making a series of small holes through the material where the volute comes.

When making a model of the back of the scroll, first take a piece of paper of suitable length and width that can be folded to follow round the scroll from under the chin to the tail. Mark a straight line lightly down the centre of this piece of paper with a knife where it may be folded in half. Cut out pieces of paper at intervals on the folded edge in the form of an inverted 'V' so that, when opened up, it forms a diamond shape through which the centre spine of the scroll can be seen. Fold the paper round under the chin and hold it in place firmly so that the centre of the paper is exactly over the spine of the scroll. Turn the instrument over and draw on both sides of the pegbox and scroll. Remove the paper and cut out.

For the pegbox repeat the same process, marking in the correct length and width of the pegbox and neck together with the fingerboard nut and the top of the fingerboard.

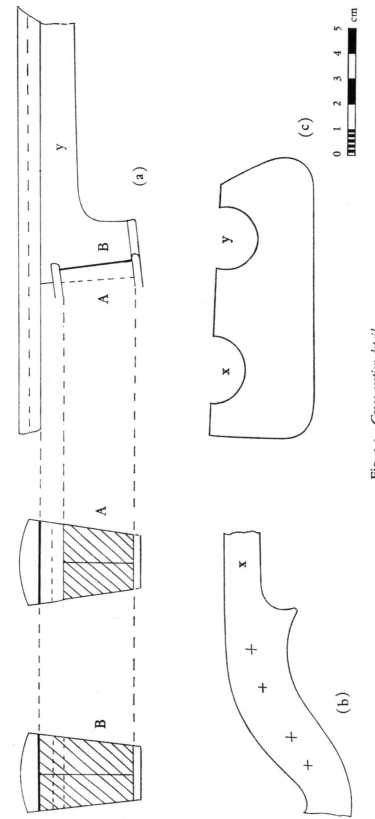

Fig. 3.2 *Cross-section detail*

To make a model for the pegholes (Fig. 1), take the scroll template and place it on a piece of paper. Trace the model from under the chin to just below the tail. Draw a line at right angles to where the top of the fingerboard will come. This line will be used as a guide to ensure that the model is placed in the same position on both sides of the scroll. The distance between the peg centres should be 15–22–15 mm. Mark the correct position of the holes and then make a small hole through the template. It is important to remember that the holes indicate the peg centres. Each string should be able to pass clearly to the nut without touching other pegs or strings.

In order to fit the neck to the body, standard measurements must be used for both the heel of the neck and the body of the instrument. Either the measurements can be drawn straight on to the heel and body, or templates can be made (Fig. 2). Transparent plastic is used for templates so that the centre line of the plastic can be placed over the centre line of either the heel or body. It is essential that the central line of the scroll has been marked on the heel. As already mentioned, when the model for the scroll was originally marked on the template, the angle of the heel, viewed from the side should have been correctly marked before sawing out. The width of the heel, looking towards the scroll, will be governed by two basic measurements: final width of the back button, 22 mm, and the width of the fingerboard at the point where the heel ends, that is to say, where the neck joins the body. The following measurements must be marked on the heel as lines at right angles to the centre mark starting from under the fingerboard: the height above the belly, 6 mm; the thickness of the edge, 4 mm; and the height of the ribs, 30 mm. The width of the button must also be marked on each side of the centre joint at the point where heel and button will touch. A line must now be drawn on either side of the button and marked to the edge of the fingerboard. Following these measurements you can make up a plastic template, making sure that the centre line is at right angles to the top edge of the template which rests under the fingerboard, and that the two angled sides are identical.

The next measurements are for the body of the instrument. The neck should be set in the centre of the top block. However, if the centre of the belly is not the true centre of the instrument, your neck could lean to one side (see p. 91). Therefore, the true centre of the belly must be found by drawing a right-angled line from the back centre joint up to the belly. Mark the following measurements on the rib: the width of the button, and the width of the heel at the point where it will touch the edge of the belly. You can take this latter measurement from the heel. Draw a line on either side from the nut to the top of the edge of the belly. The plastic model can now be made up and cut out using these measurements.

3. *The Wood*

The wood, while vital to the tonal and artistic qualities of the violin, is not of sole importance and must be considered in its relationship to the rest of the violin. Always try to match the whole violin with wood of the same quality and figuration.

When buying wood it is advisable to choose it yourself and measure it to see that it is suitable. The wood can be cut on the 'slab' which means the tree is cut up like a plank. The back is then usually in one piece. The other system used, which is also the most common, is to cut the wood on the 'quarter' in vertical wedges from a cylinder. The

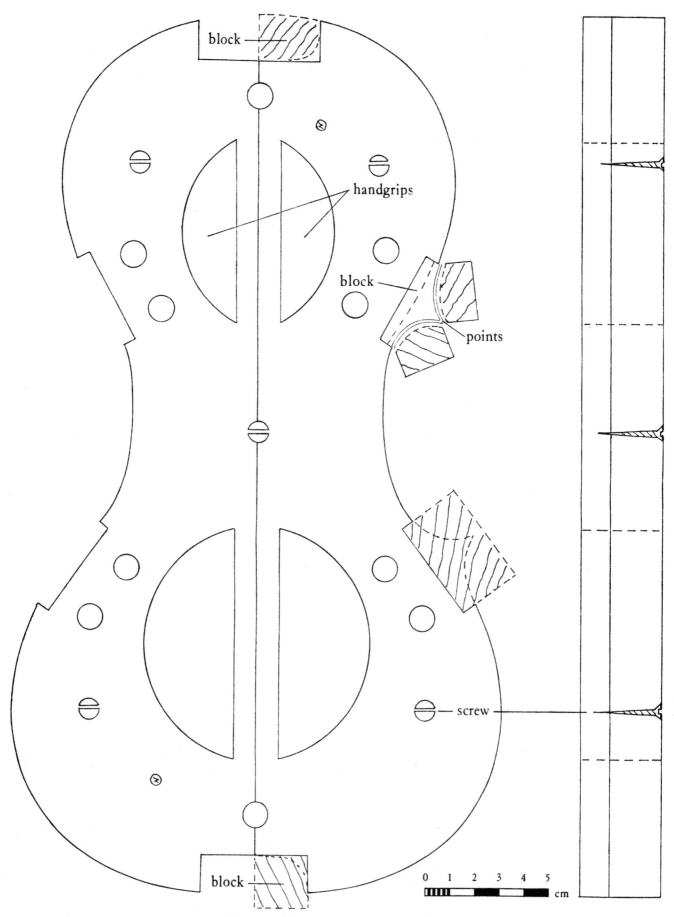

block

handgrips

block

points

screw

0 1 2 3 4 5
cm

Fig. 3.3   *Form or mould and cramping jig*

wood is split down the thick edge, from the outside edge of the tree, and these two outer edges are glued together, thus making the centre joint.[1] Spruce, preferably from the Tyrol, is used for the belly. It should be seasoned for at least five years and, ideally, split or cleft in order to reveal the true direction of the grain. Today cleft timber is difficult to find and it is invariably sawn for economic reasons. When opened up, the wood should be light, dry, straight-grained, milky white, with a bright clean appearance and free from any discoloration or resin marks. Harsh reddish dark grains should be avoided. It is better that the grain should be fine at the centre and become wider towards the outside. Due to the difficulty of finding wood wide enough for some violins and especially for violas, wood on the quarter as opposed to slab wood is used; the advantages being greater strength, evenness of tone and a better visual effect. Should the wood not be wide enough, additional pieces of wood called 'wings' can be carefully glued on to the edges at the widest points. If well done, they are undetectable.

The wood for the back is maple and traditionally comes from Turkey, Italy or Germany, although good-quality figured timber can be found in England and America. It is seasoned for from seven to ten years and the same remarks as those given in Chapter 1 concerning quality apply here. It must be remembered that the fiercer the flame the more difficult the wood is to work.

4. *The Form or Mould*

Each country has its own type of form and it is possible to detect the type of form used when looking at a finished instrument. The accuracy of the form (Fig. 3) is vital and affects the whole instrument from start to finish. The best material for the form is block-board, plywood, beech or lime. The two latter must be thoroughly seasoned as the form must not warp.

Take two pieces of wood of the same length and width: one piece of 17 mm thick and the other, a thinner piece of 15 mm thick. The thinner piece will be removed during construction. It is on this side of the form that the back will be glued. Place the thicker piece of wood on top of the other and nail together at either end. With a ruler and knife cut a line down the centre and on this line place the form template and trace round with a sharp pencil or scriber. Remove the template and repeat this process on the underside, ensuring that both the upper and underside are identically positioned. The top-, bottom- and centre-block inlets must be marked on the wood, with all their surfaces parallel and at right angles where necessary. Five screw holes must be drilled out and countersunk to take the screw heads well below the surface. Also the holes for the cramps must be drilled out ensuring that they are at right angles to the face surface. Saw out your form with a bow-saw or band-saw, cutting a perfect curve at right angles to the flat surface all along the marked line. Afterwards clean out the block inlets. Now saw out the hand grips which should not be too near the outside edges. Drill a hole to take the bow-saw blade and finish as for the outside. Open and remove the two nails. Reduce the thinner part to give the required total thickness of the form which at the top is 30 mm and at the bottom 32 mm and then re-screw together. Place glue size on the sides of the form,

---

1. See Chapter 1, p. 26. [Ed.]

avoiding the inlets, and when dry, file down. This will give strength and prevent moisture entering the wood.

5. *The Blocks*

The purpose of the blocks (Fig. 3) is to provide a surface on to which the ribs are glued, a support to hold the ribs in shape, and a surface area at the points on which the back and belly are glued. It is important that the wood, usually pine, is light and well seasoned. Only the minimum of wood must be left and the blocks must be well shaped internally to avoid impeding sound movement.

Take six pieces of pine, which are slightly proud of or larger than the form and wide enough to take the points. Whether the blocks are sawn or split, the grain should run from the upper to the under-side surface. To fit these blocks into the inlets, mark the width of the inlets on the blocks, using a table-knife to split them with the grain. All the surfaces touching the inlets must be at right angles and must fit firmly. Finish off by planing the surfaces. Place a blob of glue on the form, position the block in the recess and cramp together. It is very important to place the glue in the centre of the thicker piece of the form, as the thinner piece has to be removed later on. When dry, plane down the upper and under surfaces level with the form surfaces. Place the template of the ribs on the form. Using the centre line of the form as a guide, draw round the points. Repeat this process on the other side of the form, making sure that both sides are identical. With dividers ensure that the distances of the points from the centre line are equal. Remove the template and, using the appropriately curved gouge, cut away the centre-bout curves. The centre-bout blocks are constructed first. Make sure that the surface of the curve is at right angles to the surface of the form. Finish off the curved surface with a file in preparation for gluing on the ribs. To ensure that the ribs do not stick to the form except at the curves of the points, dry soap or wax should be applied to the form.

6. *The Ribs*

The ribs are generally made of maple, being very thin – 1.2 mm – in proportion to the rest of the instrument. The wood for the ribs can be purchased already cut into strips. First plane down the strips on one side with a toothing plane and finish off with a scraper. Repeat this process for the other side using your finished surface as a guide when calibrating to a thickness of 1.2 mm. Now decide which will be the upper, middle and lower bouts. If the flame of the wood is at right angles to the ribs then the wood may be placed in any position. If it slopes diagonally, then it is better to make them slope downwards towards the back. Try to make the flame slope in the same direction on the left- and right-hand sides of the violin. The approximate length of the ribs can be found by measuring round the form with a flexible metal tape-measure.

The curve of the bending iron should be gradual and continuous. Heat up the bending iron; a drop of water placed on the iron will bounce off, indicating that the iron is hot enough. If the ribs are accurately planed, they need not be wetted, except at the centre points. Should they need wetting, remember that when the centre bouts dry they will draw away from the form and the top and bottom bouts will draw on to the form. Before bending decide on the final position of the ribs. First, bend the centre bouts, starting at the top of the sharpest curve of the corner; a piece of thin metal or a cork or wooden block can be used to help hold the rib against the hot iron. The wood-bending technique is similar in the making of most stringed instruments and readers are referred to the description in Chapter 1, p. 22.

Place the rib against the form and ensure it exactly follows the curve of the form. The two centre bouts are glued in first. Make up cramping blocks of pine to the height and shape of the rib at the corner block to enable the cramps to be applied. First cramp up 'dry' to see that all is perfect, then dismantle. Having waxed the edge of the form, avoiding the blocks, place glue on the blocks and ribs and cramp up leaving enough wood at the points. In order to more easily make a perfect joint where the ribs meet at the bottom block, it is best to complete one side at a time. Once the ribs of the centre bouts are glued on to the form, place the whole structure on the template on the block and mark the line of the blocks both on the upper and under side of the form. Then using dividers, measure the length from all four points to the centre line on the upper side and mark corresponding points on the upper and under side. This is to ensure that all eight points are at an equal distance from the centre line. The length of the points must be made by taking a set square and placing it against the side of the rib. Join up the two marks made by the dividers with a set square. With a knife cut through the rib which should fall away leaving a clean cut. File it down and shape the blocks as before. With a deep gouge, take away a small piece from the edge of the rib so that when the other rib is placed on top, the point will be perfectly mitred. Glue the ribs of the upper and lower bouts as before. Should the mitred joint of any corner remain open, a small strip of wood may be placed between the cramping block and the point, closing it together. Now glue the other end of the upper rib on to the top block. No joint is needed for the top block, but ensure that if a gap is left there is enough wood on either side to set the neck.

The bottom-block rib-joint is made before the bottom point in order that a perfect joint can be made. Begin by taking a set square and placing it at right angles to the ribs. Join up the centre lines of the form. Cut the rib very carefully along this line with a knife, right through to the block, removing the waste rib with a chisel. Take the other piece of rib which is to form the bottom joint and hold it against the form marking where the centre joint will be. Remove the rib and at this point, as before, cut through the line of the joint, removing unwanted wood. Then file the rib so that when it is placed against the other rib it fits exactly. Glue the rib on at the bottom joint and then glue the top point. When dry, cut away the waste rib up to the mitred point that is at right angles to the form. Plane down the ribs to the surface of the form. File out any bumps from the ribs and make the angle of the points of the ribs using a file.

7. *The Linings*

The purpose of the linings is to support the thin ribs and at the same time provide a greater surface area on which the back and belly will be glued. The following method of fitting the linings into the centre blocks is the Italian system. It is important that the linings are accurately fitted and do not, after a number of years, become unglued and vibrate.

Take an evenly grained piece of pine and plane it down to 2.5 mm and cut it into parallel strips 8 mm wide, ready for bending. Wet well and bend two of the strips for the centre bouts. Bend the other four strips so that they all follow the shape of the upper and lower ribs. In order to fit the centre linings into the blocks, make a small incision of about 5 mm into both centre blocks to take the linings. Take one of the centre linings, place it on top of the ribs and mark where the incisions finish. Cut through at this point and place the linings into the bout using only slight pressure. Leave the linings slightly proud of or larger than the rib edges. The other four linings must be cut to fit without making any incisions, again using little pressure to fit them. Place a little glue on the ribs, the blocks and the linings. Insert the linings and tap them down lightly with a hammer pressing them against the ribs. Use a mirror to see that the linings touch the ribs. Position and tighten the lining cramps and clean away the excess glue which will squeeze out. When dry, remove the lining cramps and plane down the linings to the rib surface taking great care not to remove any of the rib-edges. The sharp edge of the under side of the linings must now be bevelled off. Remove the wood in a convex line taking care not to cut into the ribs or uncover them where they have been jointed into the centre blocks. The linings must be finally sanded so that their perfectly smooth, curved contours do not interfere with the inner acoustics of your violin.

8. *The Belly*

The belly is made of two pieces of spruce, either sawn or split. To decide which is to be the upper side of the belly, look at the end-grain and study the annual rings. If they are at right angles to one of the surfaces this will then be the under-side surface. The grain at the centre joint must be at right angles to the under-side surface. The Italian method for making the belly joint is as follows. First plane flat the under-side surface of the two pieces of wood. Then place the two pieces, under-side surface together, in the bench vice using a cramp to hold together the other end of the wood. Plane the two pieces of wood together to form the joint, always keeping the joint at right angles to the under-side surface. The centre of the joint should be left very slightly open to compensate for shrinkage, which will tend to make the back joint open at the top and bottom when the joint has set. Test the straightness of the joint surface with a steel rule. Apply the same test sideways, across the joint surfaces.

Before gluing, the joint is cramped together by cutting out six squares of wood (Fig. 5), two for the centre bouts and four for the corners. These will form recesses into which cramps are fitted; this provides a greater surface area on which the cramps can grip. The inlets must be at right angles to the under-side surface to prevent the cramps from slipping out. Place the outer edge in a vice in a horizontal position. On top of this place the second piece of wood so that the edges to be jointed are on top of each other. Be careful not to damage these joint surfaces. Place the first cramp in the centre on the upper surface of the belly and cramp down slowly. Remove the assembled belly from the vice and position the two outer cramps in the same way. The belly is now cramped-up 'dry' and the joint must be perfect, otherwise it may open up later on and ruin the violin. Being satisfied with the joint, remove all cramps and brush on glue which must be very hot, thin and clean. Glue both surfaces and quickly re-assemble as before. Leave to dry in a place that is draught-free. To see if the joint is glued satisfactorily, when dry, lightly gouge out three slivers from the top, middle and bottom of the joint. If the joint is not satisfactory, open and repeat the whole process.

Now that the belly has been jointed, plane the under-side surface flat. Do not reduce the thickness of the belly in the centre to less than 17 mm, nor the edge to less than 4 mm thick. Place the ribs on the under side of the belly, lining up the centre joint with the centre line of the ribs. With a pencil make a line on both sides of the instrument at the widest part of the bouts and at the norrowest part of the centre bout. Remove the ribs and square off a line at right angles to the centre joint. Take the dividers and check that the outline of the violin is symmetrical and that each side is the same distance as the other from the centre joint. When correct, mark round the ribs with a sharp pencil.

It is now time to mark the edge of the border with a pencil marking-gauge, planing it down to obtain a mark that is 3 mm from the rib to the edge of the border. The points are drawn on to the wood freehand, marking their shape slightly over-size at this stage. Cut out the belly starting at the top and working right round, but leaving the centre bouts until last and leaving the corners over-size. When following these instructions for preparing the back, remember to allow for the button at the very top of the back piece. Scribe a line from the under-surface of the belly to form the thickness of 4 mm for the border. From the line gouge away all excess wood, using a flat gouge all round the edge to make the border. Now turn the belly over and cut away the wood up to the line previously marked for the edge. Roughly shape the points with a knife making sure that the edge is at right angles to the under-side surface. Gouge a shallow and neat canal right round using a small half-round gouge. Be careful not to gouge against the grain. Plane down the centre of the belly to a thickness of 17 mm. Once again, great care must be taken not to remove too much wood from across the centre of the belly; make sure that the arching guides fit exactly. Inspect the violin belly lengthways from each end to see that both sides are even. When the desired shape is obtained, clean the whole of the belly with thumb planes and scrapers, removing all bumps and taking care not to damage the canal.

Once again go over the canal with a gouge so that it is the same depth all round and does not extend too near to the edge, otherwise it may interfere with the setting of the purfling. Make the whole of the border flat to a width of 4 mm except for the corners which should be 5 mm. Finish off with scrapers.

Now turn the belly over and with a pencil draw in the position of the corners and end blocks. Remove some wood round the inside edge up to a line which follows the linings and to the blocks where they will touch the belly or back. Gouge out three thin canals across the top, centre and middle of the belly as a guide for depth. Then gouge out the whole of the belly, finishing off to the correct thickness with planes and scrapers (Fig. 4).

9. *Cutting the Soundholes*

The soundholes (Fig. 1), together with the scroll, purfling and arching, rank high in the process of the construction of the violin and it is in these that the maker moves from the field of craftmanship into that of the true artist. Indeed, it is these features which enable the expert to recognize the maker, for the maker leaves, as it were, his signature on the violin.

The soundholes must be in proportion to the rest of the instrument and, in shape, a traditional pattern is difficult to better. Soundholes serve the purpose of allowing air to

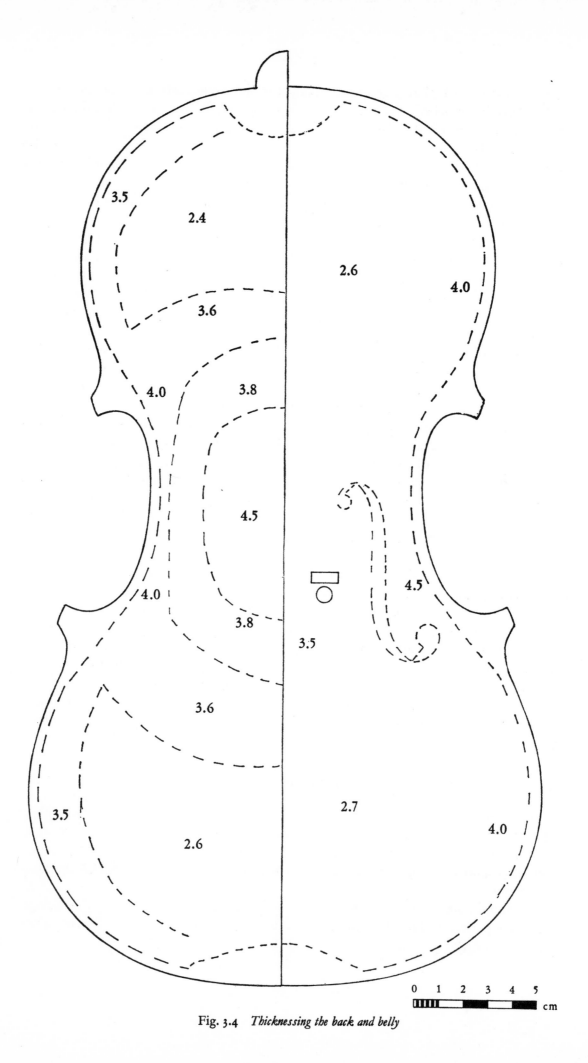

Fig. 3.4 *Thicknessing the back and belly*

be emitted while also breaking up the vibrations of the belly. If the soundholes were unequal, apart from the disturbing visual effect, they would unbalance the instrument in its relation to the bridge, soundpost and bass-bar. It is important not to make the soundholes too small in proportion as the sound would then be lower, and if they were too large the sound would be higher. If the soundholes are too far apart, the sound will be muffled, but if too close, it will be harsh and shrill!

In order to cut out the soundholes, mark a diapason of 195 mm on the centre line of the belly, measuring from the top edge of the belly. Draw a line, at this point, at right angles to the centre line. Using a piece of paper cut to an equilateral triangle, fold it in half and cut out two nicks from the folded edge which, when unfolded, can be used to sight on the centre line. On the paper triangle draw a pencil line from edge to edge forming a right angle with the folded line. This pencil line will aid the accurate positioning of the soundhole template. Place the soundhole template on the belly with the inner nick over the pencil line that has just been drawn. Place the inside edge of the template on the centre line of the belly. Keeping the pencil upright, draw round the inside edge of the template with a sharp but soft-leaded pencil, so that the soft wood will not be damaged. The distance apart of the top 'eyes' should be 42 mm. Check the distance between soundholes with dividers.

With the correct sized bit, drill a hole at the top and bottom circles of the soundholes. This is to prevent the corner splitting off when sawing out the soundholes. To saw out the soundholes, pass the fret-saw blade through the hole and start to cut out, being careful not to cut at an angle and keeping the upper edge of the blade in a forward position. Always cut slowly and lightly taking care not to snap off the points. With a very thin knife start to cut away to the pencil line being careful not to undercut on the inside. When the soundholes are completely cut out, finish off with small fine files so that both soundholes are identical. With experience only a knife will be needed and this leaves a good clean edge. No wood must show from the under surface. When viewing the instrument from above, the left-hand soundhole might appear slightly higher but this is only due to an optical illusion.

Finally, the nicks have to be cut out. Make sure they are at right angles to the surface of the soundholes and that they are of the same width, depth and angle. Now give the belly interior its final finish with graded sandpaper.

10. *The Bass-bar*

The purpose of the bass-bar is to dissipate the sound-waves from the foot of the bass side of the bridge throughout the instrument while balancing and supporting the bridge. If the bass-bar is fitted with a little pressure, make sure that it is even throughout and that neither the bass-bar nor the belly are distorted in any way. Wood for the bass-bar can often be taken from the inside edge of the belly wood before the joint is made, providing there is enough width and height left to make the belly. Again choose a good-quality wood like that used for the belly.

Take a piece of pine and cut it to 27 mm long. The grain of the bass-bar must run in the same direction as that of the belly, and at right angles to the inner surface of the belly. Plane one side flat first, turn over and after marking on the thickness of 6 mm, plane the other side down. As can be seen from Fig. 6 the bass-bar is set on the right

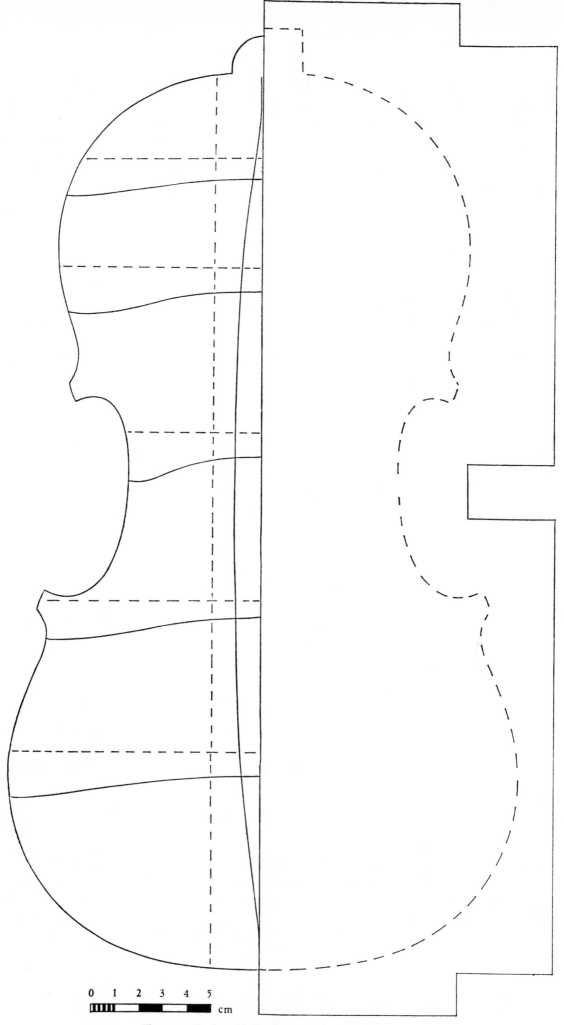

0 1 2 3 4 5 cm

Fig. 3.5   *Back and belly outlines and arching guides*

hand side of the inside of the belly. The top of the bass-bar is nearer to the centre joint and further away at the bottom. To find the correct position, divide into seven parts horizontally across the top of the belly, from the centre joint to the widest point of the rib's curve. Repeat this division from the centre joint to the widest point of the lower rib's curve. Take the bass-bar, place it on the divisions (both top and bottom) nearest to the centre joint, while also ensuring that it is in the correct position lengthways (see Fig. 6). Mark with a pencil the exact position both top and bottom, so that it can be replaced accurately. Make a mark on the bass-bar to indicate which end of the bass-bar will fit at the top of the instrument. When fitting the bass-bar, take a slightly rounded gouge and remove wood at either end so that it will sit in the belly. To achieve this, the bass-bar is turned upside down and held firmly against the bench. Using a small plane, with only a little blade showing, start from the tip and plane off where necessary, adapting it until the bass-bar fits the belly. Test its exactness by placing one thumb on the top end and the other thumb on the centre of the bass-bar and then moving it lengthways, sideways and diagonally. This work must be absolutely perfect otherwise it will come unstuck and vibrate when the violin is played.

To finally determine if the bass-bar is correct, fit three cramps, placing one cramp on the top end, one on the bottom end and the third in the middle on the nearside. Do not use force when applying the cramps, and ensure that the bass-bar is firmly seated. Dismantle and apply glue to the bass-bar only, and reset as before. Clean away all excess glue and leave to dry. Finally plane the centre of the bass-bar down to 12 mm (Fig. 6). This work must be done elegantly and the bar should be concave in shape when finished. Using a gouge, scallop the ends at an angle, and round off all sharp edges with planes and fine sandpaper. Place thin glue on the ends of the bass-bar to seal the grain.

11. *The Back*

The back is constructed by the same method as the belly except for the differing measurements (Fig. 4). When marking and cutting out the back do not forget to allow for the button at the top, and remember that the arch height of the back is 14 mm. The wood will be more difficult to work than the pine belly, due to its hardness and its curl. The back and ribs must be perfectly finished with scrapers and sandpaper before assembly. The linings must be fitted before the back can be glued on to the ribs. The thinner part of the form (Fig. 3) must be removed by unscrewing the screws. Gently lever up the thin part of the form and clean away any excess glue.

It is important to place glue size on the blocks before finally gluing and positioning the back. When the glue size is dry, sand down the ribs so that they touch the back all round. Make two pieces of wood to use for cramping-up the top and bottom blocks. Leave no sharp edges which may bruise the finished back. When fitting the back to the blocks, first see that it fits perfectly without glue, and that the border is the same distance all round, especially at the points. When you are satisfied, glue-up using a few cramps to hold the back in the correct position. Then, starting in one place and working round the back, put some thin glue between the back and the ribs using a table-knife. Hold the back and ribs apart with a small wedge of wood while applying the glue. As you proceed, position more cramps on the glued area until back and ribs are glued together, after which remove any excess glue.

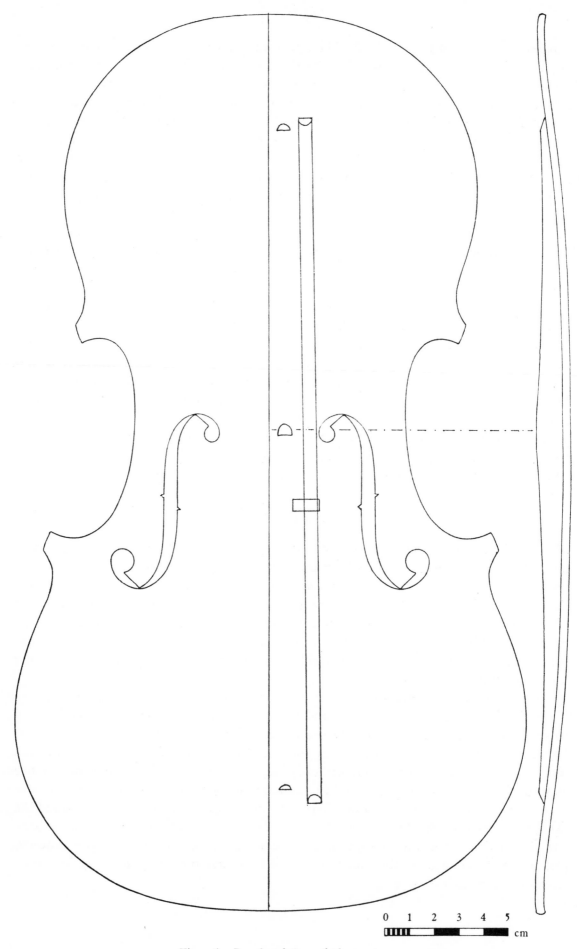

0 1 2 3 4 5

cm

Fig. 3.6   *Bass-bar design and placement*

12. *Removing the Form*

It is now time to remove the rest of the form in order to glue in the linings. Lay the instrument in an instrument rest then, placing a table-knife between the form and each of the blocks give the knife a sharp knock. The blocks should fall away from the form but if the ribs fit too tightly against the form or the blocks have too much glue on, this will prevent easy removal of the form. Lever the form out of the instrument holding it by the hand grips and in turn tapping each block until the instrument falls away into the instrument rest. Clean away all surplus glue.

Having removed the form from the ribs, the back linings have to be made and finished as previously described for the belly (p. 77). When the linings are dry, shape all the blocks by removing unwanted wood as follows. This lightens the instrument and at the same time allows the soundwaves to move more freely. Remove the wood on all the four centre blocks to form a concave shape connecting with the linings but not uncovering the centre lining. Keep the blocks parallel with the ribs. File both blocks and linings down and finish with sandpaper. When both the ribs and belly are perfectly finished internally, and your label is glued in, it is time to close up the instrument. Glue the belly on in the same way as the back. The simplest way of marking the border of the instrument is to take a pencil stub slightly shorter than the height of the ribs, sharpen it to a point. Remove one side of the pencil so that when drawing round the ribs it will make a mark that is 3 mm from the rib to the outside edge, thus forming the border. When removing wood up to the edge, do not just follow the line of the pencil but look at the contour of the edge and remove any bumps or straight places by eye.

When the edge of the border is finished and the points shaped, ensure that the edge is parallel to the rib and that all four points are of the same dimensions.

13. *Purfling the Instrument*[1]

Purfling is largely to enhance the instrument's appearance, while at the same time giving strength to the edge, especially to the belly which is more brittle than the back. The various types and sizes are, within reason, a matter of taste and it is these, together with the direction of the points, which gives an indication as to where the maker has learnt his craft. The wood used is often pear, which is stained for the black strips of the purfling. Modern purfling is usually made of synthetic fibre instead, which is easier to bend being less brittle than wood purfling. When making your own purfling, it is usual to use three wide veneer sheets, the two outer ones being stained black, and the inner one left as natural white wood. A useful veneer is sycamore which is available stained black, as well as natural, and in different thicknesses. The three sheets of veneer, which should be about 25 × 20 mm, should be glued together into a black-white-black sandwich. When this is dry cut off 2-mm-wide strips using a steel rule and a very sharp knife.

It is advisable to insert purfling in daylight as successful purfling depends on great accuracy and patience. Before using the purfling ensure that there are no defects caused by faulty manufacture. The accuracy in setting the purfling will depend on the edge

1. See also Chapter 1, p. 23. [Ed.]

having been perfectly finished. Always try out the purfling by purfling a piece of waste wood. When cutting the purfling channel in the belly it is important to follow the direction of the grain. Pine will always expand on cutting and contract when glue is placed in the channel; this is also so, but to a lesser extent, with the back. There is nothing more un- nerving than when the wood at the sides of the channel expands on applying glue, thus narrowing the channel, and one finds the purfling does not fit. If this happens, wash out the glue, leave to dry and start again.

The usual way of cutting the purfling channel is to use a double-bladed cutter, which actually cuts the sides of the canal, leaving the wood to be removed. This tool is described in Chapter 1, p. 16. If you make a mistake, it is impossible to correct. The Italian system is to use either one blade or two at a time, and gently make a faint line around the instru- ment. If incorrect, sand over and re-mark. This is a slightly slower method but with hard veins, bumps, or imperfect corners, the discerning maker can correct by eye as he cuts the wood.

Set the outside blade of the purfling cutter at 4.4 mm from the edge of the border and mark the channel, making sure that the points of the cutter are very sharp and not in a sideways position. Mark all the way round the edge. Turn the cutter round the corners freely and easily. Continue the outside line towards the point, making a guide line for the outside black point of the purfling. Make sure that the lines are parallel. With a very thin sharp knife begin cutting out so that both the edges of the channel slope very slightly towards the centre. It is advisable to leave the corners until last as practice is gained in cutting the rest of the belly first. Always cut the channel at the corners slightly smaller than necessary. Do not break away the points! After cutting the points, continue to cut a very thin line which is the continuation of the outer black purfling. This thin cut should continue in a straight line to a mark that is one-third of the width of the point, measured from the inside of the centre-bout curve. It should stop at a mark which is half the distance between the outside edge of the violin and the outer edge of the purfling. Using a purfling chisel remove the pieces of wood from the purfling channel. Avoid cutting the channel too deep and breaking through where the button will be.

Before setting the purfling, ensure that the channel is clean and accurate and that all four points have round identical curves. The purfling must fit exactly. Begin and com- plete either the back or the belly at one time. After warming the bending iron, take the piece of purfling for the centre bout, slightly dampen it and bend both corners. Starting with the inside bout, cut the angle at the point on a slope ready for mitring. Press in the corner of the purfling lightly. Measure from the point round the inside bout to the other point. Mark the correct angle at this point with a knife, leaving the purfling a little on the long side. Remove the purfling and cut at the point with the correct angle and lay the purfling lightly in the canal ready for gluing. Repeat this process on the other bout. Take the piece of purfling that has been already cut for the top bout and bend it on the iron as before. Mitre the corner with the centre-bout purfling, making sure that enough of the black is left to continue on towards the point. An easier way to mitre the corner is to place the purfling near the very edge of the bench, holding it firmly, and to cut off a diagonal slice with a knife, making sure it is not concave. When the point is mitred, both the black and white part of the purfling must match exactly. All corners must be identical. It will not be necessary to join the purfling up on the belly as it can be ended where the neck and tail saddle will be. It is advisable to make the joints of the purfling for the back on the straightest part of the back. Having mitred the corners of the top and bottom bouts on the same side, then cut the purfling at an angle so that when placed in the channel it slopes downwards to form a ramp. It is important that the slope is at right angles to the side of the purfling. Next, having completed the points on the opposite side and with the purfling in position, place one piece on top of another and mark lightly where the slope begins and ends. Remove, and cut to form a perfectly lapped joint. When gouged out there will be no trace of the joint.

The importance of making the trough after purfling cannot be overstressed. No amount of scraping and sandpapering will improve a badly made edge. The border should be flat and of the correct thickness. The trough should follow a mark which should come half way between the very edge of the violin and the outer edge of the purfling. Mark the points carefully to form a continuous curve. Take a gouge and gouge out a trough of an even depth the whole way round the instrument. At the points the trough should gradually rise and be finished to a clean round point. After the trough is completed take thumb planes and plane down to form a gradual curve from the belly to the edge.

14. *Finishing the Body*

Rounding off the outer edge is the final stage to be carried out in the building of the body, and the maker now has a very recognizable instrument. The edge really forms the 'frame' to the instrument. This stage involves the removal of the sharp external and internal edges of the border of the back and belly. The way to achieve the most uniform rounding is to file the edge away in gradual angles ending up by removing the fine line of the angles left with fine files. Take care not to remove more from the belly as it is of softer wood. Finish the points last, making sure that all eight points are identical. Keep them nicely square with a sharp clean appearance, not as though they had been carelessly worn off.

The purpose of the tail-gut saddle is to carry the tail gut over the edge of the belly and to prevent the tailpiece from touching the belly. Ebony, being hard, is used as it has to take considerable pressure in both a forward and downward direction. It is usually fitted by removing either half or the total thickness of the edge of the belly inwards and up to the internal edge of the purfling. By removing only half the thickness of the edge it is easier for the restorer to remove the belly. Then mark 17.5 mm from either side of the centre joint of the belly. Cut down to the block and just up to the purfling. Then remove the edge cutting the purfling through before lifting out. Take a ruler and at right angles to the centre joint cut across the belly to where the purfling finishes. If you are going down to only half the thickness of the edge, then mark this and remove the edge up to this point, making sure all the surfaces are square and level. If you are going down to the full depth, go down to the block. Take the partially finished saddle and find the centre of its width and mark this on the opening of the belly. Cut away the excess wood and finish so that it is slightly forced into the opening, then glue it in. Plane the saddle down to a height of 4 mm making sure it does not slope down to one side. Shape the outside of the saddle by continuing the curve of the edge of the belly as if you were making the edge before purfling. Round the under-side edge and also round the edge where the gut will touch the saddle to a half-moon shape so that the gut will pass over in a gradual curve placing maximum strain on the block and edge of the belly. Remove about 7 mm of wood from either end of the saddle to form a graceful concave slope down to the belly. Finish off with files, sandpaper and polish.

The hole to take the end-button or peg should be drilled out before varnishing. Find the centre point where the ribs are joined at the bottom of the instrument. Drill out the hole keeping the drill perpendicular to the ribs. Drill slowly to avoid splitting the blocks. Enlarge the hole using a peg reamer. Do not force in the button as it has to be removed to set the soundpost. The tailpiece will pull to one side should the button be off centre.

15. *The Scroll*

When positioning the scroll template (Fig. 1), use the grain of the wood to its best advantage. The fingerboard side must be on the thick edge of the wood. Plane down the sides so that they are both at right angles to the fingerboard surface, but no lower than the width of the eyes of the scroll which should be 42 mm. Starting on the fingerboard side, square off a pencil line right round the block of wood as near to the top edge of the block as possible, also under the chin and at the top of the fingerboard, as a guide for the model of the head. Draw round the template with a pencil and mark the volute on the scroll with a sharp point. Repeat this process for the opposite side. If a band-saw is used for sawing out the head, glue a piece of wood on to the thinner side of the block of wood so as to make that side square with the fingerboard side. Saw round the entire head. Afterwards make sure that the back and front of the scroll are square by removing wood up to the pencil line. Clean out under the chin. Scribe a line down the centre of the face and right round the back of the scroll. Take the template of the back of the head, place it on and make sure that the centre line on the template is over the centre line that has been scribed on the wood. Draw round the template. Make a pegbox template and place it on the face under the chin and draw round. At the sides, mark where the nut and fingerboard will come, and square across the face. Now cut away the wood at the sides. Cut down to the tail and turn the piece of wood round so that it can be seen how far to cut down to the pegbox. Place the piece of wood on its side and saw down to the pegbox. Continue round the volute. Make a number of saw cuts round the volute in a downward and outward sloping angle to the pencil line for the first curl and saw down to the pencil marks using a small fretsaw. Saw towards the centre of the scroll at an upward angle removing excess wood, but because of the second curl, stop under the chin. Do not cut too far into the head. With a gouge cut down and round the first curl removing the pieces of wood. Finish off with a file using the dots already made, as a guide. Repeat this process for the second curl but when arriving at the eye, do not cut down too far. Cut out the eyes at the very last moment. Make sure that the left- and right-hand volutes are identical. Smooth off all sharp angles with a file and bevel the edge round the volute. Finish off by using scrapers and sandpaper.

Next make the fluting on the back of the head. Bevel the edge on either side of the scroll from under the chin to the tail. When gouging out the fluting, see that the pegbox is well supported. Leave a spine in the centre. Starting from the crest, gouge down towards the tail, taking care not to damage the tail. Stand the head up in a vice and gouge out the top of the head, working round to the chin. A thin sliver of wood should be placed under the chin to avoid damage to the pegbox. Finish off under the chin with a knife and files and then, together with the rest of the neck, with scrapers.

To cut out the pegbox, replace the template and mark clearly where the nut, fingerboard and pegbox cheeks will be. The top width is 19.5 mm and the bottom width is 23.5 mm. With a knife cut down from under the chin to the nut, cutting along the pencil line. This is to stop the wood splitting. Decide how deep to make the pegbox, remembering that the fluting has been gouged out. Always support the scroll when cutting out the pegbox, otherwise it could snap off. With a suitably sized bit, drill at a slight angle inwards towards the centre of the pegbox. When the sides of the pegbox are finished they should be 6 mm thick and slant slightly inwards. Do not forget to cut well up under the chin to make room for the A and D peg holes. Finish off the inside of the pegbox with chisels, fine files and sandpaper, after which bevel the inside and outside edges of the pegbox.

When making the peg holes, first place the template (Fig. 1) on one side of the scroll, making sure that the fingerboard line marked on the template is placed over the line marked on the scroll. Mark the holes through the template with a pointed instrument. Repeat this process for the other side, making sure that both sides are identical. Drill out all the holes but ensure that they are upright and do not slant in any direction. With a pencil, mark the hole where the peg will be inserted. This will ensure that you do not make the hole for the small end of the peg larger than that for the thick end. Reamer out the peg holes to the required diameter. Again the holes should not slant in any direction. The final diameter of the hole will be dictated by the thickness of the peg.

16. *Making and Fitting the Fingerboard*

It is now time to make the fingerboard to the final measurements. It will then be temporarily glued on to the neck to enable the neck to be fitted. The fingerboard is usually purchased partially finished. Begin by cutting down the length to 270 mm and then planing the under-side surface so that it is flat throughout and slightly concave in the centre where it will touch the neck. Plane down and make the fingerboard 25 mm wide at the top and 43 mm wide at the bottom, after which make it gradually concave along both sides. Using a flat square, ensure that both the top and bottom are square. Make the edge 5 mm thick and then shape the top of the fingerboard throughout using the template. Again, make this slightly concave over its entire length, thus preventing the strings from vibrating against it. The top, bottom and edges should be at right angles to the under side of the fingerboard.

At this stage, the fingerboard nut must also be made. It will be the same width as the fingerboard, 5 mm thick and high enough above the fingerboard to be able to take the strings when they are fitted. The surface which is glued to the fingerboard end and neck should be at right angles to the neck face. The surface facing towards the pegbox should be sloping back towards the bridge.

To glue the fingerboard exactly in the centre of the neck, find the centre of the fingerboard at the top and bottom where the neck ends. When the fingerboard is correctly positioned, glue the nut and fingerboard temporarily on to the neck (see section 18).

The main object of roughly shaping the neck before assembly is to remove as much excess wood as possible while the head is easy to handle. The chin of the scroll should have been perfectly shaped before fluting the back of the scroll. The fingerboard will then have been glued on, and the neck reduced at the top to almost the final thickness and shape. The heel of the neck can now be shaped ready to fit the body, using the templates.

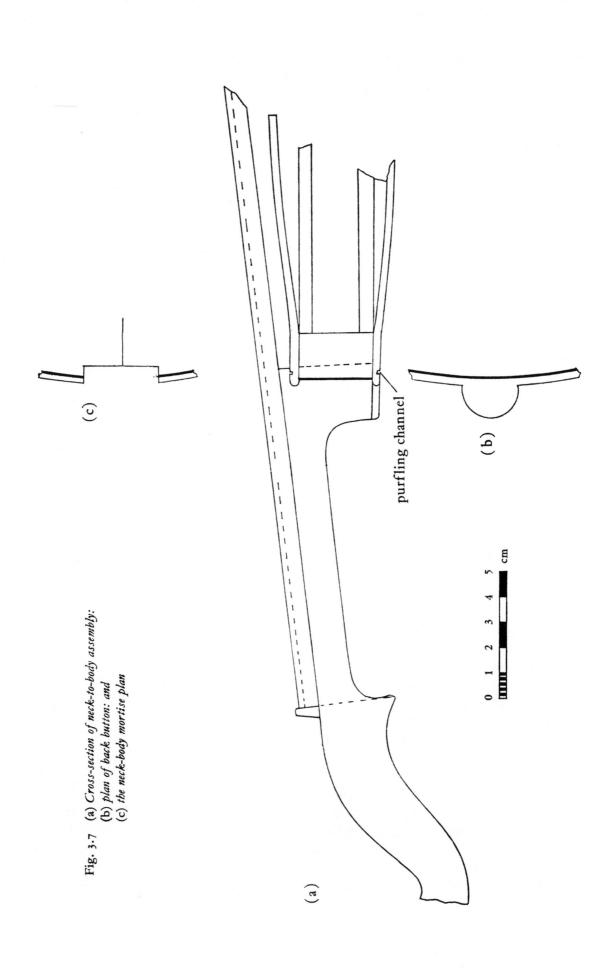

purfling channel

0 1 2 3 4 5 cm

(a)

(b)

(c)

Fig. 3.7 (a) *Cross-section of neck-to-body assembly:*
(b) *plan of back button: and*
(c) *the neck-body mortise plan*

17. *To Fix the Neck into the Body*

Take the template for the joint of the body (Fig. 7). When marking the measurements on to the body and heel, make the heel wider and the body narrower. The centre line of the model must be placed on the centre joint of the back. Draw in the angles on the ribs with a pencil. Take a knife and cut either side of the model on the ribs. Cut into the border of the belly up to the inside edge of the purfling. Lastly cut a straight line at right angles to the centre joint along the inside edge of the purfling to join up with the previous two cuts. Take a chisel and, on the inside of the cut, remove the border up to the depth of the purfling, the rib and the block to the required depth. Care must be taken not to damage the remaining purfling, ribs or border.

Now try fitting the neck into the prepared position, making sure that the sides of the ribs are straight and that when the wood is removed, it is by equal proportions from either side of an imaginary centre line. Ensure that the head is in line with the centre joint of the belly. Make sure that the following measurements (Fig. 7) are correct: the distance from the top of the fingerboard to the border of the violin, 130 mm; the underside edge of the fingerboard to the edge of the belly, 6 mm; the depth from the border into the block 7 mm; and the height of the neck continued on a line from on top of the fingerboard to the bridge, 270 mm.

To centre the neck in the instrument, place a finished bridge in the correct position on the belly. Look down the sides of the fingerboard to see that they meet up with the sides of the bridge. The only way of fixing the neck into the body is to take away a little wood at a time and continually check the measurements. When the neck begins to fit and is a little tight, remove it by giving a sharp tap on the back of the neck holding the belly between your legs, but taking great care.

The following may be the cause of an incorrectly set neck:

1. The soundholes are not centred or are not equi-distant from the centre joint.
2. The centre of the back or belly is not the true centre of the instrument.
3. The fingerboard is not set on the neck in the centre.
4. The neck is not at right angles to the centre of the instrument.

To glue in the neck, two wooden cauls must be prepared to enable the cramps to be applied. The first caul must be the same shape as the outline of the back including the button, deep enough to cover the top block and slightly wider on each side. This is so that the pressure of the cramps is spread between the nut, block and back. The second caul, which should be a wedge shape, must go on top of the fingerboard to enable the cramp to be applied at right angles. This piece should be the same width as the fingerboard where the heel ends, long enough to take the cramp, and the surface touching the fingerboard should be the same shape as the fingerboard. Both pieces should be thick enough to prevent bending, and smooth enough to avoid bruising.

Cramp everything together before gluing. Take care that the cramping blocks are not too high up towards the scroll as the neck is inclined to jump out. Size the heel with glue first. The glue should be new, hot and thin. Heat up the foot of the neck, and place the glue on the foot of the neck block and on the opening in the body. Holding the violin body between your knees, press the neck against the top block and then press firmly downwards and back towards the button. Squeeze the neck hard against the body. The back of the heel of the neck block may be hammered lightly to ensure that it is against the block. Cramp together. Clean away all glue and re-check all measurements.

When dry, the neck must be shaped and finished off, removing excess wood from either side of the heel. The button, or end of the heel, will be left at the correct width with an equal amount of wood on either side of the centre joint. The height of the button is governed by the width which must be marked on in the form of a half circle. Draw round the model for the shape of the neck removing any excess wood. Make sure that the border goes right up to the nut and that it is the same distance from the rib. Now shape the heel and neck. The neck should be 185 mm at the top, including the finger-board, and 200 mm at the bottom. A balance must be found so that the neck is neither too full nor concave. Always remember that the shape of the neck is vital to the player. When you have almost finished the neck look at it against the light, and this will show up any defects. Finally, finish with fine files, scrapers and sandpaper, damping a number of times to raise the grain.

18. *Finishing the Instrument*

Having arrived at the stage of finishing off the violin, as much (if not more) care must be taken as with the previous processes. The easiest way to finish the violin is to complete each stage in a systematic way. If there is any work to be done with a gouge or scraper do it first. Always remember that sanding will only smooth a defect rather than remove it, while at the same time giving a dead effect, especially if you remove the sharp edges on the bevel of the head or borders. Place a piece of cork behind the sandpaper to maintain an even surface and prevent the removal of the soft grain. Avoid sanding the tail-gut saddle as ebony dust will discolour the wood. When you are entirely satisfied that you have finished the violin, carefully remove the fingerboard. Should it be difficult to remove, place a table-knife under it from the heel end and gently draw the knife up towards the scroll. A piece of wood a little wider than the fingerboard must be placed on the neck. This is to protect the edges of the neck and keep it clean when varnishing. Glue it on with a little glue and put the violin away ready for varnishing.

19. *Varnishing*

This is often one of the most disputed processes in violin-making. It is, however, only one part of the long chain of processes which will determine the maker's ability. The varnish will not make a Stradivari but it could mar a well-made instrument. It is important that the varnish forms a protective layer against everyday use, is neither too hard nor too soft, is flexible and allows the instrument to breathe while not hiding the beauty of the wood. It is important to use completely clean materials with sound brushes, and to work in a dust-free room. A professional maker will usually varnish all his instruments at one time – usually between July and September depending on the weather. Choose a bright clear day as artificial light will cause reflection. Find a suitable system for hanging up the instruments. It is advisable to apply a good simple varnish rather than an elaborate highly-coloured one which would hide the natural flame and give a dead matt appearance.[1] When

1. Readers are referred to Chapter 1, p. 33, for further information on preparation and varnishing. [Ed.]

starting to varnish, the instrument must be completely free of dust. After applying any pre-varnish preparation, put on the necessary undercoat, allowing it to dry well. Should brush marks appear, do not brush them out but sand down later. If a hair or two comes out of the brush, leave until dry and then remove these with the point of a knife and sand down. When you sand down the coats and find they are not dry, the varnish will become sticky. If this occurs leave the varnish to dry thoroughly. Do not be in a hurry to set up the instrument until it is completely dry, as the bridge will make an imprint in the tacky varnish. Should extra heat be needed to dry the varnish, use a fan blower but avoid dust. Polishing to obtain a glass-like finish has been a traditional method, but I consider this unnecessary and almost an insult to a well-varnished instrument.

As varnishing is a very complex subject and a separate one on its own, I would strongly advise the reader to consult as many books on the matter as possible.

After varnishing, the fingerboard must be re-glued on permanently. Lift off the piece of wood protecting the neck surface with a table-knife. Be careful not to damage the surface of the neck. Clean off the old glue and glue on the fingerboard as before, using an ample coating of thin glue.

20. *Setting up the Violin*

Before fitting the pegs, clean out the varnish from the peg holes using a reamer. Reduce the pegs with a peg cutter so that they protrude 33 mm measured from the outside wall of the pegbox to the end of the head. Finally file and sand down to leave a smooth surface. The peg should grip in the small hole while the large hole acts as a guide when tuning. Remove the protruding peg wood from the outside of the pegbox. Round the small end evenly and then sand and polish. Drill the holes to take the strings. Make the hole the diameter of the thickest string and also ensure that the hole goes through the centre of the peg. Take a round file and bevel the opening of both ends of the hole and finish off the peg by polishing the part from the collar to the peg end.

When the strings are placed through the pegs, wind them round the pegs, turning the pegs away from you. Only a small amount of string needs to protrude from the other side of the hole, just enough to tuck under the first turn of the string to grip it. Do not allow the string to twist or bend, as if it is made of metal it will break and if gut will bruise badly. Wind the string on, keeping it neat and using as much of the peg width from the hole to the wall as possible. Do not leave an excessive amount wound round the peg in one place as it will force the space between the peg and the bottom of the pegbox.

The wood for the soundpost can be purchased as ready prepared dowel-rods, and also from wood that is unsatisfactory for a belly or from waste wood that remains when the belly has been cut out. However, ensure that the wood is of good-quality spruce. The simplest and most accurate way of making a soundpost is first to make a square rod a little wider than the final diameter. Remove the four angles from the square by equal amounts until a dowel is formed which is an equal thickness of 6 mm over its entire length. The soundpost must be able to pass through the soundhole near the nicks. The position of the soundpost is under the right foot of the bridge facing the scroll. Halve the width of the foot, and place this measurement on the belly from the back of the foot facing the tail-piece. Find the half of the foot lengthwise and place this measurement on a line with the other mark from the outside edge of the foot. The grain of the soundpost should be at

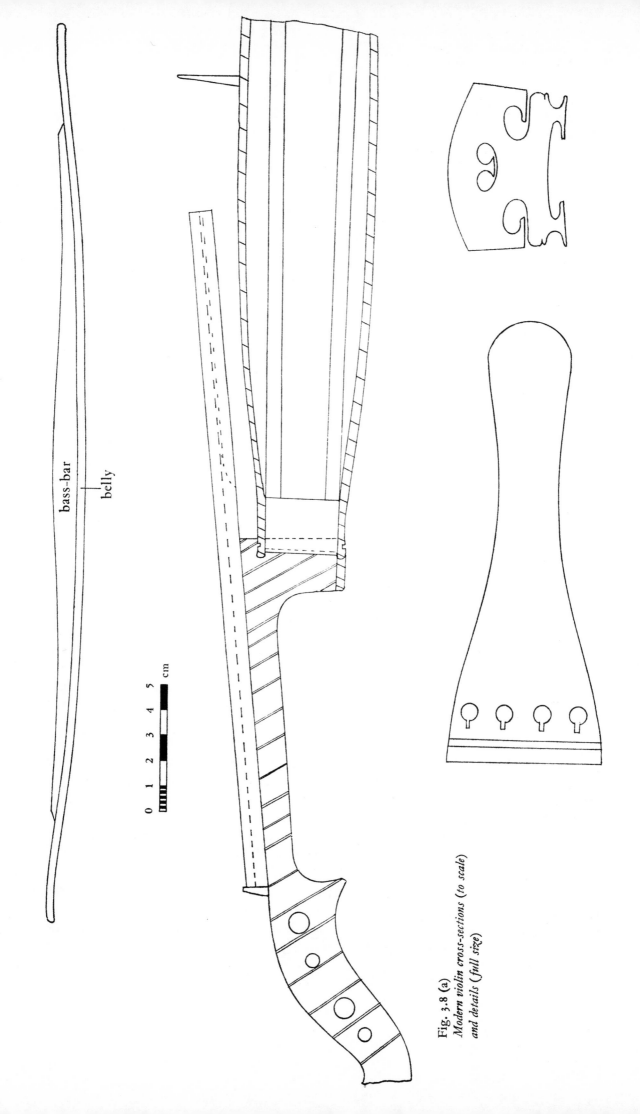

bass-bar

belly

0 1 2 3 4 5
cm

Fig. 3.8 (a)
*Modern violin cross-sections (to scale)
and details (full size)*

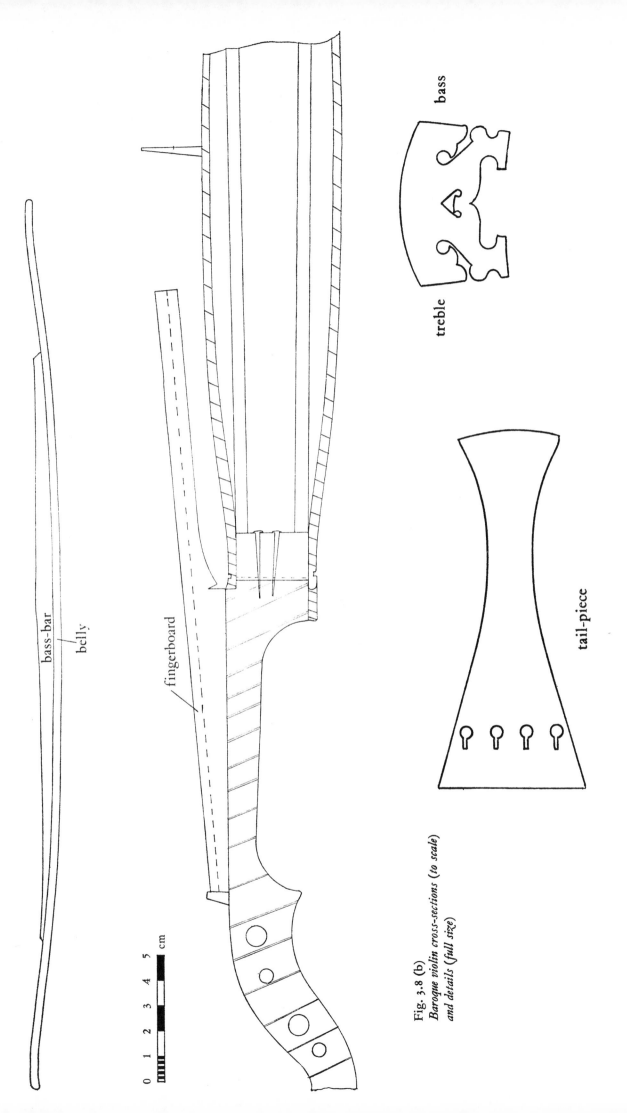

bass

treble

bass-bar

belly

fingerboard

0 1 2 3 4 5 cm

tail-piece

Fig. 3.8 (b)
*Baroque violin cross-sections (to scale)
and details (full size)*

right angles to that of the belly. The soundpost should sit perpendicular when viewed from the soundhole or the hole in the bottom block. It should sit in without being forced in, since if this occurs, it will bruise and distort the belly and back.

To find the length of the soundpost, take a piece of thin cardboard, narrow enough to fit through the eye of the soundhole. Feed it through and mark on it the under side of the belly. Transfer this mark on to the soundpost. Cut through taking care not to split the wood. Start by shaping one end of the soundpost to follow the shape of the internal surface of the belly. Check this, using a dentist's mirror. When perfect, repeat this process for the other end of the soundpost. (Both surfaces must be flat and not concave.) Take the piece of cardboard, push it through the soundhole until it touches the soundpost. Mark on where the soundhole palet ends. Place above the belly in the same position and this will show how far in the soundpost is. Fit the soundpost using the soundpost-setter pushed into the soundpost at a point half its length. Lean the soundpost inwards and draw it up with the other end of the soundpost-setter. Do not bruise the edges of the soundholes.

The next process is to fit the tailpiece gut which, if made of nylon, will be threaded at both ends. Feed one end through the hole at the end of the tailpiece (which can be bought ready-made), pass round to the other hole so that a loop is formed and the two knots are on the under side. Great care must be taken not to cross thread. If you are using the standard gut type, singe both ends after they have been threaded through and wind a piece of thin gut round each thick end. Knot well and singe these ends. Always make sure that the ends do not protrude below the tailpiece and scratch the belly. If this happens, deepen the recess with a gouge. The tail gut should be long enough to clear the tail saddle. The distance from the bridge to the bar on the tailpiece is 55 mm. To refit the end button or peg, which was temporarily fitted before varnishing, just remove the varnish from the hole using a peg reamer and fit the button again.

When fitting a fine tuner secure it so that the locking nut is firm while at the same time allowing the arm to move freely. Place a cloth under the tailpiece to avoid scratching the belly. Now the strings have to be fitted in the tailpiece. The strings usually come with either a ball or a loop at one end. If it is a loop to be fixed to the fine tuner, open the loop and place round both fingers of the tuner for maximum strength. Should it have a ball at one end, place that behind the fingers. Wind up the fine tuner so that the tone can be slightly adjusted when tuning. The remaining strings should be fed through the holes, loose end first, and drawn through so that either the ball or the knot is firm on the under side of the tailpiece. It is not advisable to feed the string through the loop and round the top of the tailpiece as this can alter the vibrating length. Should the string not have a loop, knot or ball, tie a figure-of-eight knot which will not slip through the hole. When drawing the strings up from the tailpiece to fix to the peg, allow them to unwind and find their natural position.

The purpose of the bridge is to transmit the vibrations of the strings to the belly and from there to the bass-bar and soundpost. It is important therefore that the feet exactly fit the curve of the belly. The bridge will be purchased having been roughly cut out. The wood is maple and should be hard and well seasoned. Select the side on which there are long flecks for the front of the bridge to face the scroll. The position of the bridge is between two imaginary parallel lines continued from between the top eyes of the sound-holes down to the soundhole nicks. The distance between the outside edges of the feet should be 41 mm and the feet should be placed on a horizontal line with the nick. Viewed from the side, the bridge should form a right angle on the surface facing the tailpiece with that of the belly. This will give the appearance of leaning backwards. Take a knife and begin to adapt the feet, taking an even amount from each foot so that the bridge remains vertical. The bridge should fit exactly when standing free and not twist when under tension.

After fitting the bridge, mark the width of 35 mm between the G and E strings with a groove on the top of the bridge. The grooves should be the same distance away from the centre of the bridge. Measure from the end of the fingerboard to the top of the strings and reduce the grooves to a height of 6 mm on the G string and 4 mm on the E string. When correct take the template of the curve, place it on the bridge and draw on the shape to where the grooves end. Remove the excess wood and, carefully following the shape, finish off with files and sandpaper. It is important that this arc is correct as the player has to be able to play chords as well as separate strings. The position of the D and A string is at an equal distance between the E and G string. Thin down the top of the bridge to an even thickness of 2 mm and make the rest of the bridge convex in all directions, except for the under surface which remains flat. Finish off the feet. Clean up the eyes and decorations making sure they are at right angles to the surface. Carefully file the grooves for the strings so that the strings do not bind and pull the bridge in any direction. When drawing up the strings lean the bridge backwards a little so that when the instrument is tuned the feet will fit exactly.

There are various types of chin rest available, and this must be a personal choice. Whichever type you choose, ensure that the padding on the feet is adequate and that it does not touch the tailpiece or vibrate against the belly. To fix the chin rest, unscrew the centre section and, placing it on the instrument, screw up to finger tightness using the key provided. Take care that the key does not protrude through the bar to the other side and scratch the rib. Screw up evenly and fairly tight so that it holds but does not bruise the wood.

21. *Conclusion*

To obtain perfection in violin-making it is essential to maintain a high degree of workmanship both in the accurate use of measurements and in the careful finishing of each separate process. Both self-criticism and experience are among the best teachers. While not vital, it is advisable to copy a classical maker, not to learn to imitate but to lay a foundation on which the maker will be able to form his own opinions, character and style. Unlike other methods of construction the system described in this chapter allows the maker a good deal of artistic freedom, while at the same time providing a reliable type of form which will ensure the necessary accuracy.

The Baroque Violin

The shape of the body of the violin has remained unchanged throughout its life, except for minor differences only perceptible to the expert. The most important physical changes were those to the neck, fingerboard, bridge, soundpost and bass-bar. It must be made clear that these changes were brought about by the demands of the player rather than any shortcomings of the violin. Before the seventeenth century, violinists were content to play in third and fourth positions but later, realizing there was greater scope in fifth and sixth positions, they played further up the fingerboard. This increased the pitch, the tension on the strings, pressure on the bridge and most of all, strain on the neck, therefore forcing a change in the instrument.

In the modern instrument (Plate v and Fig. 8b), the slope of the neck is obtained by canting the neck backwards and letting it into the rib and top block, thus forming a tapered dovetail mortice joint. Due to the type of joint, the neck tightens as it is inserted and, having four glued surfaces, forms a very strong and elegant joint. The maker is able to finish the heel and neck to thinner proportions, thus making playing easier, as a certain amount of wood is hidden in the top block and the joint is strong. The neck of the Baroque violin was, at least after the time of Stradivari, very slightly canted and fixed almost at right angles to the rib surface. The heel of the neck was slightly curved to follow the shape of the ribs and top block. A small piece of wood was cut out to take the edge of the belly. The neck was then glued on to the rib and nailed through the top block into the heel. The heel had to be left rather thick due to the need for strength at this point, as there were only two glued surfaces and nails to hold it in position.

It is perhaps useful at this stage to explain how the maker nailed on the neck when the body was completely finished and closed up. In the Baroque instruments four small pegs of wood were inserted in the top and bottom blocks in the centre near the purfling on the back and belly. The pegs enabled the maker from the start of construction to remove the back and belly when required. In order to set the neck, the maker needed the body to be complete to ensure that the neck was in the centre of the instrument. Therefore, he completed the instrument, prepared the neck for fitting, removed the back and belly, glued and nailed the neck in position, before finally gluing on the back and belly. The pegs were either fully or only half covered when the instrument was purfled, but were completely covered when the tail saddle was fitted. If this 'peg method' is used in making a modern instrument, they will need to be removed when the neck is fitted, which was not the case with the earlier instruments. They can be very useful in making a modern instrument as they enable the back and belly to be replaced in the exact position. More often than not, they are imitated by fitting them when the instrument is almost completed.

Another change that the Baroque violin underwent was in the construction of the fingerboard. The modern fingerboard is longer and narrower at the top and wider at the bottom. Also it is generally thinner throughout with parallel sides. It is of solid ebony, hollowed out underneath and its surface curve is slightly flatter. The fingerboard of the Baroque instrument provided the angle to the neck in the form of a wedge, being thinner at the nut end and thicker at the bridge end. To enable the fingerboard to pass over the arching of the belly, it was curved from the heel of the neck to the end. The fingerboard was made lighter by hollowing out wherever possible. Most of the fingerboards were made of maple, being lighter than ebony. They were sometimes veneered with ebony on the surface and on the edges for harder wearing. The Baroque fingerboard was shorter and the surface curve flatter. The tailpiece on the modern violin is a different pattern, being rounder and hollowed out underneath. The bridge is a different shape today. It is less ornate and slightly higher.

The internal differences of the Baroque violin (Plate v and Figs 8a and b) were that the soundpost was thinner, and the bass-bar was shorter, thinner and slightly lower. The strings were of gut with the E string wire-covered, and all of them were of a shorter vibrating length. A fine tuner on the tailpiece and a chin rest are now added to the modern instrument. The whole concept of the Baroque violin was one of lightness; an instrument in its original state weighs about 12 oz (360 g) as compared to the modern violin which weighs 15 oz (450 g).

1. *Introduction*

The development of the modern concert guitar,[1] although mainly attributed to Torres, was by no means the achievement of one highly talented guitar-maker: earlier in the nineteenth century two luthiers, Lacote and Panormo, were among the first to build lightly-constructed guitars. By reducing the thickness of the timbers, particularly of the soundboard, they introduced guitars which responded instantly in sympathy to their vibrating strings and produced sustained notes of impressive volume and tone. To strengthen the reduced thickness of the soundboard, a system of thin struts was devised which were fanned out under the lower part of the guitar's soundboard, giving maximum support yet without restricting the all-important flexibility of the soundboard. Torres not only developed this significant method of soundboard barring, but he also increased the general dimensions of the guitar and standardized its vibrating string length to 65 cm, which many of the best makers still use today. Even though hundreds of experiments have been tried to further improve the guitar, there still seem no better designs or construction methods than those used by the great makers such as Torres, Santos, Simplicio, and Hauser. Indeed, guitars by such makers offer everything that is worth copying.

The timbers used in building a top-quality guitar have become as traditional as has Torres' fan-strutting system; and for good reason. Over the years many different timbers have been used for the back and ribs of the instrument: mahogany, ebony, even ivory, and we should not forget that the Torres guitar with which the guitarist-composer Francisco Tarrega charmed his audiences was a maple back-and-sided instrument and that, earlier, Aguado said that *his* guitar was made completely of maple – including the soundboard! However, for its quality of tone as well as its magnificent appearance, it is nearly always the rosewood guitar which comes out on top. Rio rosewood from South America was the first variety used for guitar making and today one sometimes comes across early guitars by Panormo and other nineteenth-century makers in which they used the saw-cut rosewood veneer glued to pine. Bombay rosewood, another excellent variety, was a late-comer but it is now widely used by the best guitar makers because of its stability even though it is slightly less dense than Rio rosewood.

For the soundboard of the guitar there seems, once again, no adequate substitute for spruce of the *excelsa* variety. This timber has been used in instrument making for gener-

1. For the early history and development of the guitar, readers are referred to Donald Gill, *Gut-strung Plucked Instruments . . .*, Lute Society Booklets, Richmond, 1976, and to James Tyler, *The Early Guitar*, London, 1979. [Ed.]

ations and, to my mind, had no equal. Naturally, the demand for this variety has been enormous and, as a result, Sitka spruce, British Columbian pine, and cedar, have all been extensively used for guitar soundboards. Although these species may have their place in the instrument-making world, I recommend the use of *Picea excelsa*, for we are concerned here not with the making of good instruments but with the making of great instruments!

2. *Tools*

The majority of the tools used in guitar making fall within the category of woodworking tools with the exceptions of the soundhole cutter and the bending iron. However, these tools can be made by the guitar-maker himself. The soundhole cutter can be made from an ordinary cutting gauge adapted for this purpose. The bending iron perhaps is more difficult as it involves the use of either gas or electricity. For those who are electrically minded, this task offers no problems. What is required is to heat a tube, made of brass, copper or aluminium, to a temperature suitable for our purpose. I have seen a bending iron made with a bar from an ordinary electric fire (space heater). Whatever electrical device we use to apply heat to the tube, extreme care must be taken to ensure that the tool is absolutely safe and if necessary an electrician must be asked to check the insulation before we put the tool to use. I have used, in my early days, a small gas poker inserted in a tube which worked well as the heat could easily be controlled.

A word about chisels, scrapers, and planes. The advantage of finely sharpened tools must be emphasized. Badly sharpened tools are the cause of many avoidable accidents because in order to make a badly sharpened tool operative, we require more pressure behind the tool, therefore, it is more difficult to control if it slips. Scrapers should be meticulously honed to give a perfect edge, and the burnisher should be as smooth as possible and free from scratches.

The smoothing planes require not only sharp edges, but also an understanding of the use of the backing iron. When doing the final planing, this iron should be as close as possible to the cutting edge of the blade. This avoids tearing the wood and lifting the fibres. To do this properly, the backing iron must sit perfectly on the blade, otherwise fine shavings will find their way in between it and the blade and will make planing practically impossible.

If you use oil stones to hone your tools, every trace of oil should be wiped off the blade before working the wood; oil and glue do not mix!

3. *Glues*

The range of glues on the market these days is very comprehensive, too many to mention here. However, I find that animal glue still plays a major role in guitar making. This glue is unbeatable for joins of the 'rubbing' group: that is, those joins such as blocks and inlays that do not require any cramping pressure. Perhaps its greatest advantage over other glues, is that if chilled in the process of gluing it can be revitalized by applying heat, rendering it again usable. It is essential for gluing the back of the guitar to the ribs since, in cases of splitting or damage to the guitar, the back can be removed very easily by re-heating the glue joint.

PVA glues are a great help in gluing purflings and linings but these glues are not recommended for struts or bars. The best glue for these is the resin type. These resin glues are water- and heat-proof, offer a tremendous bond, and are not liable to creep like some of the PVA glues. Whatever type of glue is used, utter cleanliness must be observed while handling the joins; dust and dirt must be removed and there should be minimum handling of the gluing parts.

4. *The Soundboard*

The soundboard is the fundamental soul of the instrument, and its preparation requires the greatest care and attention. The selection of the spruce boards is of primary importance and they should be quarter-sawn, preferably from a log that has first been radially cleft which will reveal the natural direction of the grain. In musical-instrument making quarter-sawn timber is always chosen for its superior strength, uniformity and stability.

The two matching pieces selected for the soundboard are first jointed with the shooting plane, then glued and clamped.[1] When the glue is dry and the joint itself has been carefully examined, lightly plane over both surfaces of the soundboard with the smoothing plane. This will reveal the lustre and grain of the spruce and will enable you to choose the most attractive surface for the outside of the soundboard. Having decided on this, take the template of the soundboard outline and mark round this on the opposite side of the soundboard, using the joint line as the centre line. Cut out the shape, being careful to make the cut about 1 cm round the outside of the pencil line; on to this narrow border are later glued the soundboard offcuts (p. 105). Returning to the side of the soundboard chosen for the outside surface, proceed with a very sharp cabinet scraper and graded papers to bring the surface to a perfect finish. When this has been achieved, use the outline template to mark the exact centre point of the soundhole, ensuring that the position of the template corresponds with the marked outline on the other side of the soundboard.

A ready-made rosette can be bought but, if one is more adventurous, rosettes to one's own dimensions and design can be made. The process of rosette making is described under a separate heading (see p. 127). Once the rosette is at hand, set your circle cutter (see Chapter 5, Fig. 3; circle cutters are also available from most luthiers' suppliers) exactly to the inside radius of the rosette's circle and mark this carefully on to the outside surface of the soundboard, using, as your centre, the centre point of the soundhole already marked. When this circle has been scribed to a depth of not more than 1 mm, set the circle cutter to a radius that exactly corresponds with the outside edge of the rosette's circle and scribe this in the same way on to the soundboard, using the same centre point as before. The waste wood between the two scribed circles must now be carefully removed with chisels to a depth of 1 mm so that the rosette itself will fit snugly into the recess with only the slightest pressure. A portion of the rosette will, of course, be covered by the fingerboard at a later stage and, when you are finally applying the glue and fitting the rosette permanently into place, you must ensure that the break in the rosette pattern is positioned so that it will later be covered by the fingerboard. In three or four hours the rosette will be set and dry.

1. One method is described in Chapter 2, p. 50. [Ed.]

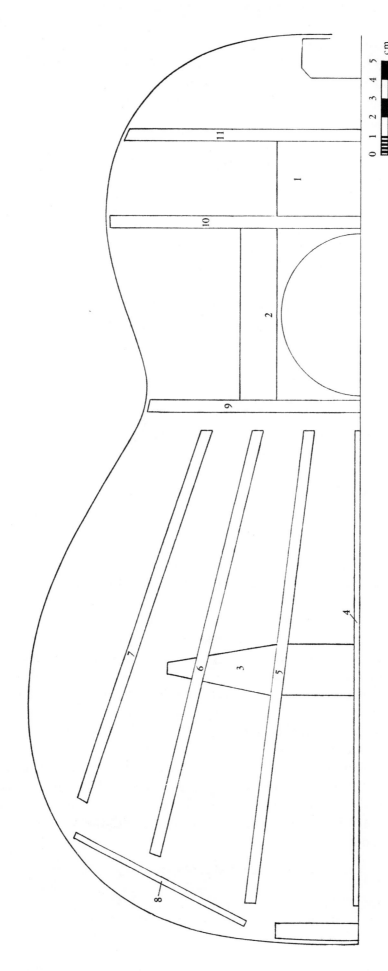

Fig. 4.1 *Soundboard and barring layout; numerals indicate gluing sequence*

The rosette must now be scraped down so that it is flush with the soundboard surface. This work is done with the sharp scraper taking pains to avoid scuffing or digging into the soundboard surface; sandpapers are to be avoided in this operation because the darker dust from the rosette will be ground into the soft spruce which is very unsightly and impossible to remove.

The soundboard is now laid face down on a clean surface and the crucial business of planing and scraping the soundboard down to the required thickness commences. There is no hard-and-fast rule about the thicknesses or where the variations of thickness, if any, should occur. The quality of the wood is the deciding factor. One literally has to apply the rule of thumb to determine the thickness. The wood has to be flexed with the thumbs to ascertain the elasticity and strength value of the soundboard. Too thick a soundboard will inhibit the sound and too thin a one produces a brittle sound.

The soundboard should be light, yet strong enough to put up a resistance to the tension-compression forces. It must be well braced to avoid flapping. I suggest a thickness of 2.5–3 mm as a general guide, but in fact the maker is really on his own and up to a point is in the lap of the gods when preparing the soundboard. It may be facile to bring in the word 'intuition', but perhaps intuition and experience are not a bad mixture. On tapping the soundboard it should sound clear, low in pitch having no predominant overtones.

Before we cut out the soundhole we must draw around the guitar-shape template (Fig. 1) on the inside of the soundboard. While the template is resting on the soundboard, small pieces of the offcuts of the soundboard should be glued following the outline of the template. This will help to obtain the perfect shape when the sides are glued to the soundboard. Mark with a soft pencil the placement of the struts and bars on the inside of the soundboard according to Fig. 1. The soundhole wood is now removed, using the circle cutter set at about 2 mm less than the rosette's narrowest radius.

The struts and bars have different functions. The fan struts must keep the part of the soundboard that they occupy properly under control. That is to say, the soundboard must be made to respond uniformly throughout; the struts, jointly with the soundboard, must find the perfect balance of flexibility and tension. They must be sufficiently strong to offer resistance to the tension and compression to which they will be subjected. This is the secret of a responsive 'breathing' movement. Too heavy struts will cause the guitar to 'gasp' for breath.

The three transverse or harmonic bars, have a dual purpose: to stop the soundboard from collapsing, and to control some of the overtones. These again require sympathetic handling to make them just the right strength.

The under-fingerboard plate must be glued with the grain running across that of the soundboard and parallel with the harmonic bars above and below. The purpose of this flat piece of spruce is to add strength to a part which has a tendency to sag inwards as well as, in cases of very drastic dryness, to crack on both sides of the fingerboard. The other important reason is to add 'meat' to that part of the fingerboard and to avoid the nasal sound that would otherwise be produced.

The inside of the soundhole is now lined with two thin plates of spruce alongside the hole, following the grain of the soundboard. The main reason is to eliminate the weakness created by the insertion of the rosette and to stop the buckling of the rosette. These plates need not be much wider than the rosette itself. Once these two plates have been glued and set, they should be planed to 2 mm in thickness. The under-fingerboard plate no. 1 must be left flat, whereas the two plates numbered 2, either side of the sound-hole, should be shaped to a feather-edge finish. When doing this job a chisel with the corner rounded off and a strip of masking tape placed alongside the edges of the struts will help to avoid damaging the surface of the soundboard. The under-bridge plate shown in Fig. 1 as no. 3 should be shaped as indicated and glued with the final thickness of 2 mm at the centre, tapering off to nothing at the edges. The excess resin glue should be cleaned away with warm water and a fine bristle brush.

The fan struts must be proceeded with as already mentioned, beginning with the centre struts. A simple device like the one shown in Fig. 2 will prove invaluable in the gluing of the struts. When you have glued the fan struts and the harmonic bars, make sure that the surplus glue has been cleaned off.

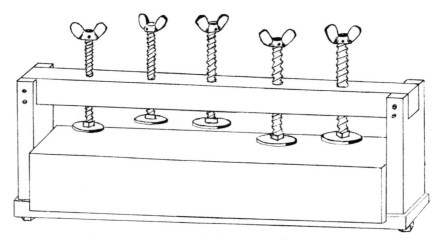

Fig. 4.2   *Cramping jig for fan struts and transverse bars*

5. *Shaping the Fan Struts and the Harmonic Bars*

The struts and bars should be of the finest spruce available. They must be cleft to gain maximum strength and the annual ring growth should fall at a right angle to the glued surface. The shaping of the struts and the bars must be done once they are glued on the soundboard. This must be undertaken with considerable caution, as it is one of the most vital jobs. Tackle this job slowly with a relaxed attitude. The best tool for the shaping is a 10-mm or 12-mm chisel with rounded corners. The idea of leaving the shaping of the struts and the bars until they are glued to the soundboard is twofold. On the one hand, their being equal in length helps the gluing procedure tremendously and, even more important, their remaining whole until after gluing gives the opportunity to adjust the thickness to the degree of flexibility required.

In the final shaping of the struts will be seen the importance of using those that have been cleft rather than sawn. By doing this we ensure that the fibres are long, i.e. what is known as the grain is neither short nor diagonal. The cleaving must be done two-dimensionally in order to secure the maximum strength within the dimension of the strut. The final thickness is determined, as already mentioned, according to the flexibility we want to impart in the soundboard. It must be taken into consideration that the centre struts require the most strength. It is in this area, immediately in front of and behind the bridge respectively, that the tension and compression of the soundboard is at its greatest. The tension and compression diminishes from the centre outwards, therefore we must make these struts perhaps 1–2 mm thicker than the struts at the edges of the soundboard.

It is almost as impossible to give a firm rule for the final dimension of the struts and the bars, or for the final 'tapping sound' of the soundboard. The struts must have perfectly round, smooth edges and should taper wedge-like at each end (see Fig. 5).

It is usual to finish the harmonic transverse bars by scalloping at the extreme ends and by making the top surface rounded and very finely smoothed. Finishing the inside of the guitar as well as the outside is of great importance as it is a proven fact that the wood surfaces reflect sound in a way not unlike light reflection. Every surface has to be given the maximum freedom to reflect sound.

The inside edge of the soundhole must be rounded and smoothed, taking care not to distort the shape. A shaped piece of wood used in the fashion of a cork-block rubber will ensure that we do not dig up the soft wood leaving an uneven edge. The soundboard is now put aside and we proceed with the neck.

6. The Neck

The ideal wood for the neck is Honduras cedar, or Honduras or Cuban mahogany. This mahogany is slightly heavier than the Honduras cedar but it offers the same qualities. It is stable and strong, yet light and easy to work. Ideally, the timbers for the neck should be cleft wood, particularly the depth side, however this is almost impossible to obtain these days. When selecting wood the grain should be parallel with the face of the fingerboard side. Short, diagonal grain should be avoided for, apart from being weaker than the straight-grained wood, it is very much more difficult to tool, and liable to warp.

The neck has to be constructed in a way that will give the maximum help for the left hand. The thickness has to be so adjusted as to give the left hand the freedom to move up and down the fingerboard with ease, yet it must offer resistance to the string pull at the same time. Contrary to what some experimentalists say, a well-thought-out neck, in the wood stated, will be perfectly stable and rigid in spite of the continuous stress.

The scale length has now to be decided. If using the standard scale length of 650 mm, a piece of Honduras cedar or mahogany would be needed of about the following dimensions: 42 cm long × 6.6 cm wide × 2.4 cm thick.

The heel must be built up to 84 mm, the depth of the guitar's ribs at the neck join. The dimensions are as shown in Figs 3a and b. The direction of the grain in the block must run in the same direction as that of the ribs of the guitar.

When we make the slots in the heel to take the ends of the ribs of the guitar, allowance must be made for the curvature of the rib at the joint with the neck. This is very important as failure to do so will throw the ribs out of shape when we bring them together. The cut into the neck should be done with a fine tenon saw at a deviation of four degrees from the right angle parting from the centre line of the neck. Mark with a short curve the thickness of the rib on the neck itself. Make the slot cuts by resting your saw blade against a block of wood, which is already shaped to give you the correct cutting angle; make this cutting block in such a way that the brass back of the tenon saw rests on the top of the block, thus giving exactly the correct depth of cut. Once you have made the first cut move the block along to proceed with the other cut to make it wide enough to take the side. A piece of veneer must be inserted to fill in the first cut to ensure that the saw does not slide back to the first cut and make the cut uneven. Clean out the widened cut with a fine chisel, making sure that the base of the slot is clean and straight.

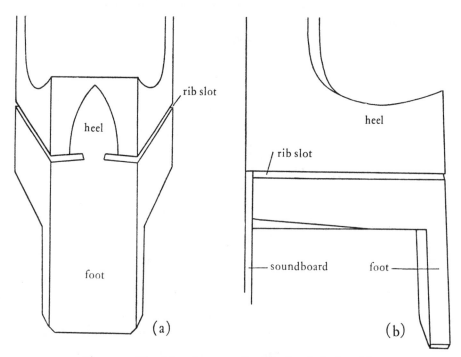

Fig. 4.3 *Plan (a) and cross-section (b) of neck, heel, and foot*

From the front part of the heel-neck assembly (Fig. 3a) that will be glued on to the soundboard pare away the thickness of the soundboard, plus a 0.5 mm allowance for glue and wood expansion, to make sure of having the neck and the soundboard flush with each other when we come to level the neck and the soundboard plane. Then a centre line is scribed on the neck from top to bottom. This mark will be an insurance against setting the neck wrongly, that is, not following the centre line of the soundboard.

The heel and foot sections of the neck must be well sandpapered. Using the white of an egg, proceed to brush-seal the end-grain of the neck and lower block with a liberal brushing. The egg white is a very good size and will help to smoothly finish the end-grain parts of the block. When dry, using fine glasspaper or sandpaper, smooth those areas concerned and then brush on a good coat of varnish or french polish. This will help to seal the end-grain of the foot block and so reduce the risk of splitting. The shaping of the heel is done at the same time as shaping the neck. I prefer to put the neck aside at this stage and proceed by preparing the ribs of the guitar; the shaping of the heel I leave until a later stage (see section 14, p. 120).

7. *The Ribs*

Once we have selected the rosewood for the ribs or sides of the guitar, which are usually bought in matched pairs about 75 cm long, proceed to plane them to the desired thickness. A well-sharpened plane and a fine scraper are all we need. The wood must be planed in a direction away from you, that is away from the device holding the wood and with the grain.

The thickness depends entirely on the quality of the wood. Make sure by flexing the wood with the thumbs across the grain, that it does not buckle like veneer. The wood must also have enough resilience to offer resistance to blows and knocks. An average thickness guide would be 2 mm to 2.5 mm for rosewood. If using any other type of timber for the sides the thickness will depend on the density and elasticity of the chosen timber.

The ribs should be planed straight on one edge. The distance from the neck-joint to the centre of the waist is marked on the outside of the ribs. When cutting the ribs allow yourself 2 mm extra on the following widths: 82 mm at the top neck-joint of the ribs, 88 mm at the waist, and 92 mm at the bottom of the ribs. If the ribs are wide enough, the surplus wood can be used to make the purflings or the inlays. Check to ensure that the grain of both ribs matches. This is an important point as we can easily bend them in such a way that the figure of the wood on one side would no longer match the other.

There are various processes, wet and dry, to bend and shape the ribs. It must be understood that the wood has to stretch and be compressed. The best means of bending the ribs to shape is to make the wood pliable by steaming, as follows: the ribs are immersed in a container of water for two hours. Afterwards they are taken out and placed in between two solid planks and weighted down or cramped together, and left for another hour.

Care must be taken not to scorch the wood when applying it to the bending iron, particularly at the waist. A piece of wet veneer between the iron and the side will help to prevent this. Working with the template of the instrument by your side, begin the bending which must commence at the waist. Carefully place the rib perfectly square to the perpendicular of the bending iron if using a vertical iron, or perfectly square to the horizontal if the iron is horizontally operated. The wood must not be forced, but held with firm pressure against the bending iron until one feels that the resistance is being undermined by the heat. As the work progresses from the waist, it must be checked periodically against the template on both edges to ensure that both sides are true to the form.

It must be stressed here that, as we are building the guitar without a mould, the execution of perfect shaping at this stage is vital. But do not worry if you do not accomplish the task at your first attempt; experience is a slow-growing friend. A well-shaped rib should rest flat on a flat surface and it should lie square to the surface.

It may be necessary, after having shaped the ribs and having put them aside for a few days, to reshape them, since wood bent in this way tends to remember its old shape. The ribs should not be wetted again, although the piece of wet veneer may be helpful.

8. *The Back*

The back must be of the finest rosewood available, quarter-sawn if possible and well seasoned. The join must be executed in the same fashion as that of the soundboard.

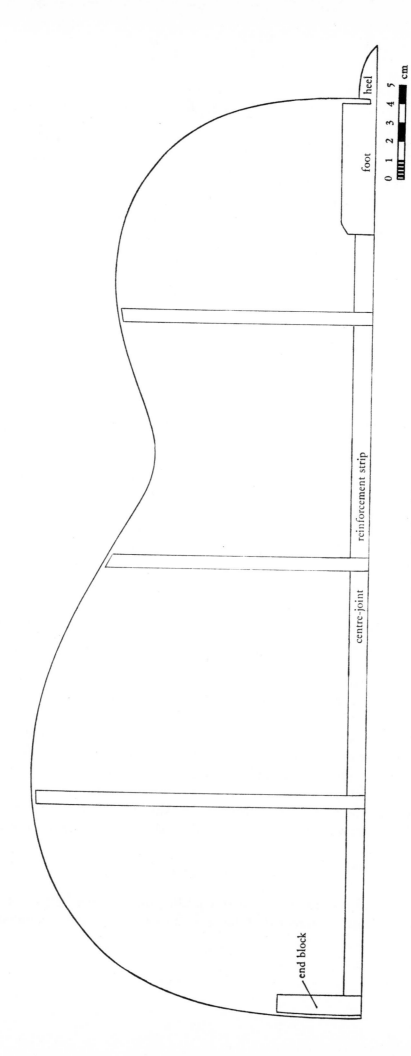

Fig. 4·4 *Back and bar positions*

Before cutting the back to the approximate shape the surfaces must be cleaned, and also planed to ascertain which is the best side for the face and which end must be by the heel. If we have two halves where the grain does not run parallel but runs diagonally, make the convergence at the heel of the neck so that when the two halves of the back are jointed the grain flows outwards to become wider at the lower half of the instrument.

Running your plane over the rosewood boards will quickly reveal the direction of the grain and, having made sure which way to handle the back, you must plane it to the right thickness. Again there is no firm rule for the ideal thickness which is governed by density and hardness. The back must not be made too thin as this will create areas which will flap and which will help to break the uniformity of purpose. When tapped, a high-pitched sound must be avoided; as with the soundboard, try to obtain the lowest possible sound without making a 'flapping' back. The pitch of the back will rise when the bars are glued in position, so test the sound before they are glued on. Here again we are treading on thin ice when considering the pitch of the back. Violin makers sometimes use an A or a G tuning, when thicknessing the backs of their instruments, and this practice is also favoured by many guitar makers.

The principal function of the back is to reinforce and help the soundboard in its job to amplify the sound, but it must fall, in order to be helpful, within the range of frequency of the soundboard. The back must be a 'servant', that is it has to take orders from the soundboard. The bars control the output of harmonic response. I avoid the high overtones of the back by ensuring that the bars are glued on the back at the points where they do not enhance the high partials. I place the bars slightly off centre of the back length. The top and bottom bars are also glued slightly off centre of their respective positions as shown in Fig. 4.

The transverse bars are usually made from mahogany, Honduras cedar, or wood of similar character. It is essential that, whatever wood is used, the grain runs parallel to the length of the bars and that they are straight and true. This will be appreciated when the wood is planed down, for the best wood is that which planes more or less the same, working from either end. The ideal way to obtain this is by splitting the wood and then by planing one side and working from that point. Short-grain wood must be avoided.

A reinforcement strip is glued on the centre join in the inside of the back. This strip seals the inside join of the back and adds a little support to the long span of the back. It should be thin, feather-edged and with the grain going along *with* the grain of the back.

The transverse bars are usually about 6 mm in width by 13–16 mm in depth. They are scalloped at the ends in the same manner as the transverse bars on the soundboard, and this is carried out when the bars have been glued to the back. The transverse bars are shaped so as to give the back a gentle arch. This arching strengthens the back.

Mark the position of the bars and fit them on to the central strip; this strip must not be cut to accommodate the bars. The press shown in Fig. 2 is invaluable when gluing these bars. In order to use this press a piece of wood must be given the corresponding curve of the back and used as the base for the gluing press. After gluing, the surplus glue should be cleaned out and the bars left to set.

9. *Inlay for the Back*

Inlays are very simple to make. They are pieces of veneers of different naturally-coloured woods glued together to form a pattern. The combinations are numerous therefore I will confine myself to the method of inserting them in the instrument.

The back central inlay is sometimes the thickness of the back and is glued in the centre of the back as the two halves of the back are brought together. The sections must be flush with each other as otherwise difficulties will arise when planing the back to thickness. However, I prefer to scratch a channel out of the back once the back has been joined together, and then to let in the inlay. I believe this is the safest and easiest method as far as the join is concerned.

Once the back has been thicknessed accurately, the centre must be found. A straight-edge is laid on the back, exactly where one of the sides of the inlay is to be, and firmly held in place with cramps. If we burr a chisel with a burnisher in the same way that one burnishes a cabinet scraper, the job will be much easier. Proceed to scratch out the wood that is occupying the area where the inlay must be laid. The chisel must be slightly narrower than the inlay and to compensate for this, we move the straight-edge slightly once we have scratched one side to make up for the difference in the width of the chisel. The strip of inlay must be tested in the groove before spreading any glue. A good dab of animal glue, a hot iron and a small hammer is all that is needed to glue the inlay down in the groove. This is the usual veneering procedure.

10. *Assembly*

We have our form, soundboard and neck as well as the ribs ready to hand, and these are all assembled on a flat work-board or form.

The form must be about 10 mm wider than the guitar with enough extension at the top for the neck to rest on. A hole is made exactly where the centre of the soundhole lies and a centre line is drawn from top to bottom of the form. This is the guide-line for the centre join of the soundboard and neck to fall on; the centre line of the soundboard must coincide with the centre line on the form.

The soundboard is laid upside down on the form and must be held firmly in position. This is ensured by a piece of wood 3.5 × 2.5 cm, long enough to go across the two harmonic bars by the soundhole, and screwed from the outside through the hole made in the form (Fig. 5). With the soundboard flat and firmly held in position continue by cutting the ribs to length. This is done by placing the ribs on to the soundboard and following the contour of the guitar shape. It is at this point that we realize how important are the small pieces of wood which were glued earlier to the outline of the instrument (see p. 105). Cramps are used to hold the ribs down while we are doing this job. After making sure that the ribs follow the contour and that they are perfectly square to the soundboard, mark on the ribs the centre-line intersection of the soundboard at the neck joint end and bottom-joint end. Mark both ribs and then calculate the angle of the neck grooves for the rib joints. Take into account the width left in the centre of the neck between the grooves that take the ribs. Taking half of this width we must measure off that amount into the rib and from that point mark the angle on the rib that must exactly correspond with the angle inside the groove. The ribs must be cut as a pair and if a mistake is made in cutting the angle the rib must be scrapped. With the block end cut made, we are now able to fit the ribs into the groove; when we are satisfied that they fit in a glove-joint way, the neck may be glued on to the soundboard.

Having rebated away the part of the neck block that fits on to the soundboard, now make sure that the centre line of the neck is a continuation of the soundboard centre line. The neck must be given a set, that is, it must lean slightly forward towards the front of the guitar; this is explained further on p. 115. Apply the glue and cramp it firmly until the glue sets.

The ribs must be cleaned inside with a scraper and glasspaper and they must be free from dust in order to have a clean surface for the glue when we press-glue the lining blocks. The end block is glued on to the soundboard allowing, when we do so, for the thickness of the rib between block and outside line of the guitar shape drawn on to the soundboard.

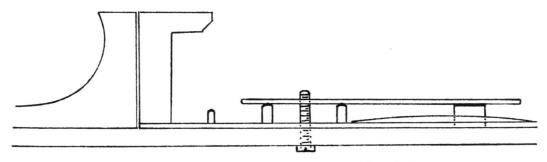

Fig. 4.5   *Neck and soundboard-to-baseboard holding device*

There are various ways to make the inside linings. The idea is simply to provide more gluing area than the thickness of the rib itself and to add strength to the contour of the guitar. Some makers use a continuous lining while others use the kerfed system which is a continuous lining with saw cuts at 1 cm intervals, cut four-fifths into the wooden strip to facilitate bending. I prefer the single-block system for the soundboard and a kerfed lining for the back. The advantage of using the single blocks for joining the ribs to the soundboard is that it enables the maker to adjust the ribs to the outline in a more comprehensive way in the dry, that is, with no glue involved. In this way we allow ourselves some flexibility and can ensure that the ribs are perfectly placed and squared. The blocks can be glued individually using an animal glue. The blocks are kept warm by placing a few at a time on the flat side of a hot iron, which will ensure that the glue will be hot enough when we rub-glue the block. A space of 2 mm between each block is a reasonable distance, although some makers choose to glue the blocks together in a continuous line.

If we follow this method it is to our advantage to ensure that the blocks follow each other in their natural sequence, as they were before they were cut. If this is not done we will find there are differences between them as they are brought together from different parts of the strip of wood. This unevenness looks very unsightly and cumbersome. The 2 mm-gap method hides these small discrepancies and makes the blocks look more harmonious.

One wedge-shaped block must be glued on the end of each transverse bar (harmonic bars) to give these bars the necessary strength needed for the support of the soundboard.

How does one determine the final depth of the guitar? This is not an easy task for there are as many variations as there are guitar makers. The size of the guitar determines, to some degree, the depth of the ribs. A large-bodied guitar will perhaps be happier with rather narrow ribs, if we are looking for the balance between treble and bass. On the other hand, a smaller guitar will require a rather deeper rib to compensate for the loss of air volume. However, this also depends upon the note that we have from the instrument without the back on. The response of the instrument on tapping will show us how it is for pitch. If rather high and with too many loose high partials we must ensure that the back is disciplined to fall in line with the soundboard as stated before (p. 111).

When the ribs have been planed to the required depth, proceed with gluing the linings. This gluing process can be made easier by making a simple cramp out of channelled aluminium (u-shaped in section) and a thumb screw. In order to make the cramping operation easier, the linings must be left square and the tapering on the inside done once they are glued to the ribs. The surplus glue must be cleaned away with a damp cloth and the linings left to set. When dry, using a sharp knife and clamping the guitar on its side, we give the linings their final shape. Finish with glasspaper to ensure a smooth finish.

Before the back is ready to go on the guitar, the bars must be shaped. This is done when their position has been marked on the guitar itself. To do this, place the back with the bars facing the inside of the guitar. Ensure that the centre line of the back coincides with that of the bottom block and with the centre line on the foot. Also check that the top end of the back is exactly on line with the outside of the ribs at the heel.

All this done, hold the back in position with a weight, and with a very sharp pencil mark the bars on the linings and side as well as marking underneath the bars on the outside of the sides. Remove the back and, with a small square, run the lines perpendicularly on the linings to mark the bar positions. Mark the depth of the cut on the linings, only about 5 mm. Using very sharp tools pare away the wood of the lining where the bars are going to be fitted.

On the back transverse bars we have marked only the outside edge of the ribs. From these lines we must go in the thickness of the ribs plus 0.5 mm; this is to make certain that the bars do not touch the ribs. Cut the bars as explained previously and shape them to the final size, scalloping them like the harmonic bars on the soundboard, and rounding them at the top edge as smoothly as possible with glasspaper.

This finished, lay the back on the instrument again and mark the point where the inside centre strip meets both the foot and the end block. The area of the back which is to be occupied by the foot can be marked on the back by measuring the distance between the heel and end block with dividers and transferring this measurement to the back itself. Clean the surplus wood away from the reinforcement strip at the foot position and at the bottom end-block position, and thoroughly clean the inside of the guitar. If using a label, now is the time to fix it on the inside of the back, beneath the soundhole.

Before finally gluing the back, a form must be made to fit on the inside of the soundboard over the fan struts, exactly on the spot where the bridge has to be fitted. This will be inserted as a cramping block when we come to glue the bridge on the soundboard, and it will ensure against an uneven soundboard surface and give a flat rigid surface when gluing the bridge.

All is now ready to glue the back in position. Animal glue is the best for this purpose together with a few violin or cello cramps. Fit them dry: that is, proceed as if gluing the back so that every screw cramp is adjusted ready for use. Take the cramps off and apply the glue to the ribs and linings. A warm flat iron will be needed to help glue on the back;

the same method as that described in Chapter 2, p. 56, can be used here. At the foot a deep-throated cramp will be needed, although care must be taken not to apply too much pressure on here, which might result in the heel block collapsing.

Having left the glue to set overnight, remove the cramps and release the guitar from the form or work-board. Proceed to clean the surplus wood from the back and sound-board edges as well as giving the ribs a going-over with the scraper to erase any irritating bumps that may be visible. This finished, place the guitar on its back and draw the centre line from bottom to top of neck.

Now it is time to check the rake of the neck, bearing in mind that at the twelfth fret the clearance of the string from the fret top must be around 5 mm at the bass side and perhaps 3 mm at the treble side, this again depending on string tension. The bridge saddle must have a height at its centre of 8.5 mm, 8 mm at the treble, and 9.5 mm at the bass from the soundboard. An ideal action should give a string height of 10.5 mm at the treble, and 11.5 mm at the bass, when measured from the soundboard surface to the underneath side of the strings. With these reference points one is able to determine the raking of the neck. Bear in mind that the height of the string over the soundboard must be as uniform as possible to reduce any possible difference in string length, taking the fingerboard as reference for string height. The more we keep the strings parallel over the fingerboard the less we increase the tension when fingering the strings in the high positions and so minimize the discrepancy in pitch difference at the twelfth fret position and above.

11. *The Head*

The basic principle to have in mind when setting the head, is the need to give the strings at the nut sufficient down-bearing to avoid back-feed and to clean-cut the vibrations of the strings at that point. I must mention that too acute an angle will result in increasing the pull on the head and therefore on the neck itself. A setting of the head of 14° is a good compromise; it will give us the necessary down-bearing and help the neck to remain straight.

From the neck/soundboard joint (this being the position of the twelfth fret), mark on the neck half the scale length we are using and add 2 mm to mark the joint of the head. I make the splice-joint in the neck/head join because, aesthetically, it is much more rewarding than the widely used scarf joint.

The head is fitted to the neck by means of a v-joint which is accomplished by leaving the pyramid part on the neck itself and cutting out the corresponding part on the head (Fig. 6). This is a tricky joint but beautiful if well done. It calls for accuracy and patience, and sharp tools are essential. Using a template, I knife-mark the v-shape on both head and neck. The end-grain of the head must be kept at right angles to the face of the head, and the 14° angle is given to the pyramid extending from the neck itself.

We have to make a form that follows the setting of the head which is cramped on the face of the neck. This will give us an anchor for the cramp when we come to glue the head on to the neck, as well as a reference so that our head keeps at the correct setting while the glue sets. Apart from the aesthetic point mentioned above, this method ensures that the wood grain is kept parallel to the length of the head, whereas if the head was made out of the same piece of wood as the neck, the wood on the head might be some-

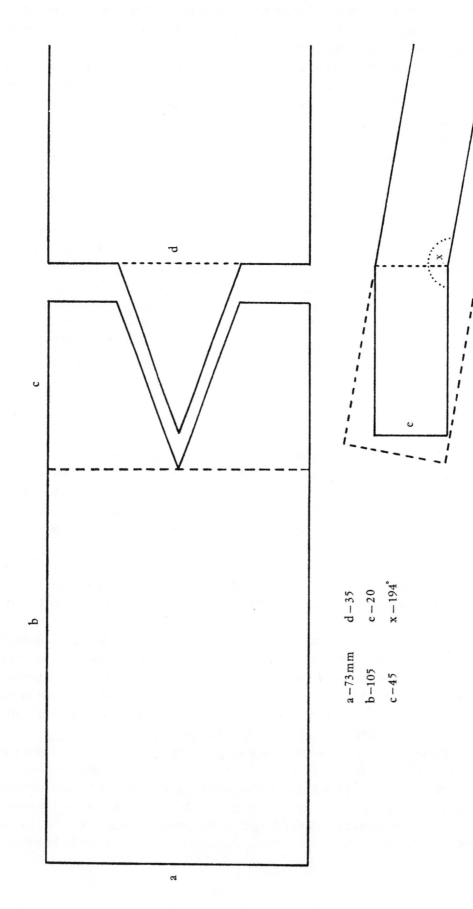

a – 73mm d – 35
b – 105   e – 20
c – 45   x – 194°

Fig. 4.6 *Neck-bead splice-joint*

what slanted and therefore weaker. Once we have glued the head in position it is then usually faced with ebony or rosewood veneer, prior to giving the head the final shape and opening the slots for the machineheads. The design for the head is idiosyncratic to every maker. Two things to consider are simplicity and soundness of design. A template will be a great asset when shaping the head (Fig. 7).

The holes to take the rollers of the machineheads are drilled before opening the slots. It is necessary to have the machineheads on hand in order to do this job accurately; the rollers are unscrewed and the plates are held in position and marked out. The final thickness of the head is 20 mm. The width of the machinehead plates is about 19 mm, and as the machineheads are located exactly in the centre, this will leave us 0.5 mm at each side. The final thicknessing must be left until we have opened the slots and shaped the head. This extra thickness will help to eliminate the damage in case of possible splintering.

The holes for the machineheads must be slightly larger than the rollers so that the rollers can turn freely with as little friction as possible. What is most irritating about poor-quality machineheads is their inability to respond evenly on turning. The poorly-machined cogs and worms will not control the string tension, on the contrary, the roller will move by leaps and bounds, making the tuning rather trying. Therefore the main priority of the machinehead must be functional accuracy, and design although important must be a secondary consideration. Unfortunately, first-class machineheads are difficult to obtain, and only recently have quality handmade machineheads become available once again.

12. *The Fingerboard*

The fingerboard should be made of ebony. Having decided to adopt the traditional string length of 650 mm, mark on the neck 325 mm from the neck-body intersection to indicate the location of the nut, as described on p. 115. The standard width at the nut should read 52 mm and the width at the body joint in the region of 64 mm. To check that the fingerboard is aligned it must be securely held in place on the neck. Then with two straight-edges, one on each side of the fingerboard, ensure that at the bottom of the guitar, the distance from the centre joint of the soundboard is exactly the half-way point between the two straight-edges. Mark the shape of the fingerboard on to the neck and run a pencil down to the soundhole to mark the semi-circular end of the fingerboard where it meets the soundhole. The surplus wood is cut away and the fingerboard fitted. Immobilize the fingerboard when gluing by the use of two dowels. This is achieved with the help of two headless pins driven into the neck on which the fingerboard should be laid as if you were fixing it permanently in position. The pins will give us the centre of the dowels and these must be inserted in the upper neck surface, carefully avoiding boring too deep into the fingerboard. Remove the pins before drilling the holes for the dowels and then glue the fingerboard in position.

It cannot be stressed too strongly that the fingerboard is one of the most important parts of the guitar. A well-worked-out fingerboard will not only determine the ease with which the guitar may be played, but it has a substantial role to play in the sound-quality of the guitar itself, as well as in the intonation. To elaborate at length on this subject is beyond the scope of this chapter, but a few points will help to elucidate some of its functions.

By far the most critical aspect of the fingerboard is the accurate calculation and

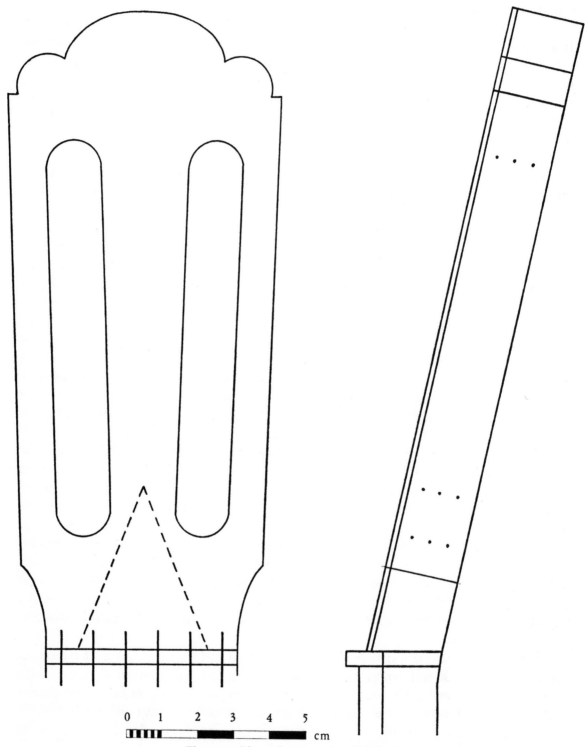

0   1   2   3   4   5
                        cm

Fig. 4.7   *Plan and cross-section of the head*

placement of frets, explained below. We are concerned here with the setting of the fingerboard in relation to the bridge. This is particularly critical as the down-bearing pressure on the bridge-saddle determines, in no small degree, what kind of sound we have; too much down-bearing will result in a tightening of the instrument and the result will be a banjo-like sound, as the high partials will come into prominence.

It must be understood that we need more clearance at the bass side of the fingerboard than at the treble side. This is because the excursion of the bass strings is greater. Thus, in order to allow the bass string to work without buzzing, we have to increase the height of the saddle at the bass side or we must reduce the thickness of the fingerboard at the bass side. I favour the latter method, for in this way we keep the saddle down to a reasonable height. This is accomplished by giving the fingerboard a slant from treble to bass, that is, the fingerboard, instead of being parallel throughout, is slanted, leaving the treble side 1.5 mm thicker than the bass side. This slanting must start from the topmost part of the fingerboard, where the nut is situated, and must be diagonally flat to the very end of the fingerboard at the bass side of the soundhole. The accumulated difference in height at the extreme ends of the fingerboard at the soundhole end must be a difference of 1.5 mm. This method allows us to reduce the height of the saddle on the bass side by exactly the same amount.

I true the fingerboard and fret it once it is glued on to the neck; however, there are some makers who glue the fingerboard already fretted. This method is rather chancy, for a slight movement of the timbers will result in the fretting being inaccurate which in turn must be, when possible, counteracted by doctoring the frets with the possibility of making the fret spacings unequal within themselves. Both methods offer their advantages and here again the personal approach and the result will be the deciding factor.

The fret spacing is worked out mathematically by using logarithms or a pocket calculator. What we are concerned with is dividing the string length into particles of the musical scale. Equal-tempered fret spacing is based on the result of finding the square root of 2, that is the division of the octave into twelve sections.

The figure is 1.059461 and if we divide the scale length of 650 mm by 1.059461 the result is 613.52 mm which is the distance from the bridge *front* to the first fret. Again, proceed by dividing 613.52 mm by 1.059461, which gives 579.06 mm; this being the second fret position, and so carrying on the same procedure of division up to the nineteenth fret.[1]

The only difficulty involved in this method is that of ensuring that the measurements are accurately transferred to the fingerboard. This is done by marking these measurements on to a wood or metal template shaped like the fingerboard. Using the template, these figures are then transferred to the actual fingerboard.

Before making the saw cuts on the fingerboard which take the frets, check that the saw cut is the right width for the frets. Then make the cuts and bed-in the frets. It is

1. In calculating fret positions the divisor 17.817 can also be used. The string length is divided by this number and the result gives the position of the first fret from the nut; the fret measurement is then subtracted from the string length and the result is then divided again by the divisor, and this process continues until the desired number of fret positions have been reached. The divisor, 17.817, gives an exact half of the string length (i.e. one octave) at the twelfth fret and close to two-thirds at the nineteenth fret. The calculations described will also give accurate fret positions for viols and lutes, where equal-tempered fretting is required; further information on different temperaments can be found in Appendix 11 of *John Dowland* by Diana Poulton (London), 1972. [Ed.]

simple to perform our task on the neck; however, on the floating section of the fingerboard, between frets thirteen and nineteen, we are in a different region. It is here that one realizes how essential it is to make an accurate cut and to have the right type of fret. Every tap on the fret with the hammer must drive the fret home. Re-tapping on the same section of fret wire is fatal; it will be to no avail as the subsequent tapping will help to lift the fret again and not to bed it. If this happens, we could use a G-cramp to bed them in properly. A wooden block must be placed inside the guitar and it must be thick enough to clear the height of the harmonic bars.

The frets should be trued over the entire fingerboard surface. An ordinary dry honing stone will do this job perfectly. Once they have been trued, they should be rounded, either with the fret files designed for this purpose or with an ordinary fine file. Self-adhesive tape placed in between the frets will prevent the scouring of the fingerboard during this procedure. Raw linseed oil is sometimes used to darken and protect the fingerboard.

At whatever stage you choose to fret the fingerboard, the fingerboard itself is usually glued to the neck after the purflings have been fitted (see section 14 below).

13. *Shaping the Heel*

It is at this stage, when the guitar has been completely assembled, that I prefer to shape the curved heel of the neck. Some guitar makers shape the heel before the ribs are fitted into the slots but this is a matter for personal choice. The heel of the guitar and its shape will greatly influence the aesthetic success of your instrument: the curve must be bold but elegant. When you have designed satisfactory curves for the front-edge and sides of the heel, cut two thin templates to these shapes which will be applied to the heel itself as the carving proceeds. These will ensure that both sides of the heel are symmetrical and that the front-edge of the heel agrees in profile to the curve you have designed. Cut the profile curve of the heel with a bow-saw to within 1 mm or 2 mm of the marked curve. Then proceed to pare away the surplus wood with gouges, files, and rifflers; frequently use your templates to check that not too much wood is being removed. Complete the heel-shaping processes with graded sandpapers, dampen to raise the grain, and finally smooth with flour paper. When every blemish has been removed from the heel, apply the white-of-egg size, as with the foot of the neck in preparation for french polishing.

14. *Inlays and Purflings*

Once the head is glued our attention must turn to the making, fitting and gluing of the inlays and purflings. Before starting, check that the soundboard and back are clean and check the sides for bumps.

Inlays can be made in many different patterns. These are made by sandwiching together thin naturally-coloured veneers (not dyed) until we have the thickness for the design required. The inlays must be delicate in form, and to achieve this we have to use very thin veneers. I usually make my veneers from wood-shavings taken from a specially prepared piece of holly or hawthorn. For this we require a straight-grained, knot-free piece of wood, and a very, very sharp plane – preferably a jointer or jack plane. A certain amount of control over the planing is needed, as well as experimentation with thicknesses, until you arrive at the final, required thickness. These shavings will come out of the plane curled up but when ironed with a hot iron they will then be suitable to be made into the sandwich.

With harder woods like rosewood and ebony this procedure is not possible because of their hardness. These woods are often used for purflings and have to be scraped to bring them to the right thickness. A simple device to help us make these veneers thinner is to anchor an ordinary scraper on to two solid supports on a flat piece of wood and to draw the veneers through repeatedly until we have the required thickness.

Once we have prepared all the veneers, glue them together to form the pattern using a heat-proof glue (synthetic resin). This is essential since, when we come to shape them on the bending iron, the shaping required can be carried out without the glued inlays coming apart.

The purflings are usually made of a hard-wearing wood such as rosewood or satin-wood. The function of the purfling is something more than a decorative device. In the first place it seals all the open grain in the soundboard and back, and it protects the wood from splintering. Secondly it adds strength and rigidity to the rim, helping to maintain stability as well as giving the instrument a well-finished appearance.

It is advisable to have the purflings cut to size and shape before proceeding to make the rebates in the edges of the guitar to take the purflings. The best tool for cutting the rims is a cutting gauge, which works on the same principle as an ordinary marking gauge, except that it must be adapted to negotiate round the waist of the guitar. The blade must be extremely sharp and semi-circular in shape in order to avoid the cutter wandering in its tendency to follow the grain. This is a very important point, particularly where the soundboard is concerned. On the ribs, instead of using a cutting gauge, I favour a scratching gauge so that the cutter scratches away the wood, making a channel. This is a great help, particularly in avoiding splintering the ribs when we are paring away the surplus wood where the purfling must fit.

I glue both the purfling and the inlay at the same time. Although this demands complete accuracy it is in my opinion the best method. This is accomplished by paring away the wood from the edges of the guitar for both the inlay and the purfling and then gluing both, as I have said, at the same time, using string right round the guitar pressing on the corner of the purfling and holding them in place. For this a form like the work-board is needed which is slightly larger than the guitar, with round-headed screws fixed on the edges to anchor the string. This is a very simple method, but by far the most effective.

I start from the waist going up until I reach the joint with the neck taking about 100 mm in length at a time. Then I proceed from the waist down to finish at the bottom of the guitar.

The inlay must be thoroughly bedded down in the groove, which is done by the pressure of the string bound round the guitar body. The joining of the two purflings at the bottom can be done with a butt joint or a mitre joint. I prefer the mitre joint as this can be made almost invisible, whereas the butt joint is always more-or-less visible. The surplus glue must now be cleaned away.

Apart from the join at the heel, the same procedure is carried out with the back. I usually make the heel section of the inlay an integral part of the back, so a rebate for the inlay must first be cut round the top edge of the heel to take the purfling. The purfling and the inlay follow round as for the rest of the back and the central inlay right up to the top of the heel.

The inlay on the guitar ribs is usually fitted after the purflings and the top and back inlays have been glued and cleaned. The side inlay is positioned so as to cover the join of the purfling and the rib. In this way, if we have been unlucky with this join, the error can be righted by covering it with the side inlay. When using the old-fashioned scratch gauge for this purpose, take care to control the depth and the width. The inlays must be shaped as closely as possible to the guitar's rib shape, testing them in the groove before applying the glue. Proceed as in veneering (Fig. 8).

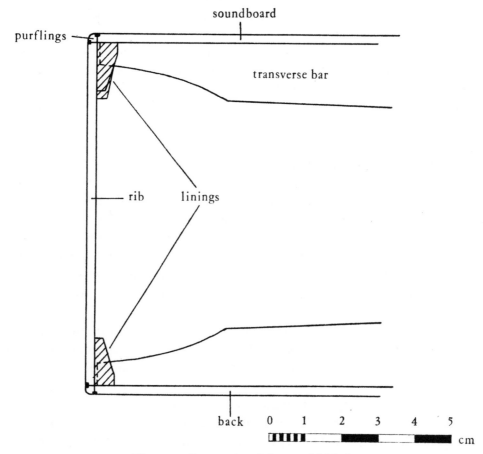

Fig. 4.8 *Cross-section of the assembled body*

15. *Shaping the Neck*

The tools used in shaping the neck are the spokeshave, chisels, gouges, and a knife. We have to work carefully, checking the thickness regularly to keep within the figures given as follows (which include the fingerboard):

Nut 21 mm
3rd fret 22.5 mm
6th fret 24.5 mm
10th fret 27 mm

These thicknesses apply to Honduras cedar and mahogany but other timbers classified as hardwoods could, of course, also be used. However, I have not experimented with other timbers for the neck so I am unable to give any recommendations on that point.

The neck should be semi-circular in shape and for this purpose four templates are required: the first template to go below the nut, the second template to go under the third fret, the third template to go under the sixth fret, and the fourth template to go under the tenth fret. It is advisable to make a fifth template for the side of the heel, to be certain that both sides of the heel are identical in shape. It is a great help, when shaping the heel, to work with the grain and not to disturb the end-grain too much, otherwise, particularly if the wood is soft, we will have a tremendous job to make this part smooth enough for polishing.

I finish the shaping of the neck using various grades of glasspaper. I half-wrap a piece of glasspaper around the neck, and with the hands holding the glasspaper on each side of the neck I run the glasspaper backwards and forwards on the neck with a downward pulling motion. This method will help to achieve the roundness on the back of the neck and eliminate any bumps and unevenness. Once we have finished shaping the neck, the head should be given the final thickness, and both the head and the neck should be rubbed with a damp cloth to raise the grain. The final smoothing should be done with flour paper.

16. *Nut and Saddle*

I use ivory to make the nut and the saddle. It is expensive but is unbeatable when compared with other materials, although good-quality bone is a very fine substitute. The nut is fitted as accurately as possible and should be rounded at the top ends. I fit the strings at 9-mm intervals from centres and the grooves to take the strings should be deep enough to keep the strings securely in place. The strings should run smoothly in the grooves and care must be taken not to round the front edge of the nut, otherwise the vibrating string will not be clean-cut and the result may be unwanted buzzing and loss of tone quality. The nut is 4 mm thick and the height will be determined by the type of fret used. The strings should be high enough to clear the frets; the bass side clearance should be 2.5 mm and 1.5 mm on the treble side, measuring from the underside of the string to the top of the first fret.

The saddle should also be fitted as accurately as the nut, and once we have worked out the appropriate height (see p. 115), the top edge should be rounded, very smooth, and burnished to ensure that the strings run evenly while the instrument is tuned. The saddle should be 2.5 mm thick (Fig. 9).

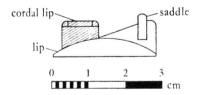

Fig. 4.9 *Cross-section of bridge and saddle*

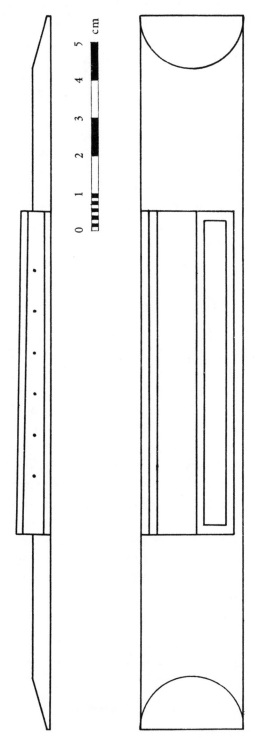

Fig. 4.10 *Plan and side elevation of the bridge*

17. *The Bridge*

The bridge itself should be made of rosewood, cleft and straight-grained, with the dimensions as given in Fig. 10.

The lip at the rear base of the 'cordal block' has the vital function of moving the strings away from the glue join of the bridge to the soundboard. This is the most vulnerable point, and thus moving the 'axis' of the pull of the strings from the very edge of the bridge inwards we can thus strengthen the joint. If possible the edges of the cordal block, the sections where the strings are tied round, should have some hard-wearing edging. Ivory is a good material. This prevents the strings from digging into the rather softer wood and so minimizes the wear. Before preparing to shape the bridge to its final shape, it is advisable to cover the underface of the bridge with self-adhesive tape, in order to keep the gluing area perfectly clean.

It is when one comes to gluing the bridge in position that one realizes the importance of the block of wood that was made to fit on the inside of the soundboard beneath the bridge (see p. 114). Place the block in position and hold it with two 'props' inside the guitar from the back to the soundboard. The props should be exactly placed so that they hold the piece of shaped wood exactly underneath the bridge. The fitting of the props must be carefully controlled so that they do not disturb the shape or arching of the soundboard. This done, the bridge should be laid on the soundboard and its exact position marked.

The safest way to ensure that the bridge is glued in the right position is to make a template of plywood, or some thin wood, of the right length from nut to saddle with a lip glued to the template to fit into the groove made for the saddle. To compensate for the increase in tension in the higher register, I add 2 mm to the given scale length so that, for a 65-cm string length, the bridge will be positioned 65.2 cm from the nut. I find, for my guitars, that 2 mm is a perfect adjustment, and this must apply to many other guitars too.

For gluing the bridge I use a combination of deep-throated cramps and the old-fashioned technique of go-bars: the cramps for the bridge wings and the go-bar in the centre. To do this, place the guitar on a soft surface of felt, taking extreme care to lay the guitar so that it rests exactly on the points where the cramping blocks (p. 114) touch the back. This insures against any damage that may occur if we put pressure where there is no support.

With the bridge laid on the soundboard, place the template on the fingerboard and fit the lip of the template into the saddle groove on the bridge. Find the location for the template and, checking that the bridge is exactly in the centre of the soundboard, mark the corners of the bridge on the soundboard with a soft pencil. Remove the template and, either with cramps or go-bar, secure the bridge on exactly the same place as before. I use two small dowels to locate the bridge whilst gluing. With a fine drill bore two holes inside the saddle groove while the bridge is in position. Care must be taken not to drill the holes so that they go through the fan struts as this will weaken the struts. Glue the dowels into the bridge; then double-check that the bridge is in the right position by placing the template as before. The soundboard must be thoroughly cleaned, using a very sharp cabinet scraper, before gluing the bridge.

I glue the bridge with a resin glue such as Cascamite before varnishing or polishing the soundboard. This allows me the opportunity to adjust the soundboard, after trying the guitar for sound, by either scraping or using finishing papers where needed.

18. *Cleaning and Polishing*

In the final cleaning of the guitar prior to polishing, I recommend that the back and ribs should be finished before the soundboard; carefully avoid letting the rosewood dust creep on to the soundboard. Whilst sandpapers are used elsewhere, do not use them for finishing the soundboard for two reasons. First the fine particles of dust are forced into the pores and tend to blur the wood; secondly, even if used with great care, sandpapers tend to scratch and, although the scratches are very fine, they will be most difficult to remove. For this job I recommend a sharp scraper which will rake the dust particles that remain in the pores out of and not into the soundboard. Small bumps, that are undetectable unless the contrasting light and shadow throws them out, must be eliminated at this stage. If these bumps are left on the guitar the polish will give them prominence and will result in an ugly patch on the instrument. An electric light may be used to show up these irregularities, and again used, when neatly rounding the edges of the instrument, to show up any ridges.

Some of the wood used in guitar-making, such as rosewood, is very open-grained. In order to achieve a perfect surface, therefore, it is essential to fill in the open pores to give a flat continuous surface. A solution has to be found that fills the pores and remains in place. Pumice powder mixed up in a volatile or evaporating agent is a good medium. This coloured filler should be applied to the back, sides, neck, and head but *not* to the soundboard. The soundboard should be left unfilled but if colour is desired this should be carefully controlled with spirit- or water-based dyes using a wad of cotton wool; alternatively, use a coloured varnish.[1] Try the colouring on a piece of scrap wood of the soundboard until you can skilfully stain the wood without causing patchiness.

I apply egg-white instead of water, prior to polishing the guitar, in order to emphasize the grain; this also helps to fill in the pores in the soundboard as well as bringing out the beauty of the wood. When the egg-white has been applied, and dried, it should be burnished very carefully with flour paper, well worn in order not to scratch the soundboard again or to make it patchy.

Much has been written about varnishes and their uses in musical instrument making, yet we are still in the dark about the effect, beneficial or otherwise, on the tone of the instrument. Contrary to some opinions, I do not believe that the varnish or polish is the determining factor controlling the tone quality. However, I do believe that the finish affects an instrument in some small degree, though not enough to be noticeable, unless the quantities of varnish applied reach the proportion of absurdity, as is the case in some of today's instruments where the finishing coats form three or four thick layers.

The polishing of the guitar has a two-fold advantage; first, as a preventative against moisture absorption and, secondly, as a surface protector in addition to enhancing the beauty of the wood.

Although varnish has been used for centuries, the present-day guitars are either

---

1. See Chapter 1, p. 33f. [Ed.]

french-polished or spray-finished with lacquer. However, we are concerned here with the traditional french-polish finish which is a solution of shellac diluted in methylated spirit and applied with the old-fashioned 'rubber' method. This is a difficult process – a separate craft in itself – that probably takes as long to learn as any other professional craft, and one where proficiency is only reached with experience.

The basic principle is simply to spread the polish evenly all over the instrument until a substantial coat has been applied. This job is carried out with a 'rubber', a wad of cotton wool or wadding wrapped inside a piece of fine linen. The wad is soaked with polish and, with the linen well wrapped round the wad, the wad is then flattened. The pad or rubber must be lubricated with a smear of raw linseed oil to prevent the rubber sticking to the polished surface as you proceed; it is also vital to keep the rubber moving otherwise it will stick to the tacky surface and ruin the finish. I strongly advise some practice in french-polishing before starting on the instrument.

Varnishes fall into two categories: oil-bound or spirit-bound; these are mixtures of various resins dissolved either in oil or spirit. The formulas are limitless, however, and various reliable varnishes can be purchased from reputable dealers.

Unless we have some means of precipitating the drying process of the oil varnish or are prepared to wait months for the instrument to dry, it is better to keep to the spirit finishes; that is to french-polishing or spirit-varnishing. The reason why oil varnish takes longer to dry than does spirit varnish is that methylated spirit evaporates while oil oxidizes. Oxidizing depends much more on the favourable atmospheric conditions than does the drying of spirit varnish. We have heard how the violin makers used to hang their instruments to dry in the open air; however, what applies to violins does not necessarily apply to other instruments, least of all in unfavourable climatic conditions. While both 'plates' of the violin are free to move with the vagaries of the weather (dryness-moisture), guitars are restricted and inhibited by the system of struts and bars. Unless we can ensure that the atmospheric conditions are identical to those of the workshop in which the instrument has been constructed we will find ourselves in great difficulties.

19. *Rosette-Designing and Making*

It is in the designing and making of the rosette that the guitar maker will show the seal of his personality. Patterns are numerous and the making involves a straightforward approach and lots of common sense. The majority of amateur guitar makers, and certainly a few professionals as well, use the mass-produced rosettes. These rosettes are made with dyed woods and, although well made, they lack the character and the nobility of the rosettes made with naturally-coloured woods. The difficulty in using naturally-coloured woods as compared with the dyed veneers is no less, but the result is much more pleasing.

There are various methods of making rosettes and here I will describe the way I tackle my rosette-making and hope that this will encourage others to make their own rosettes. This method provides a number of rosettes of the same pattern.

A round form or tube is needed which must be 4 mm larger in diameter than the soundhole. We shall build the rosette round this tube. We also require a flexible strip of 16 swg aluminium, long enough to go round the tube and the rosette plus about 100 mm more at each end. This is used as a cramping device when gluing the whole rosette together. This aluminium strip has to be made into a keyhole shape, and the narrower end has to be securely fixed to a block of wood about 50 mm wide (Fig. 11).

Once the motif has been decided, we must prepare the corresponding 'sandwiches' of veneers. Every section of the motif must have its corresponding sandwich. These sandwiches are brought about by gluing veneers together in a pre-arranged sequence in such a way that, when we bring together the slices – one from each sandwich – they will create the motif within the block. For those who know of Tunbridge ware, there will be no difficulty in understanding what I mean.

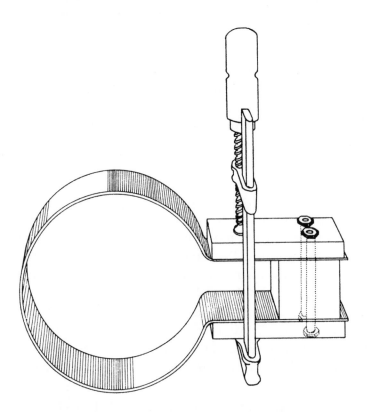

Fig. 4.11 *Cramping device for gluing and holding the rosette.*

We must, when gluing the veneers into sandwiches, be extremely accurate in achieving the same thicknesses for each individual block. The reason is that if different thicknesses are brought together they will throw the motif out of true. So to achieve uniformity of thickness the same pressure must be applied to every sandwich. If using PVA glues, allowance has to be made for the sandwich to dry, and it must be protected from warping. When dry, they have to be cut into thin slices, the same thickness as that of the veneers – probably the most difficult job of the rosette-making procedure. I use a very fine circular saw blade for this procedure, but even so this is a tricky enterprise. However, the slices could be cut thicker and then trued using the same method as is used in the thinning of the veneers. These thin slices are glued together and again a system has to be used to ensure the right uniformity of pressure throughout the whole length of the block.

When dried, these blocks must be tapered radially so as to fit round the form. This taper has to be accurately worked out if we are to achieve a perfect fit. Take extreme care in removing exactly the same amount of taper from each side of the block, otherwise, when we bring them together, the discrepancies will show rather clearly and spoil the motif. The taper could be made by the use of the shooting board; a system has to be devised with the right amount of tilting to achieve the right angle for the taper, planing one side and then adjusting the procedure for the other side.

Long pieces of veneer have to be selected to make the inner and outer layers of the ring. These veneers are wrapped round the tube in the selected order and, with the help of the aluminium device, cramped together, after animal glue has been applied to the veneers. One section after another is made, each one by exactly the same method, and each section or block is rub-glued to the one next to it. It is while fitting and gluing these blocks into the circular tube that we shall realize how vital it is to have made the taper perfect. The blocks or sections will not form a complete circle, and it is this break in the pattern which will be covered over by the fingerboard. I start gluing the blocks exactly in the middle of the circle and carry on from there until complete, building up on both sides of the central block. Once this job is accomplished, the identical section to the first section must be glued round the blocks to complete the design.

The whole rosette must be cramped and left to dry until you are sure that the glue humidity has evaporated. It can then be removed from the form, and slices for individual rosettes may be cut as required. It is advisable to keep the remainder of the rosettes on the form until needed. For those who wish to make a single rosette for a single instrument, it may already be clear that one tapered block or section can be sufficient if the block is carefully sliced and assembled on a flat surface in the same manner as described above.[1]

20. *Stringing and Tuning*

Choosing the strings for our guitar is a matter for some consideration as there are strings of different tensions and gauges. One has to be prepared to spend some time trying different strings until one is satisfied which strings suit the instrument. Experimenting with the strings can be done once the guitar has been strung and tuned.

The stringing should start with the lower string, bottom E, followed by the top E, the 2nd string, the 5th, 4th, and 3rd, in that order so that the guitar and its component parts are not submitted to any unequal strain. The tension should be gradually brought up to modern pitch, $A' = 440$. The guitar should be left to settle for a couple of hours and then tuned again. Guitars take several days to build up the tension required, and the strings have to be given the chance to stretch and settle as does the instrument. If you decide to experiment with different string gauges they should not be removed all at once, but one by one, and the new string should be tuned before the removal of the next string.

1. A further description of rosette-making can be found in Irving Sloane's *Classic Guitar Construction*, New York, 1966, p. 80f. [Ed.]

5

The Harpsichord

MICHAEL JOHNSON

1. *Introduction*

I remember, some years ago, having just finished my first harpsichord – a walnut-veneered, pedalled instrument, complete with plastic jacks and leather plectra – asking Jane Clarke to give me an opinion. After playing the instrument for a while she remarked that it was not a bad harpsichord, but I would be well advised to seek out an original old instrument to copy. To this day I am most grateful for those words of advice which proved to be the turning point in my career.

This chapter will therefore be devoted to the traditional harpsichord and I shall go on to describe my approach to making a French double manual. First, however, I will describe how I set about measuring an old instrument.

Should you be fortunate enough to examine an instrument that is undergoing major restoration work, you may find that the bottom board has been removed and you will be able to see how the instrument has been framed and barred. This is the usual way to make any repairs to the soundboard, etc. Take this God-sent opportunity to measure in detail exactly where the soundboard barring is placed and also the position of the framing. Failing this, you might make a careful inspection with a lamp through the rose or sound-board leaders, though this will not enable you to take any of the vital measurements. Otherwise, it is possible, but expensive, to have the instrument x-rayed. I have a most helpful friend who is a vet! Several museums now offer a further alternative by making invaluable x-ray plans available.

There are of course some excellent books too, Hubbard's[1] comes to mind, which will provide a great deal of information, should you have to frame and bar the instrument without those important details mentioned above.

Read and study carefully all the information you can lay your hands on before building what will in fact be your own frame and soundboard barring. This should, however, be so close to the traditional design of the period you are copying, that your harpsichord will produce the sound you would expect from a period instrument.

2. *Drawing a Plan*

You will of course have access to the case dimensions and thicknesses and these should be accurately recorded. Search for chips in veneers, or parts that have not been lacquered,

1. Frank Hubbard, *Three Centuries of Harpsichord Making*, Cambridge, Mass., 1965.

to decide what are the woods to be used, for it is most important to use traditional materials if you want to capture the character and tone of the original.

After taking out all the jacks, and having ascertained they are original, you should make a full-scale drawing of one of them showing accurate details of the length, breadth and thickness of both the blank and the tongue. Note whether the tongue varies on the 4-ft jacks and, most important of all, where the axle pin is situated. By removing the keyboards you can take accurate details of where the balance pins are; for the fulcrum point of the keyboard is all important to the final touch. It determines the distance a key will dip in order to complete its work. Another important detail to observe, is how the keyboards are balanced.

It is advisable to measure the speaking lengths, and gauge every string, though I doubt whether you could be sure that the strings are original. Should you find any maker's string-size numbers, make a note of these, for although the diameters would not be metric measurements as we know them today, they should show where gauges are changed on the original instruments. Makers usually mark the pin plank, behind the bridge, where they change gauge.

Be sure also to take the measurement from the nut to the plucking point of each of the jacks – the first and last note of the compass and the plucking point of each 4-ft jack – for reasons which will become obvious later.

With some good-quality brown paper, carefully cut out to shape a length to fit inside the case and completely cover all the soundboard area, including the gap for the jacks and tuning pin plank. If you have been accurate in shaping this, you will be able to stretch the paper flat by sticking it to the inside of the case with masking tape. Then, with a wax crayon (or better still, cobbler's heelball, if you can get it) rub over the bridge pins, hitch pins, nut pins and tuning pins. Whereupon you will have a very accurate detail of the 8-ft scaling. You have already measured the speaking lengths of the 8-ft strings, but the rubbing will give you accurate details of the length of the string behind the bridge to the hitch pins and from the tuning pins to the plank bridge. It will also give you the angle of side draft at these two points.

Before starting to make the instrument, it is advisable to first make all the templates. Of course these can be used again and again, but even if only one instrument is being made, the templates should be well prepared just the same. The main plan ideally should be done on 4-mm plywood of good quality. Take the rubbing of the original scaling and, with the help of your measurements, cut out the shape of the instrument less the thickness of the case. It is a good idea to sandpaper the plywood board and give it two coats of white undercoat or emulsion paint at this stage, so that your pencil markings are clear.

As you already have measurements of the thicknesses of case parts, you do not need them on this pattern. Now put on to the plan the details of the plank, gap for the jacks, the size of the 8-ft hitch pin rail and, if any, soundboard-cap mouldings. Carefully place the rubbings of 8-ft bridges etc. over the plan, checking all the time with the measurements you have taken, and prick with a sharp point the position of the hitch pins, bridge pins, nut pins and tuning pins. On removing the rubbing you should have details of all the 8-ft scaling.

With a 1 mm drill bit carefully bore a hole through each prick mark and join up these holes with a pencil line. Now even your plan starts to look like a harpsichord!

The next stage is to put in the plucking points by measuring them on to the plan in the same way that you took them from the original instrument. Draw lines through the gap for the jacks, representing the plucking points to each register of jacks.

With the measurements you have taken of each 4-ft plucking point, it is now possible to mark in the 4-ft nut pins, and from there the measurement of the speaking lengths will give you the detail of the bridge pins and thereby the path of the 4-ft bridge.

You will also have measured the length of each string and angle behind the bridge, so you can now plot the hitch pin band to the 4-ft choir. The bar that retains these pins is the 8-ft cut off (see Fig. 2).

The 4-ft tuning pins will have come out on the rubbing, so you can bore the 4-ft scaling holes with a 1 mm drill bit and pencil in those strings. The 4-ft strings should be spaced away 0.5 mm from the 8-ft string above it, otherwise the 4-ft damper will foul the 8-ft string when playing. By now you will be tired of boring 1 mm holes, but mark the centre of the rose on the plan and finally bore this small hole. With a pair of compasses you can draw the area to be cut from the soundboard to take the rose.

Now fill in all the details on the plywood board such as framing, soundboard bars, 4-ft and 8-ft cut-off bars, and the area of soundboard to be glued to the liners; also the soundboard leader or leaders in the case of instruments other than Italian harpsichords. The leader is the piece of framing retaining the soundboard at the gap. The keyboards can also be drawn in, and you should then have a master plan showing where everything goes.

With another piece of painted plywood, draw a side plan of the keyboard to scale with all other details appertaining to the keyboards and key frame, etc. Yet another piece of painted plywood should show a plan of the side view of the case, where the soundboard liners go in relation to the bottom boards, plus their dimensions; where the upper framing goes in relation to the soundboard liners and their dimensions, and where the lower framing goes. Of course this plan will show the depth of the case including the thickness of bottom boards.

Go back to the master plan and, between every six pairs of strings on a line 1 mm behind the bridge pins, bore holes with a 2.8 mm drill bit. From these holes you will dowel the bridges to the soundboard, thus enabling accurate location. Do the same for the nuts, spacing them evenly over the area, as only five dowels will be necessary here. Be sure to bore the holes in the master plan at right angles, because now you have to make separate templates for the 8-ft hitch pin rail, bridges, 4-ft hitch pin rail and plank.

This template is made by placing some 7-mm plywood under the master plan and marking through with a pin that just fits the hole. You will now see that if the hole in the master plan is not at right angles, the under piece will be marked incorrectly.

With a band-saw or bow-saw you can now cut out separate templates for the bridges, etc. These should be made to cover the whole area of the bridges to be glued to the soundboard and all holes must be bored with a 1 mm drill bit. The same applies to 8-ft hitch pin rails and 8-ft cut-off bar. You will also need an area plan of the wrest plank showing where to bore each hole for the tuning pins as well as where to place the nuts on the plank bridges.

3. Bent-side Former

All that remains, before work can commence on the instrument, is to make a bent-side jig.

It is advisable to make a solid former on which to laminate the bent-side, but if only a single bent-side is to be made, it does seem rather an expense and a lot of work. A simple former can be made by cutting to the curve of the bent-side three pieces of 25-mm pine 10 cm longer than the bent-side and 25 cm deep. Do this by screwing the three boards together, so that you cut them identically.

When you have achieved the correct shape, increase the curve at the front by approximately 1 cm, gradually losing it into the bend and then towards the tail by approximately 5 mm (see Fig. 1). This is to allow for the laminate to spring back a little which it is sure to do. Join up the three boards with spacers of 25 × 25 × 350 mm every 150 mm or so at the bottom of the former.

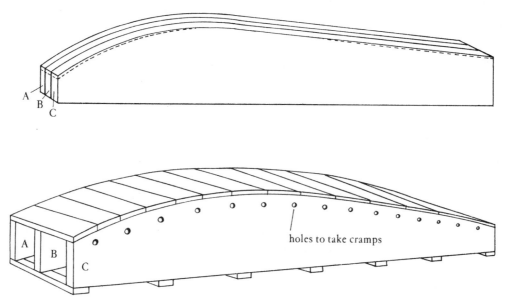

Fig. 5.1 *Laminated bent-side former, constructed from three or more boards. The dotted cutting line shows extra curve to allow for spring back.*

Each separate piece will have to be planed slightly to angle so as to fit around the curve and the surface cleaned off smoothly to shape again on completion.

Bore a large hole every 160 mm in the outside pieces so that you can get cramps in to put pressure on the laminates.

4. *Casework*

In the past I have used many different woods for the cases of my instruments, but I find poplar the best for the main case. As we are concerned here with a French instrument, poplar will be very much the correct timber to use for the case. You may however, wish to use lime or even pine and by doing so you will not be committing a mortal sin!

Firstly the main boards for the case must be sorted out and planed to thickness. For extra stability it would help if you could use quarter-sawn timber for the spine and treble side as it is so difficult to produce an instrument where these two areas remain square and flat. The tailpiece usually comes out of the board that produces the treble side and with luck you will get enough out of this plank to use as a front piece to which the name slip screws on.

134

The final thickness of the case to be made will determine the thickness of boards you will buy. A useful tip is to buy 33-mm boards for a 16-mm-thick case. After carefully surfacing the 33-mm boards, ask a timber merchant with a large band-saw to cut off from the surfaced side a 7mm-thick board. If this is done to four boards you will be left with four 7mm-thick boards, each one surfaced on one side and ready to bring to thickness from the sawn side. You will have left four boards of approximately 23 mm to 25 mm thickness which should leave enough timber to surface and thickness to the 16 mm required for the main case parts.

The 7-mm boards can now be thicknessed so that together they make the 16 mm needed for the bent-side laminate. This should be glued as soon as possible, for poplar worked as thin as you now have it tends to curl and move about. Once it is glued and in the bent-side former, it cannot move and it will be convenient to leave it in the former until you need to fit it.

For all the gluing operations to case and structural parts, namely all areas that come under strain, you will need a reliable plastic resin glue (Cascamite or Aerolite 606). You may wish to use animal glue, which is of course how the original instruments were put together. If you do use animal glue, however, it will need to be kept constantly hot and all surfaces of wood to be glued will have to be warmed with an iron before gluing. This is to prevent the glue chilling before pressure is applied.

Continue to prepare the wood for the case from the boards left over after removing the laminates; decide which one will make the spine and cut it to approximate length. This of course should be the best board. Then cut to length the two pieces for the tail and treble straight piece. You will also have to find a narrow piece for the front of the plank on to which the name-slip fits. Surface and thickness these timbers to the required dimensions and put aside. Be sure to lay them flat and allow air to get at all areas by separating the boards with small sticks. This way they will stay flat and not twist.

Prepare an oak plank to the correct thickness and dimensions for the soundboard leader (Fig. 2), and veneer both top and bottom with soundboard wood. You may think it odd to veneer both sides of the oak. However, it is most necessary as you must avoid warping.

The timber for the key-bed frame can now be prepared, as well as all the wood needed for the bottom and upper framing. You will need a good-quality lime for these parts and it is advisable to get a close-grained lime for stability. Some lime grows too fast and apart from being open-grained, it tends to be soft and spongy.

Whilst working with the lime, the mouldings to the inside of the case can be made. You will find a moulding block attached to the circular saw very helpful here, or a router with a cutter specially made to your moulding; you could even use the old-fashioned wooden moulding plane. Although the case is to be made in poplar this wood does not mould well, and I find it more satisfactory to rebate the top edge of the case and let in lime mouldings.

Having made the mouldings, you will know just how much rebate is needed to the top inside edge of the spine, tail bent-side and treble side. This rebate can now be cut together with the rebate to the bottom inside edge that will take the bottom boards. Some makers fit the bottom board directly under the case and clean off flush with the sides. If this is the way you choose to work, you must of course make allowance in the depth of the case sides. However, I prefer to rebate the bottom board up in order to save the end-grain showing through the lacquer at a later date.

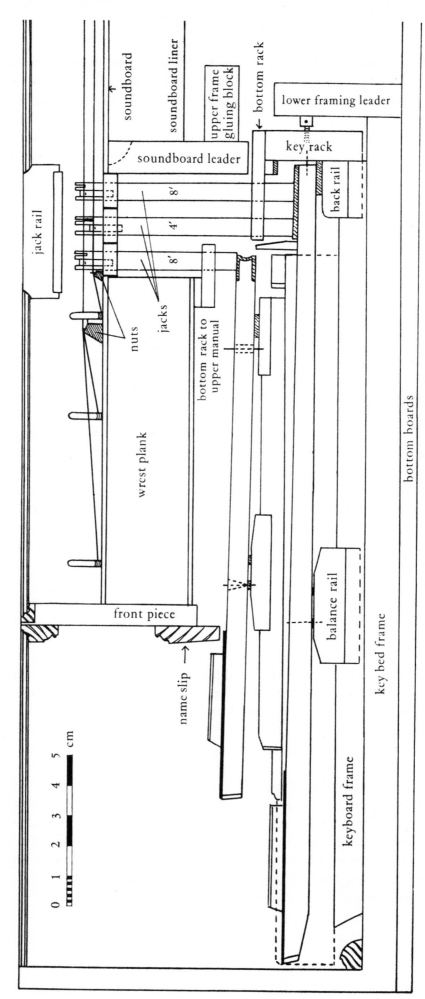

Fig. 5.2 *Keyboard- and action-design for a French double-manual harpsichord*

soundboard

soundboard liner

upper frame
gluing block

bottom rack

lower framing leader

jack rail

soundboard leader

key rack

8'

back rail

4'

8'

bottom rack to
upper manual

nuts

jacks

wrest plank

bottom boards

front piece

balance rail

name slip

key bed frame

keyboard frame

0 1 2 3 4 5 cm

The keyboard frame can now be made up in the prepared lime. Half-lap joints can be used at the corners, should you wish; however, I prefer mortice-and-tenon joints. Glue to the back of this frame the leader and the lower framing, whereupon you will now have the part made which will form the distance the spine will be from the treble side. Tenons can now be cut into the ends of the plank, making the shoulders exactly the same distance apart as the keybed, then the tenons can be made to fit perfectly in the spine and treble side in their correct places.

The soundboard leader has now to be let into the spine and treble side, thus forming the gap for the jacks. Do not make the mistake of fitting it level with the plank. It must be lower than the plank – the thickness of the soundboard, say 3 mm. I have included a line drawing of these parts, which bears no resemblance to any particular instrument but serves to identify such details as these.

Having cramped up all the work dry and checked that everything goes together correctly, the spine can be cut to length at the tail-end to form a mitre with the tail. This must be done with great care and is not easy because the angle of the tail has to be considered. Also the treble side can be cut to length in the same way. The mitres must be made to match on the bent-side as well, and once these have been done, blocks glued on the outside faces of the case with a dab of animal glue will enable you to cramp the case together dry. The mitres will be simple to make if you have the use of a radial arm saw. However, without such sophistication, they will need hand-sawing and planing to fit.

In order for you to get a good pressure on gluing the mitres of the case, you will need to fit a tongue or something similar to stop the joint moving – chopped off panel pins between the gluing surfaces is a simple way to check this type of joint from creeping under pressure.

All is now ready for gluing, but before doing so, remove the wrest plank and mark it out from the plank plan. It is now a simple job to bore the tuning-pin holes under a drill press, thus saving a hand-drill operation once the wrest plank is glued in.

There are quite a lot of joints to be glued and cramped at this gluing-up stage, but plastic resin glue (Cascamite) will give you a little time for adjustment before it sets. Be sure, however, to have plenty of hot water available to clean off surplus glue once the pressure is up, keeping a square at hand to check that you are not gluing the case 'in winding' or out of square.

One of the problems is planning work that can be done whilst waiting for the glue to set. Therefore it goes without saying that a lot of time is saved by careful thought and preparation. As you are waiting for the glue to dry on the main case, it might be a good idea to get out the timber for the bottom board.

5. *Frame and Linings*

Having selected the timber for the bottom board, we return to the case – the bottom-board frame is the next operation. These frame members should be slightly let into the spine and bent-side before being finally glued. They have a two-fold function; firstly, they keep the bottom boards flat and in plane; secondly, they help to keep the case square under the string tension. Once the bottom frame is in place, the soundboard liners can be glued to the inside case with cramps.

The bent-side soundboard liner can be steam bent to shape or laminated in a similar way to the bent-side. Should you choose to laminate this part, be sure to space the leaves to be glued the thickness of the case away from the bent-side former. If you do not, the curve of the liner will be that of the bent-side. The shape of the liner must carry on from the inside curve of the bent-side if it is to fit.

Although it is not necessary for the liners to be jointed at the corners, advantage should be taken of the way the butt joints are placed.

The tail liner should be fitted first and glued so that it butts up to both the spine and bent-side. It is advisable to make the section a little thicker for this part and I take the liner down to the bottom boards. This of course is determined by the number of strings mounted on to that area, but usually there are between thirty to thirty-eight strings and the strain is a direct pull towards the plank; it therefore needs a little help. The liners to spine and bent-side should then be butted up to the tail liner which would stop the tail liner coming forward should it want to. Finally the short liner on the treble side can be fitted.

A strip of timber to give you a gluing area should be fitted behind the soundboard leader now. On to this bar the treble top framing will be mounted. The framing around this area must be most carefully joined. It is responsible for the distribution of tension through the bent-side and, if faulty, the instrument will be sure to twist under strain.

The framing of a harpsichord is designed to keep the soundboard and bottom board parallel under the tension of the strings. It is surprising how much strain the case can accept. However, once the parallels of the framing move, the case will twist and all stability is lost.

Having built the main case and fitted the mouldings, the other small parts should be made. I see no reason to detail this work as it is straightforward woodwork; music desk, stand or legs etc., will be of your own design or copied from an original according to your abilities.

6. *Bottom Boards*

Once again the timber used for this part varies from maker to maker. Lime is quite acceptable, as is poplar or pine. Personally I do not like using plywood or blockboards, but one of the finest makers I know has used them extensively. My own choice, however, is pine which I like to be light in weight and very dry. The wood should be surfaced and thicknessed to a little over 12 mm in order for the finished board to be 12 mm thick after cleaning. It is not a good idea to use boards wider than 100 mm, for even though limiting the width in this way will involve more jointing work, the end product will stay flatter.

Glue three or four boards at a time and allow them to dry before adding on further boards. I suppose the obvious way to cramp together boards of this nature is with sash cramps. You must, however, be sure to keep the boards flat under pressure and I find too much pressure is generally exerted by using sash or G-cramps; so I will describe a method I use which is most successful.

Cramp a long straight board, approximately 21 mm thick and 100 mm wide along the side of your workbench to act as a stop. Having shot the edges of the boards to be glued,[1] and placed them against the stop, place a straight-edge to protect the edge of the

1. For methods of preparing soundboard joints, see Chapter 2, p. 50. [Ed.]

last board. This straight-edge also distributes the pressure. A further board similar to the stop board is then fixed to the bench top leaving a gap of approximately an inch. Into that gap you place double wedges of wood every 250 mm or so, and by tapping these wedges together a very even and efficient pressure can be achieved. This is also the most efficient way to glue soundboards together, so you will be gaining valuable experience for that operation.

The bottom boards can either be fitted now or left until the soundboard is glued in. However, when you do put in the bottom boards nail them up with the addition of a little animal glue, so that they will not be too difficult to remove, should repairs to the soundboard or framing become necessary in the years ahead.

7. *Soundboard*

The soundboard must be the heart and soul of the instrument, upon which all will depend in the final analysis. It goes without saying that only the finest-quality timbers should be used. Many different soundboard woods are available and I have used most of them. Cedar, British Columbian pine and Sitka spruce are useful woods provided the right quality is obtained, but I must point out that Sitka seems a little lacking in fundamental tonal qualities, producing a noticeable harmonic 'fizz'. By using one of the European spruces you will be assured of good results: *Picea abies* or *Picea excelsa* are the most common.

The selection of boards for the different areas is a personal one, and, I hasten to say, my way is only the right way for me! Much experiment has to be done before one can hope to get anything like the qualities you admire in an old instrument. I am, however, sure that the good harpsichord maker must learn to master the soundboard before all else and I hope the following suggestions will help you to avoid some of my early mistakes.

Carefully, with a very sharp plane, surface all the boards to be used in the soundboard, marking the grain direction on each board as you plane it. It is most important to glue up these boards with the grain going in the same direction. Should you make the mistake of getting one board the wrong way round, it will pick up and tear every time you plane the surface and look most unattractive. When all the boards have been surfaced, they can be brought from the other side to thickness. I find approximately 5 mm a useful thickness for the gluing stage, as there is enough meat left in the boards to keep them flat.

The grain will now be easily seen and you can sort out the wide grain from the close. The board with the widest grain should be the first board on the bass side and placed next to the spine. Twelve hard grains to the inch would be ideal for the bass boards. However, should the spruce be firm and tight to the touch, you can go as low as eight or nine.

There should be a gentle increase in density and the grains should get closer as you progress through towards the treble side of the soundboard. Do not be afraid to part boards of uneven grain, thereby keeping the grain selection even. It is not a bad fault to have as many as twelve or thirteen joints in a soundboard. Indeed it will probably be more stable for that treatment.

Having selected the boards you feel are right, they should be numbered so that no mistake could be made when gluing up.

Your previous experiences of gluing up boards with double wedges and straight-edges will pay off now. It is far more difficult to glue 5-mm boards than 12.5-mm ones, but by now you will be more able to tackle this job. Once again the secret is to glue a few joints at a time, placing a little weight – such as planes, boxes of screws etc. – on the boards as you apply pressure and this will stop them coming up. Do not make the mistake of trying to force a badly-shot joint together by pressure. It will not react properly and will only produce a curly unstable soundboard.

I glue the soundboard up on the bench top with a sheet of brown paper to stop it adhering to the bench. The brown paper stays there until all boards have been glued, but you must slit it down in between each board to be glued, otherwise it tends to stop the pressure of the wedges getting to the joint.

For all the gluing operations on the soundboard, use animal or Cascamite glue. Avoid PVA or any glue that will creep under strain. It is also important to clean off the surplus glue with a damp cloth as soon as pressure is applied.

When all the boards have been glued, the master plan should be placed on top and cramped or weighted to make sure it stays in position. A pencil line around the edge will give the shape in which the soundboard has to be cut. Before removing the master plan, bore with a 2.8 mm drill bit all the dowel holes for the 8-ft bridge, 4-ft bridge and 8-ft hitch pin rail; also the small hole which determines the centre of the rose.

Saw the soundboard to shape with a bow-saw or coping-saw so that it fits into the instrument. The top surface can be cleaned down now with a plane in preparation for the underside to be thicknessed. One should only attempt to get the board flat at this stage. The best way to do this is by planing diagonally across the boards and it is most essential to have the back iron of the plane set very close to a very sharp iron for all soundboard planing so that the plane iron will not dig in to the soft pine. No more than 0.5 mm of blade should overhang the backing iron.

Once the top surface has been planed flat, the operation can be repeated to the underside. You should now have a board of uniform thickness of some 4.5 mm.

Finish the surface of the soundboard by carefully scraping it down with a wide, very sharp cabinet scraper and sandpaper with medium-grade garnet paper ending up with fine and finest grade. Use a flat piece of wood or cork as a paper block, large enough to take half a sheet of sandpaper.

It is difficult to say what the final thickness of the soundboard should be. This will depend on the density of the wood used. A tight and firm spruce board can go thinner than a softer board; only experience will help you here.

Turning to the underside, reduce the treble to not more than 3 mm thick and taper off all the edges of the soundboard so that they also are not more than 3 mm. The graduation of these thicknesses will have to be constantly checked with callipers.

The tapering can go into the soundboard 7 to 8 cm – a little more at the point of the tail. Once that has been done, scrape and sand off the underside of the soundboard. Sanding must be done with the grain in order to avoid deep scratches which will certainly show and disfigure the final appearance.

8. *Bridges*

We can now move on to the bridges, and I suggest you fit the 8-ft and 4-ft bridges before proceeding to bar the underside of the soundboard, as you will get a much better glue line to the bridges if you work with a perfectly flat soundboard on the bench. If you have barred the underside first and have to block-up to allow for the barring, the job is more hazardous.

I strongly advise that you use a quarter-sawn board for bridges whether they are to be of pear or sycamore. Use your bridge template to mark out the curved saw line before cutting the bridge from the plank. When sawing, keep the grain running straight through the bridge as much as possible. Of course this is not possible on the bass hook, nor is it possible at the treble. The bass hook can be left but it is advisable to scarf a new piece of straight-grained wood at the treble. The joint should be made approximately two octaves in from the treble end and it should be angled to cover a good 5 cm.

Before squaring the sides of the bridge, surface and thickness it, thus eliminating any twisting in the board. By placing the bridge template under the blank, the dowel holes can be bored to correspond with those in the soundboard. You will now appreciate the need for accuracy in making the template!

Before removing the template, mark a line down the front of the bridge and on the edge of the template so that you can transfer the template to the top surface in the same place.

The marking out for the bridge pins can now be made with a pin through the template holes. The holes can then be bored in the bridge, but do not make the mistake of boring these too small. The pins must be firm, but as they are fine pins – approximately 0.72 mm – they will easily bend should you have to drive them home hard. Measure the pin you will be using with a micrometer and bore the hole with a number drill one size smaller. The reason for marking out the bridge this way is to enable you to use a drill press for boring the holes, therefore assuring they are all accurately upright.

The next job is to plane the bridge to the correct height from soundboard to strings. The bridge on a French instrument slopes from as much as 2 cm in the bass to as little as 1.3 cm in the treble. That taper can now be planed on to the bridge from the top surface.

Finally, with a spokeshave and compass plane, remove the wood behind the bridge to form the correct triangular shape (see Fig. 2). You will see from my line drawings of bridge sections that there is yet another angle which allows the pin to form the speaking length. This angle can be made when the bridge is glued to the soundboard.

The principle is exactly the same for both 4-ft bridge and 8-ft and 4-ft nuts. Also the 8-ft hitch pin rails are produced in the same way, so there is little point in describing the making of these parts further. There is one exception, however: the 4-ft bridge if planed to its correct taper in square section is fine enough to effectively steam bend to shape.

When you have made the bridges to both 8-ft and 4-ft choirs, and the bridges to the plank, it is advisable to check them on the master plan. If your location dowels are correct the bridges will fit both plan and soundboard. You will soon see if the bridge pin holes do not line up with the pencil line representing the string on the plan; better to be sure now than when the bridges are glued on.

Gluing down bridges is not an easy task because you cannot get cramps for the job. The best way to get the pressure is by using go-bars. These are lengths of ash or similar wood sprung between a ceiling and the piece of wood you are gluing, thus forming a type of wedge. You will need a good support fairly low in height as go-bars are not so efficient over about a metre in length. They can also be quite dangerous if too long, for they have a nasty habit of springing off bridges or bars and damaging the soundboard. Pressure can also be achieved by cramping a length of timber across the bridge from each side of the bench. You will need a great many cramps, should you do the job this way. Pressure will be needed every 15 cm or so and you will need two cramps to produce one area of pressure. However, should this be the only way you can do the job, you must glue the 4-ft bridge first. Obviously, if you fit the 8-ft bridge first it will be in the way of the wood strips unless you block off.

9. *Rose Hole*

Once the bridges have been fitted, the rose hole should be cut. A simple way is to make a cutter from a broken hacksaw blade and fit it to a block of wood. At a point the exact radius away from your cutter blade, you must bore a hole and drill a pin through.

By placing the pin in the small hole you have bored in the centre of the rose, the cutter is used as a compass to cut out the rose-hole area from the soundboard. This must be done slowly, or the grain in the soundboard will tend to force the cutter off course and produce an oval shape (Fig. 3).

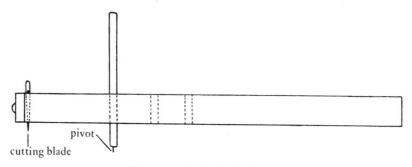

pivot

cutting blade

Fig. 5.3 *A simple circle cutter*

10. *Soundboard Barring*

On turning the soundboard over, the transverse or harmonic bars can be fitted and you will have to make some spacing blocks to lift the bridges clear of the bench top. These blocks should be placed under each bar position and must be the same length as each bar. Several different woods have been traditionally used for this job. Some makers have used lime and some poplar; however, I like to use spruce quartered in a similar way to the soundboard.

It is advisable to mark out where you want to glue each separate bar with a pencil line, and once again to put them up dry before gluing. Glue them to the soundboard in square section and when dry flute away the edges. This way you are helped by the thickness of the wood in getting even pressure to the glue line at the two ends. The ends of these bars have to be let in to the spine–soundboard liner. I do this operation before moving on to fit the 4-ft cut-off bar to the soundboard. When it comes to letting the 4-ft cut-off into the liner and leader, you then know that the other bars will not be in the way. The 4-ft cut-off is dealt with in the same manner and should not produce any difficulties.

The last piece to be made for the underside of the soundboard is the 8-ft cut-off bar. This not only serves as a bracing to take the strain of the 4-ft strings as it retains the 4-ft hitch pins, but it also separates the 8-ft soundboard from the 4-ft.

I have made these cut-offs in lime, Sitka spruce, pine and poplar, but have found that poplar gives the most satisfactory results. The great value of poplar is its strength relative to its mass. Although poplar is very light, it is extremely rigid and strong. These are very useful advantages for this particular part of the soundboard.

With the template made originally for this part, mark out from a poplar board the area you will need. Once again be sure to get the grain running with the length, and to do this you may have to scarf twice, letting in two straight-grain pieces in the treble. Poplar, regrettably, is not an easy wood to work and from our point of view is cursed with many small knots and imperfections. It will pay to be most selective when choosing the wood for the cut-off, so pick out as clean a piece as you can. When the scarf joints have been made and the cut-off cleaned to its shape and size, it should be surfaced and uniformly thicknessed to approximately 28 mm.

Let the bass end of the cut-off into the spine liner with a half-lap joint, removing the wood from the underside of the cut-off and from the top edge of the liner. After reducing the thickness of the cut-off bar from its underside to 15 mm in the treble, tapering back towards the bars about two octaves, it can be let into the leader. If this work has been well done, the cut-off will rest in position with the help of a little packing underneath it on an upper frame member.

By marking on the inside case where the cut-off bar is fitted, it will be possible to place the soundboard in the case and line up your template on top of the soundboard in the same position as the cut-off. The detail for boring the 4-ft hitch pins can now be made with your marking pin through the template holes. But, what is more important, carefully bore two holes with a 2.8 mm drill bit through the template and soundboard into the cut-off bar about 12.5 mm from the spine with a similar hole at the treble end. On removing the soundboard you will then be able to place the template in exactly that same place over the cut-off which will enable you readily to see if you need to remove any more wood in order to give the bridge room to work in the treble. It will also enable you to glue the cut-off to the underside of the soundboard on the bench, using dowels through the holes to give you an exact location. You will be sure of getting a good glue joint this way, which is of the utmost importance, for it has to take quite a lot of strain. The stability of the 4-ft choir depends on this one piece of wood.

Having checked that the soundboard with all the barring and cut-offs glued to it fits easily but positively into the case, the rose can be fitted (see section 11, below).

Gluing the soundboard in is an exciting stage to have reached, but do prepare this stage well. It must be put up dry first. Once again, I would use go-bars for this operation. However, sash cramps every 30 cm or so will do just as well. Be most careful if using cramps not to apply too much pressure.

11. *The Rose*

Unlike the rose in a lute, the harpsichord rose is never carved into the soundboard using the soundboard wood. The rose is always let into a hole made in the soundboard to receive it.

The Italians made their roses out of parchment and leather which were gilded and decorated after fitting. However, Flemish, French, and most European makers of the seventeenth and eighteenth century, cast the rose in plumber's lead.

To do this you require a top and bottom mould of iron into which you can pour the molten lead. The lead is poured in and left for a few seconds, then the bulk of lead is drained out before it can fully set leaving a thin skin with a hollow centre. This was the way toy soldiers were cast some years ago. If the rose were cast in the solid, it would prove quite a weight on the soundboard.

I must admit to cheating here, as I cast my rose in resin into which I add a small quantity of brass powder to give it a similar weight. I often wonder if Taskin and Ruckers would have used such materials had they been available! I like to think that they would.

To make a mould to produce these castings you will need to get a positive of the design you wish to use. If you can get permission to taken an impression from an original rose, make a negative with dental wax or something similar. From the negative you can cast a positive in plaster of Paris. The mould is then made by placing the plaster cast in a box or tin and pouring in latex rubber. When the latex has cured you will have a mould from which you will be able to cast as many resin replicas as you wish. Final decorating with gold leaf will leave your plastic rose, if I may use that terrible word, undistinguishable from a lead one!

12. *Stringing*

Physically, stringing is a simple operation and most players manage to replace broken strings on their instruments with little difficulty. However, a few tips might make life easier and help to give a more uniform appearance to the job.

Harpsichords have separate strings to each note; unlike a lot of pianofortes and early keyboard instruments, where the string returns at the hitch pin to make a second string. It is therefore, necessary for an eye to be made at the terminal point of each string. Although producing the eye itself is not difficult, care is needed to produce 183 of them as near identical as possible so that the job looks professional.

I have included a drawing of a simple eye-twisting tool which I cramp to my bench (Fig. 4). However, before I use the tool, I pre-form the loop which fits on to the hitch pin. This I do by driving a hitch pin into the bench and simply bending the wire round it. The loop is then placed in the hook of the tool and, by holding both the string and its tag with a pair of smooth-jawed pliers, the hook is revolved to twist the eye. You will need twelve turns to give sufficient stability to the eye under tension. All you need to do to ensure that every eye comes off identically is to hold the string with the pliers the same distance away from the hook each time. If you measure the length of wire behind the wrest pin hole before you wind the coil on the tuning pin, you will achieve the same number of coils on the tuning pin for each string. Do not hammer the tuning pin into the pin plank and then thread the string on. Spin the coil on the pin in your fingers and drive the pin home when you have reached the hole in the plank.

Deciding the correct gauge of string for each note comes with experience. You have to try the gauges and listen to the way they speak if you do not have a scaling to work from.

As the speaking length gets longer, the tension for any given gauge at a fixed frequency gets higher. Therefore the reason we have to increase the gauge of strings as we proceed from treble to bass, is because the speaking lengths are reducing in relation to the frequency. Some Italian instruments use just scaling some three octaves or so from the treble. That means they double the speaking length for each octave; by doing so the string gauge remains constant. As soon as the ratio of speaking length becomes lower than 2:1, the tension has to be replaced by increasing the gauge and thereby the mass.

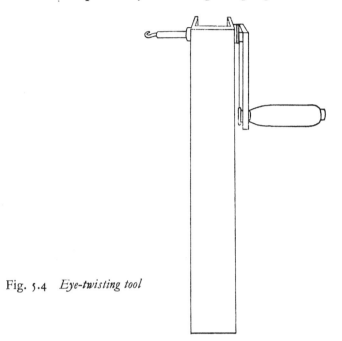

Fig. 5.4 *Eye-twisting tool*

It therefore follows that if a string keeps breaking because of too much tension, the remedy is a *thinner* string to reduce tension, and not a thicker one because the string is not strong enough. The problem of breaking strings does not arise until you reach the changeover from steel or iron to brass or copper in the bass. If, when you reach that area, the thinnest copper or brass string persists in breaking, you will have to use more steel and go into the bass strings lower down. The reason for breakages to copper or brass when the diameter of the string is the same as the steel, or even heavier, is because the specific gravity of brass is higher than that of steel. I could write a chapter on this subject alone and ask forgiveness from the scientist for over-simplifying.[1]

In the final analysis, it is how a particular gauge string sounds on the instrument you are building that is what really matters. To this day I always string each harpsichord I make by listening to each string in turn and changing gauge when the instrument tells me to.

Pitch is yet another interesting feature. Taskin worked at a pitch over a semitone flat (A′ = 409) to ours today. Stringing an instrument at that pitch results in the use of heavier gauges to maintain the tension. This in turn alters the character – only a little, but the small amount is an improvement.

1. For some valuable research into this subject, see Friedemann Hellwig, 'Strings and Stringing: Contemporary Documents', *Galpin Society Journal*, XXIX, 1976.

13. *Keyboards*

The making of keyboards and actions is a skill on its own and seems to be in a different category to cabinet making. Not all harpsichord makers make their own actions, and should this be your first instrument it may be wise for you to get the keyboards made elsewhere. There are several firms that specialize in this work. It is also possible to get both plastic and wooden jacks from suppliers.

However, for those who want to make their own keyboards and jacks I will venture some advice.

The keyboard should be cut from a blank of quartered lime. The choice of lime is of the utmost importance; it should be hard in texture; perfectly knot-free and straight grained. Make up the blank by gluing together boards to cover the total width of the compass using the same technique employed in making bottom boards etc. It is of no importance where the joints come, providing the joints are perfectly shot; and far better to have joints than an uneven grain and therefore unstable blank.

Once the blank has been planed to thickness on both sides, the keyboard frame should be made. This can be made from lime or poplar offcuts. However, the balance rail that retains the fulcrum pins must be of a hard wood; oak, sycamore, or beech would be ideal.

Marking out the keyboard on the blank is a little complicated, but I suggest you start by putting in the fulcrum point line from bass to treble. Transfer the scaling of the strings to the rear of the key-blank, so that you are sure that the keyboard, when cut out, will have a key in between the respective 8-ft strings. Then, at the front end, pencil in the cutting line for each natural. Octave span varies with different makers both old and new. A useful octave span to use is 161 mm. This gives an individual key width of 23 mm and is fractionally wider than Taskin's octave span of 159 mm.

To mark out the accidentals you will need to space evenly the C sharp and D sharp in between C, D, and E; and the F sharp, G sharp, and A sharp evenly between F, G, A, and B. When this has been done, square off and line up with a point just behind the fulcrum. It is almost certain that the key will not be straight to the end, so any drift towards bass or treble can be lined up from behind the fulcrum to the mark at the jack end of the key.

French harpsichords have ebony naturals and ebony accidentals capped or veneered with ivory. Flemish and English instrument makers covered the keyboards with bone or ivory in the same way as modern piano makers. Whichever you choose, the covers have to be cut out and individually fitted to the blank at this stage. If the front of the key is to be moulded, the moulding should be made and glued to the front of the blank before gluing on the covers. If, however, arcades are to be used for fronts, be sure to leave the cover overlapping the front of the key enough to glue on the arcade when you have separated each key.

A simple arcade cutter can be made from a 16-mm spade bit. You will have to reduce the point as small as possible and grind the facsimile of the arcade to the flat sides. Strips of arcades can then be cut using the drill press and, when sawn off, can be glued to the key fronts after the blank is cut out.

Once you have glued on the covers and cleaned them off evenly, the scribe lines can be made. These are the lines that determine the head of the natural. There are usually three of them and the one farthest away from the key end is the cutting line to release the accidental (Fig. 6). A good way to cut the scribe is to shape a point in a marking gauge so that it becomes a small scraper; this will enable you to scratch the line using a marker gauge in the normal manner.

Now the blank can be placed over the key frame in the correct position and the fulcrum holes bored through the blank and into the balance rail of the key frame. The keys cannot fail to fit the frame this way.

Fig. 5.5
Cross-section of arcade cutter bit

Some keyboards have a slotted rail at the back in order to guide a pin placed in the end of the key. This should be made before the blank is sawn out so that you can mark where the saw cuts should be made from the centre of each key lever. An easier way of solving this problem is to bore another row of pins, approximately 160 mm behind the balance or fulcrum pin, making sure to leave room for the coupler dogs and jacks. The upper manuals have to be back-pinned this way!

Piano balance pins can be used, but you will find making them from 4-mm silver-steel rod very satisfactory and much cheaper. Personally I find piano balance pins much too thick and heavy. The drill hole must of course be slightly smaller than the diameter of the pin to be used, in order for the pin to fit tightly in the frame. The hole in the key can then be opened up to fit closely after chiselling the tapered mortice (Fig. 6).

You will need a small band-saw to cut out the individual keys from the blank. Firstly, separate the blank into sections of three and four keys together. This is done by sawing in between all the B and C keys and all the E and F keys. After this has been done, the accidentals can be cut through to the scribe. Careful sawing along the scribe with a fretsaw will release the accidental shaft. You will be left with a comb which, after cleaning out the fretsaw cuts to the scribe line with a sharp chisel, should be separated on the band-saw to produce each natural key.

Each key can now be fitted to the frame after planing the sides clean. It is normal practice to round off the sides of the ebony cover from the front to the first scribe line. This can be done with a fine wood file (not a rasp) or a sandpaper block. You will find it a help to roughly shape the ebony round with a cabinet maker's small scraper before filing or sanding.

Accidentals or sharps are cut out from ebony and veneered with ivory or bone. Of course plastic will do for this cover. However, I hope I am never placed in a situation where I have to use plastic materials for keyboards.

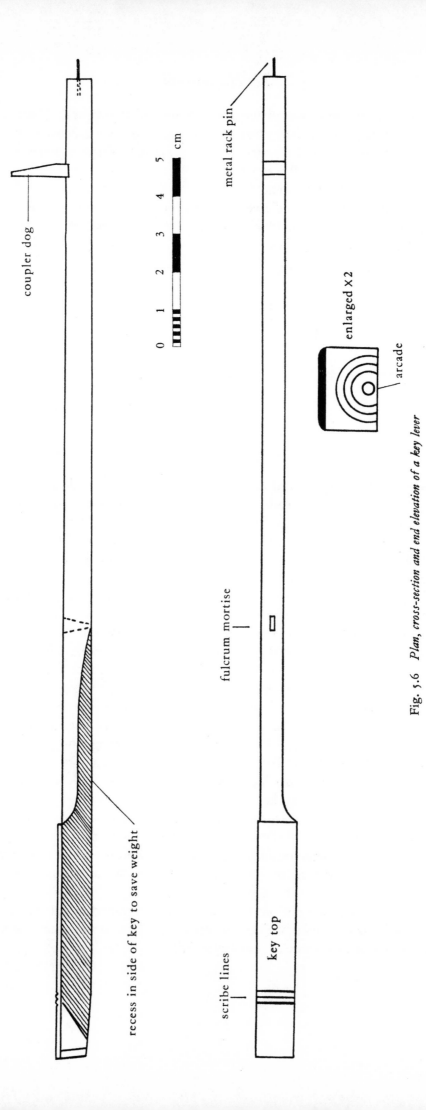

coupler dog

recess in side of key to save weight

0 1 2 3 4 5 cm

metal rack pin

fulcrum mortise

enlarged ×2

arcade

scribe lines

key top

Fig. 5.6 *Plan, cross-section and end elevation of a key lever*

When you have made the sharps for the keyboard, remove most of the ebony on the accidental shaft left over from the natural covers. It helps if you leave a very thin veneer on the shaft, otherwise you will be able to see the white wood of the lime shaft behind the sharp.

You will be well advised to tooth-plane both the under surface of the sharp and the fine veneer of ebony left on the key shaft before gluing on the sharps with animal glue. Glue the sharps to the keyboard with all keys on the frame using the rub glue joint principle. No pressure is needed provided you have created a good butt glue joint.

Ebony if finely sandpapered will burnish to an effective finish with a good wax. Contrary to what one would expect, burnishing wax is better achieved with a coarse rag rather than a soft one. Indeed professional cabinet makers use sacking or a brush to obtain this finish.

On reading through these few words on keyboard making, one might consider the operation rather simple; it is not, and great care is needed to produce a really fine keyboard. This comes from practice and experience; so I strongly advise you to gain the experience by making simple keyboards such as Italian etc., before attempting a French double.

14. *Jacks*

Jacks are not as difficult to make as they might at first seem. You will need some equipment to do the job well, however. A simple type of lathe will be needed to bore the necessary holes for hog bristles and axle pins. A punch tool will have to be made to provide the mortice to retain the plectra. I have made a drawing of a simple tool (Fig. 7) to accomplish this operation.

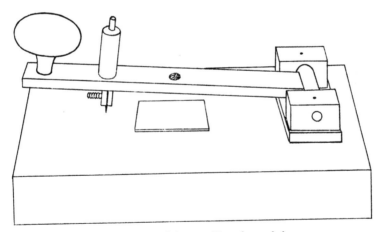

Fig. 5.7   *Tool for punching plectra holes*

The most common woods used for making jacks are pear for the blanks and holly for the tongues. You will not improve on these woods, but you can use beech for the blanks and pear or sycamore for tongues if you wish.

I find the best way to produce the blanks is to surface and thickness a board of pearwood to the exact width of the blank, usually approximately 12.5 mm. After shooting the 12.5-mm thickness perfectly at right angles, I saw off a strip 3.5 mm thick using a very sharp planer saw blade on the circular saw. I proceed through the board producing quantities of such strips, but I shoot each one before sawing off. You are then left with all the strips planed on three sides. I hand-plane the surface, that has the sawn face to fit the rack perfectly, after sawing the jack blanks to length from the strips.

Assuming you have cut to length the blanks, planed them in to the racks for each individual key, numbered and placed them in that order on a tray, the next operation is to remove the wood from the blank to take the tongue, and this is done with a slotting saw 4.5 mm thick on the circular-saw bench. These saw blades can be bought from any good firm supplying engineers' tools etc. It is advisable to obtain one 150 mm in diameter in order to get a good angle to the cut at the root.

By fencing and stopping off round the blade, you can now feed each jack blank to the saw and remove from the top down 4.5 mm of wood to accommodate the tongue. This cut must be made to one side of the jack in order to leave enough wood to the other side to take the flag damper.

With the jack in position in the rack the flag damper should be behind the plectra. It is therefore obvious that each register of jacks will need a new fence setting.

If you start with the furthest away 8-ft jacks – these usually pluck the long 8-ft string towards the bass – the fence setting can be left for the 4-ft jacks as well, for they pluck in the same direction. However, as the 4-ft strings are under the 8-ft ones, it will be necessary to make the cut deeper. The cut will need to be deeper by the distance the 4-ft strings are away from the 8-ft ones. This is approximately 6 mm on a Taskin instrument, but you will find it advisable to give yourself 8 mm at least.

The fence setting will have to be moved nearer the blade for the front 8-ft jacks. This can be achieved by turning over one of the rear 8-ft jacks so that the wide side to take the damper is to the left of the blade. You will then be able to set the fence to the thinner wall, whereupon the setting will be correct for the last rank of jacks. Of course the depth stop returns from the 4-ft one to an 8-ft cut.

Tongues are made from a blank shaped with the grain going with the length of the tongue.

Because you have created the distance the 4-ft strings are away from the 8-ft choirs by a deeper cut on the slotting saw, the tongues can all be the same length.

Holly comes in narrow boards, so regrettably you will only be able to get ten or twelve tongues from each blank. Be sure to make more than enough blanks before cutting out the tongues. Great care is needed on separating the tongues from the blanks. They need to fit the recess in the jack blank perfectly: not so tight that you spread the wall of the jack when putting them in, but tight enough not to fall out.

Before placing the tongues into the jacks, bore the hog-bristle holes to all the pear blanks. I do this by sliding the jack towards the drill which is fitted to a small lathe. Necessity will be the mother of invention here and you will devise some means of boring these fine accurate holes.

Next, the mortice to take the plectra can be made in the tongues, and also a fine cut should be made on the back of the tongue to direct the hog bristle. I have detailed these operations in a drawing (Fig. 8) as they are too complicated to explain with words.

The tongues can now be placed into their respective jacks and the axle-pin boring done. Do not bore this hole right through the jack; it needs to only just spot the wide wall of the jack having passed through the narrow wall and tongue. When you finally fit the axle pin you will be able to drive it into this wood, whereupon it will hold firm. The hole you are boring for the axle is therefore larger than the pin and will give freedom for the tongue to work. I find a 0.35-mm drill bit just right for the hog-bristle holes and a 0.65-mm drill bit will take axle pins made from 0.63-mm copper or brass wire. Should you decide on these diameters, a dressmaker's pin will hold each tongue in place until you finally drive home the copper or brass pin. Make sure that once the axle hole has been bored, the right tongue goes into the appropriate jack, so do not get them mixed up.

Obviously the tongue is too tight to work in the jack at this stage, for it is a perfect fit. I remove the excess wood by resetting the slotting saw to remove some of the wood to the thicker wall for the damper. You can, of course, plane off the sides of the tongue

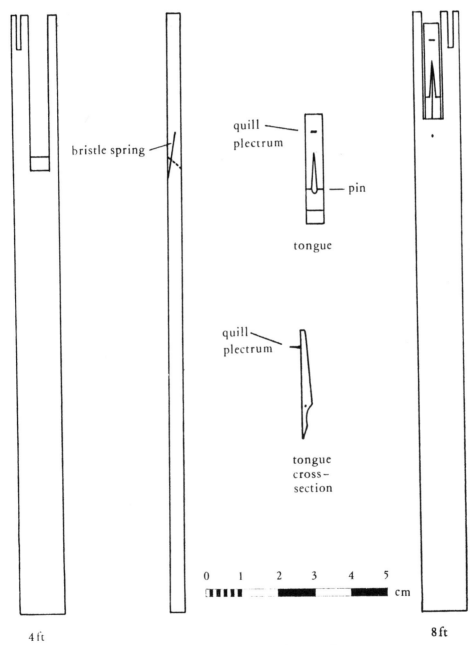

Fig. 5.8 *Four-foot and eight-foot jacks*

until it works freely, if you wish. Do not make the mistake we all have made here of fitting the tongues too fine. Leave plenty of clearance to allow for swelling in damp conditions etc.

All that remains now is to assemble the jacks by driving home the axle pins and fitting the bristles. The damper slot should be made, if possible, with the band-saw or similar machine that leaves a serrated edge. This will hold the felt in place when fitted and save you from having to use felt so thick that, in order to stay in place, it will spread on the pearwood and foul the tongue.

15. *Setting up the Action*

You will have heard players and makers alike talking about separation. They would not, I hope, be discussing their domestic affairs, but be referring to the comfort of the action. Separation is the process of setting up and cutting all the quills perfectly to the same degree under the strings. These are most important details to get right; without them you will never achieve a good touch. It would be almost impossible to play a note on the instrument with any control if, with all the registers on, the quills all plucked at the same time. To obtain the necessary comfort and control for the player, we stagger the plucking on each register. Once again there are different orders and ways of doing this, but I will deal with the most common one.

The 4 fts pluck first, so I suggest you quill those jacks so that the plectra are just under the strings at rest. You will need a little play in between plectra and strings, or repetition will be impaired. The entire register should be quilled and regulated so that the quills just protrude beyond the strings. It will also pay to roughly voice them at this stage, but I will deal with voicing later on.

The 4-ft register usually works from the lower manual and the next rank to pluck will be the lower manual 8-ft choir. Having fitted and regulated the length of quills to that rank of 8-ft jacks, adjust the length of jack so that they pluck after the 4 ft. The operation is repeated to the final 8-ft choir but your adjustments to this rank will have to be done through the couplers, because this is the choir that works from the upper manual for solo work, or through the lower manual via the coupler for 2 × 8 ft. A three-ranked French instrument usually has a key dip of about 7 mm, so if you have produced a comfortable touch from the lower manual 8 ft working at the bottom of this dip, and have a good separation between the other 8-ft and 4-ft choirs, you will have met all requirements. If with all three ranks on, you depress a key evenly through to the bottom of the touch, and can count the separation at the normal speed of saying one, two, three, you should have all that is desired.

16. *Voicing*

Players often refer to an instrument as being badly voiced, when they mean it has been either badly regulated or set up, that is, separated. Voicing simply means making the sound even and correct. This is achieved by removing quill from the underside to reduce sound and fitting a stronger quill to produce more sound. There are several ways of removing the quill and you should experiment to find the way which works for you. I scrape away the material with a very sharp cutter made from broken high-carbon hacksaw blades. The edge must be kept so very sharp and you will need to strop on a leather after scraping every quill or so. If you allow the edge to get blunt, it will scrape off the material instead of smoothly peeling it away. Other makers cut away quill with a scalpel and some file it away. I am a firm believer in the right way being that which works for you and produces the results, so do try all ways.[1]

I do hope you have gained some help from this chapter. There really are no mysteries, only careful thought and hard work which at the end is so rewarding. I also hope you have caught the bug; for that is what it is! A bug that lasts for life and for which there is no cure; indeed, who would want one?

1. For further advice on harpsichord maintenance and tuning see Howard Schott, *Playing the Harpsichord*, London, 1971, appendix. [Ed.]

6

Restoration & Conservation of Historical Musical Instruments

FRIEDEMANN HELLWIG

1. *Introduction*

This chapter can only serve as a general introduction to the most important and most common problems arising from the conservation and restoration of musical instruments, and for this reason I include the treatment of wind instruments which are not otherwise discussed in the present volume. I am concerned less with offering practical instructions to would-be restorers and encouraging makers to take up restoration, but more with helping to protect the small number of instruments that have survived from earlier centuries. My main aim is to provide owners and restorers of old instruments with information on their preservation as a precautionary measure against unnecessary repairs.

I have dispensed with any detailed descriptions of technical procedures; anyone interested can consult H. J. Plenderleith's and A. E. Werner's *Conservation of Antiquities and Works of Art*,[1] which indeed is the standard handbook for general conservation techniques, many of which apply also to the constructional aspects of musical instruments. Furthermore, no technical literature is cited with the discussion of specific methods or treatments; instead the reader should refer to the books and periodicals listed in the bibliography. The A A T A and R I L M bibliographies are a particularly indispensable source of information.

2. *Motivation for Treatment*

The decision that an instrument should undergo some kind of treatment is usually based on its unsatisfactory state of preservation. This may be caused by a number of factors, separately or in conjunction, the most frequent of which I shall discuss briefly here.

a. *Deterioration through neglect*
Neglect is the most frequent cause of damage. Once an instrument is regarded as worthless, the ensuing lack of care or unsuitable storage is almost certain to lead to severe deterioration. There are also sad instances in early and more recent times of instruments having been handled in a thoughtless manner, resulting in major accidents and serious mechanical damage.

1. London, 1956. Second revised edition, London, 1971.

b. *Biological attack*

Many instruments stored in attics or damp cellars have suffered irreversible damage through woodworm attack and growth of fungus.

The term woodworm comprises the larvae of a number of flying insects the most common of which is the furniture beetle or *Anobium punctatum*. The fertilized female *Anobia* deposit their eggs, which are large enough to be detected with the naked eye, near the surface of the wood in cracks or sometimes just inside old worm holes. After a few weeks the young larvae ('worms') emerge from their eggs and immediately start tunnelling their way into the wood and filling the galleries with bore dust. For a period of two to four years they remain in this stage, slowly growing until the larvae mature and change into pupae. This happens near the surface of the wood through which they bite their way into the open air leaving the characteristic flight hole. After a few weeks the life circle starts again with the deposit of new eggs. The damage done by the larvae of such wood-boring insects is immense with much old furniture, with wooden musical instruments, timber structures in houses and public buildings being infected in varying degrees.

In musical instruments the damage is especially serious with parts contributing to the sound, like soundboards or bridges, and with mechanically stressed parts like wrest-planks of keyboard instruments or necks of stringed instruments. The insides of stringed and keyboard instruments are ideal rearing sites for furniture beetles.

The damage caused by fungus appears less drastic to the eye; it should, however, not be neglected. The fungus, a vegetable growth, sends a network of cells into the fibres of the wood, receiving nourishment from it and thus destroying the host. The best-known group of species is the mould which is detected by the eye only in its final stage by the growth of the 'sporophore' for the production of spores. All fungus growth is accelerated by a high humidity level and raised temperatures (as in the case of mushrooms out of doors), and with a reduced motion of the air.

Observed woodworm attack and mould growth should lead to an immediate treatment to prevent further spreading of the pests.

c. *Environmental factors*

LIGHT Though light is indispensable to life it has destructive powers on various materials used in the making of musical instruments. When strong incident light is absorbed at the surface of an object, its radiation energy is transformed into warmth which may locally cause a rise of temperature and with it a reduction of relative humidity resulting in the shrinkage of wood and other hygroscopic material. This is especially likely to happen in glass showcases exposed to sunlight.

The radiation energy itself also has a chemical effect, its strength depending on the wavelength or colour of the light. Blue, violet, and ultra-violet (invisible radiation beyond the violet end of the visible spectrum) have the greatest destructive power: many organic pigments and dyes fade, some darken on exposure to it; this applies to colouring matter as well as to naturally coloured materials like wood. Many varnishes, lacquers, and oils turn yellow or become insoluble with the course of time. These effects are due either to chemical breakdown of certain organic compounds or to oxidation and 'crosslinking' in connection with the oxygen of the air.

Dangerous radiation sources are sunlight and, to a certain extent, fluorescent tubes.

AIR POLLUTION   Another factor which has received worldwide attention during past years is the rising amount of atmospheric pollution. Gases like sulphur dioxide, especially, have a corrosive effect on most metals; the strength of the corrosiveness corresponds to the nature of the metal, the amount of moisture present, and the concentration of the gas itself. However, with objects kept indoors the rate of decay is low.

d. *Warping of wood*

All organic materials with hygroscopic properties display dimensional alterations in accordance with their moisture content which depends on the surrounding humidity level. Wood from freshly cut trees will therefore shrink until its moisture content is in equilibrium with the relative humidity of the air. The rate of shrinkage depends on the direction of the grain: it is greatest along the annual rings as seen in a cut across the tree, and a little less across the rings, but is hardly perceptible along the length of the stem. The same effect can be observed with pieces of wood cut from well-seasoned lumber, subsequently exposed to a lower humidity level. The opposite takes place when wood is kept at a higher humidity level (Fig. 1).

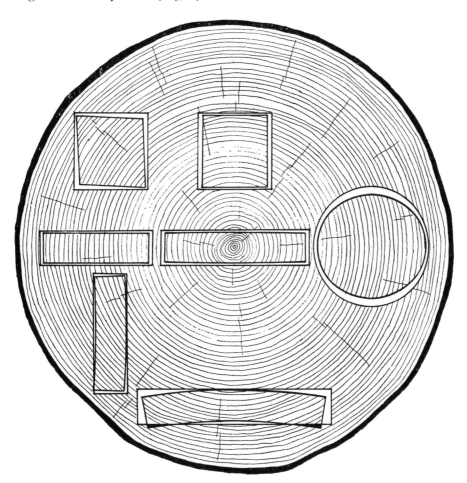

Fig. 6.1   *Cross-section of a tree showing how cut lumber is likely to be affected by shrinkage according to its position within the tree's annual growth rings*

A consequence of these observations is the need for strict humidity control in rooms where delicate wooden objects such as musical instruments are stored.

In many instruments certain parts have supporting bars which, in order to work best, have their grains in a direction mostly at right angles to that of the piece to which they are glued. A change of humidity and consequently of the moisture contained in the wood leads to different expansion rates according to the different directions of the grain. Since only a certain amount of stress can be taken up by the wood, cracks are the result. Examples can be found in practically all soundboards of lutes and guitars, backs of guitars and viols, soundboards of keyboard instruments, etc.

Another problem is that of excessive moisture during the playing of a woodwind instrument. The immediate surrounding of the bore absorbs a high amount of moisture leading to a rapid expansion while the exterior surface remains unaltered, and in some instances the tube will crack (Fig. 2).

Ivory, which is also an organic hygroscopic material, shows basically the same properties with still more inclination towards cracking.

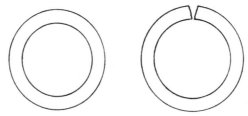

Fig. 6.2   *Typical cross-section of a woodwind instrument showing how the tube may be cracked as a result of moisture from playing. Note that the crack is wider at the outside surface.*

e. *Corrosion of metals*

Corrosion is a destructive electrochemical process which takes place on the surface of a metal and which gradually effects the material's inner layers. The rusting of iron, and the development of green patina on copper or copper alloys, are well-known examples of the decomposition of the metals. Corrosion can occur where two different metals are in contact in the presence of a conductive solution of an acid, a base, or a salt. As in an electric cell the baser metal is dissolved and turned into a salt while the less base metal remains intact. Examples of such pairs of metals are found within every alloy, even within a 'pure' metal alone, between metal and solder, between plated and unplated metal, etc. Even a heavily worked metal can form a pair with a less worked one. A conductive solution is easily formed from present moisture and carbon dioxide or oxygen from the air.

Various forms of damage from corrosion have been observed; pitting is the most frequent effect, giving, on first appearance, the impression of an evenly decomposed metallic surface. In fact, almost any really old piece of metal looks like a lunar landscape when viewed through a microscope. Often corrosion causes cracking along the boundaries of inner-metallic structures. These cracks are minute; they may, however, spread like a network and cause a sudden mechanical breakdown of a piece of metal under strain. This can occur in metal of all ages and I have also observed it occurring in nineteenth-century instruments. Inadequate cleaning methods seem to be a frequent reason for such cracking. The increasing brittleness often observed in old brass instruments is to a large extent due to the process of corrosion here described.

f. *Deterioration through playing*

Unlike so many other historic objects musical instruments need to be played to be of the greatest interest to music lovers, players, instrument makers, and organologists. However, there is no doubt that using the instruments shortens their life.

Constant handling causes abrasion which is so troublesome, for example, in the case of the veneered fingerboard of a Baroque violin. Constant strain is imposed on an instrument by the tension of its strings, which is about 25 kg in a violin, between 300 and 600 kg in a harpsichord, and several tons in a mid-nineteenth-century grand piano. Though many instruments do not seem to have suffered much from string tension over the course of a hundred or more years, certain British pianos show definite signs of distortion in their case work. In many grands from south Germany and Austria the wrestplanks have been bent and pulled towards the soundboard; in a number of harpsichords the gap between wrestplank and soundboard rail has narrowed for the same reason. The deteriorating effect of string tension can also be noticed on soundboards and necks of lutes and guitars, and in a number of bowed stringed instruments.

The moisture effect on woodwind instruments while they are played has already been described. The use of metal wind instruments will increase the risk of corrosion through the excessive amount of saliva and condensation. I do not want to advocate that original instruments should never be heard again. However, if the physical aspect of instruments is to survive for another fifty, hundred, or more years then the playing of them has to be restricted. From this point of view the decision of one museum to release the strings of their keyboard instruments and to bring them back to pitch only for special events like concerts or the production of records is understandable.

g. *Alterations to instruments*

Since instruments were primarily made to be played, their usefulness is subject to the effects of evolution in music. Thus many an instrument became outdated with the augmentation of keyboard compasses; with the addition of courses to extend the range of the lute; with the development of new keywork on wind instruments; with the change of tonal ideals, etc. Many instruments had to be altered so that they could meet the new musical and technical requirements. Alterations based on the genuine historic development of music should seldom motivate the alteration of an instrument. For example, a viola d'amore converted to a viola at the beginning of the nineteenth century should not necessarily be changed back into its original state, since the viola head, neck and fittings represent in themselves an important period of instrument making. If, however, the alterations or repairs were executed to meet a collector's expectation of an extraordinary item, they may well be removed (unless they are so absurd that they became an historic document of a special kind).

3. *Protection from Damage*

a. *Handling, transport, storage*

The safeguarding of precious old instruments should be the primary aim, making costly and risky restorations unnecessary. Precaution is the best preservation.

Handling has to be done with the greatest care, always removing traces of use such as rosin dust from the violin belly or surplus moisture from the bore of a wind instrument. When an instrument has to be transported it should – at least in the case of smaller objects – be put in a strong case capable of absorbing a heavier shock; for transport by mail, ship or plane the case should be insulated against the effect of external moisture by lining its inside with oil paper and filling the surplus space in the box with a shock absorbing, hygroscopic material like woodshavings or crumpled newspaper. In no case should the instrument be placed in a moisture-tight plastic bag, as condensation easily takes place with the change of temperature. This can be avoided by using a bag made of cloth. A word of warning may be necessary against the use of carrying-belts for lifting heavy unprotected keyboard instruments: very often these belts cause pieces of veneer to flake from the edges of the instrument.

When an instrument is not in use it should be kept away from any possible damaging influence. If it is small enough it should be put in a suitable case or stored away in a cupboard where conditions will be more constant. In larger collections the instruments should be kept in a room with specially controlled temperature and humidity.

b. *Climate*

One of the most important factors of preservation is that of climate. As has been shown above, the various materials used in the making of musical instruments demand different conditions. Therefore a satisfactory compromise has to be found. Under mid- and north-European conditions a temperature range between 15°C (60°F) and 20°C (68°F) seems commendable at relative humidity levels between 50 per cent and 60 per cent. These figures take into account the sensitivity of tin and tin alloys to low temperatures and they avoid excessive warmth together with high moisture contents which may promote mould and fungus growth. The swelling or shrinkage rates of material like wood are within permissible limits.

In museum practice the climatic values have to be narrowed down to 14–16° at 58 (±3) per cent relative humidity in moderate climates or to about 20°C at about 50 per cent relative humidity hot climates. These values can be regulated to some extent, of course, by adjusting heating systems, or by protection from outdoor influences such as light and sunshine using blinds and curtains.

Temperature and humidity are measured by thermometers and hygrometers respectively. The latter can be constructed in various forms: the most common ones operate by using a bunch of human or animal hair which expands or contracts with the change of humidity. The dimensional changes of the hair are transferred to a scale which allows direct reading of relative humidity values. This type of hygrometer is inexpensive and robust but requires calibrating every month. This procedure takes only a short time and is easily executed: the entire hygrometer is wrapped in a damp cloth; after at least ten minutes the hygrometer should indicate 95 per cent, or must otherwise be adjusted to this value by means of a small screw found at the back or side of it; for better control the hygrometer is wrapped up again to check the corrected value.

Other humidity-measuring equipment works on chemical principles (making use of the changing colours of cobaltic salts) or physical principles: reduced temperature in a moistened thermometer in relation to one in dry condition can be used for the calculation of the relative humidity in the surrounding air (psychrometer). The former method is inexpensive but inaccurate, the latter very precise but expensive.

For private individuals combined thermometer/hygrometers seem most to be recommended. They can be bought either as simple indicating apparatus or as an apparatus recording both temperature and humidity on to a cylinder which is covered with a sheet of calibrated paper. The cylinder makes a full rotation in one week at the end of which the paper is replaced by a new sheet. This apparatus is ideal for long-period control.

In case the conditions of humidity are not in accordance with the above-mentioned values, the room must be artificially humidified or dehumidified. The best humidifiers evaporate water which is then blown into the room by a fan; a hygrostat controls the humidity level by switching the apparatus on and off. Apparatuses producing clouds of water droplets are unsuitable because they cause calcareous deposits on instruments, furniture etc., unless they are filled with distilled water. Dehumidifiers function on the principle of refrigerators with the humidity condensing on cooling coils.

To a certain extent the humidity can also be regulated using changes in temperature: lowering the temperature will make the relative humidity increase and raising the temperature will reduce the relative humidity.

It is a fatal error to open windows in cold winters in order to allow in 'moist air' to cure humidity problems. The outdoor air which indeed may have a suitable relative humidity at outdoor temperatures will show a very low relative humidity when warmed up to room temperature.

c. *Light*

The effect of light is partly connected to climatic considerations. Sunlight, when absorbed by a musical instrument, or similar object, will raise the local temperature and at the same time reduce the relative humidity. Likewise and even more dangerous, is the damage done to colours and many organic materials by blue light and ultra-violet radiation. Instruments should, therefore, be protected from direct sunlight and strong fluorescent tubes; even under normal lighting conditions damage as described may occur. A value of as little as 50 lux is recommended for long exposure to daylight or to fluorescent tubes.

d. *Choosing a restorer*

A most important point regarding the protection of old instruments from further damage is the right choice of restorer once a treatment seems necessary. Few painters possess the technical knowledge and skill necessary for the conservation of old paintings; likewise only a few instrument makers have the knowledge and experience necessary for the restoration of musical instruments of previous centuries. There are no reliable criteria as to what makes a good restorer. There exist, however, a few indications: a responsible restorer will not rush at a treatment but will discuss with the owner all the possible consequences of a treatment; he will take the time necessary for a careful conservation; he will deliver with the completed instrument all the little bits and pieces he did not put back during the repair; he will hand to the owner a full restoration report; he will give advice on the future care of the instrument.

4. *Restoration, Conservation*

a. *General principles*

The actual work on old instruments should be governed by a few basic principles:

Never gain your first conservation experience (as owner or restorer) on instruments of high quality. In the course of several restorations executed on less valuable and less problematic items you will augment your organological experience and technical ability to the benefit of the more precious objects.

Any treatment has to be preceded by a thorough examination of the instrument. Without such you may easily proceed too far with cleaning or disassembling an object that poses unexpected difficulties.

The old must be preserved. At first reading, this appears simple enough. However, many an instrument has been ruined by hasty replacement of such parts as seem to be in a state unsuitable to function under the stress of playing conditions. Worm-eaten wood, complicated fractures or heavy corrosion should be accepted as a challenge to the restorer to preserve and restore by means of modern conservation techniques, but not to renew without thought. If, after careful consideration, there seems no alternative to replacing in order to restore playability, the question should be discussed with other colleague restorers and the owner. One should not forget that if today there is no alternative, an alternative might be found tomorrow in another laboratory. So better not renew today.

All the restorer's work should be reversible. He can rarely be absolutely sure that what he does will prove to be beyond doubt the only answer to a restoration question. In ten or fifty years time the restorer's successor might be glad if he can remove the former restoration without trace.

The restorer should not renovate an instrument too thoroughly. He should not try to enhance its beauty through highly glossy polishes, spotless removal of wear marks or exaggerated cleaning of the insides. The result might equal that of a nineteenth-century replica. Many traces of earlier alterations may contribute to an explanation of the instrument's previous history.

b. *Examination before treatment*

The general examination before the disassembly or treatment of an instrument is perhaps the most fascinating job, which also satisfies the restorer's professional curiosity. The tools used may comprise magnifying glasses, microscopes and on a more sophisticated plane infra-red, ultra-violet and radiographic equipment. Magnifying glasses with a magnification of 2 to 6 times and having a large viewing field are most suitable. Of the many types of microscopes, a stereo microscope with a magnification of 4 to 40 times is ideal for the surface examination of paints, varnishes, metals and many other materials.

Infra-red (IR) equipment makes use of 'light' wave-lengths longer than the visible spectrum; it can in many cases penetrate surface layers of paint or other material and is reflected or absorbed by structures hidden to the eye. The image can be recorded by a camera on specially sensitized film, or by means of a special television camera connected to a monitor.

Ultra-violet (UV) techniques have proved very helpful in the musical-instrument restorer's laboratory. The wave-lengths used are shorter than the visible spectrum and adjoin to its violet end (hence ultra-violet). This radiation makes a number of materials fluorescent in visible colours different from those observed in ordinary light. They can be photographed on ordinary black-and-white or colour film. Special types of fluorescent tubes or quartz lamps serve as the radiation source. If the fluorescence is to be photographed, a yellow-light filter has to be used for black-and-white films, a uv haze filter for colour photographs. In addition to fluorescence techniques, uv photography can be utilized for reflex/absorption examinations. Typical examples of the application of uv techniques are the examination of old varnishes and lacquers (distinction between original and recent retouching), the deciphering of otherwise illegible inscriptions, the study of hardly visible glue marks, etc. (see Plate xiii).

With the aid of x-rays the inner construction of an instrument of practically any material can be analysed. Special apparatus is required which is only found in well equipped museum laboratories or scientific institutions. Medical x-ray apparatuses are less suitable because of their voltage range which gives unsatisfactory contrast for wood. X-rays are a powerful examination tool which can be applied to all kinds of musical instruments and which have been shown to be indispensable with woodwind and certain brass instruments, lutes, early guitars, some types of bowed stringed instruments and especially with keyboard instruments.[1]

c. *Aims of treatment*

The result of the general examination largely determines the aim of a restoration. Not every treatment must necessarily aim at playability. Though to restore the original function of an early musical instrument will appeal strongly to both the owner and the restorer, it may seem questionable in a number of cases. The tonal qualities of a harpsichord which has been transformed from a ruin without soundboard or keys to a perfect playing instrument may call forth high praise. This instrument, however, is not an authentic instrument with regard to its most important parts. It has not been restored but renewed. Its sound, therefore, is the outcome of a well-executed modern effort and is by no means a tonal document of an earlier century.

If an instrument has been fully preserved, yet severely weakened through woodworm attack, corrosion or other causes of deterioration, a treatment might aim at the conservation of its construction, rather than at the restoration of its function which could be fatal to its future preservation. In a number of instruments there are open questions in regard to certain organological or constructional aspects: the restoration to playability should only be considered as a course of action when answers have been found to at least the major problems.

Often there is more to think about than just the alternatives: playable or unplayable. Instruments which have been altered in the past pose the greatest problems. As a rule, alterations made in order to adjust the instrument to new musical requirements of the past should be left untouched; perhaps the best example in this category is the lute which, during the seventeenth and eighteenth centuries, was frequently converted to a theorbo or had extra courses added. If, however, alterations were made so that an instrument

1. See F. Hellwig, 'Die röntgenographische Untersuchung von Musikinstrumenten' in *Maltechnik-Restauro*, 1978, Vol. 2.

would be more attractive to collectors of little competence one would be inclined to remove these. In general one should be very cautious about taking out what seems unsatisfactory. In addition, many traces which could hint at the original state of the instrument get inevitably lost during the removal of an alteration. In the course of time people will probably become more interested in these alterations because the alterations themselves have their own significance.

Here are two examples from my own museum experience: a viola da gamba, signed Gregory Karp, Königsberg 1694, consisted of a satisfactorily preserved body with a head dating from about 1900, according to an art historian's judgement. The neck was shaped like that of a violoncello with dimensions and characteristics of execution inappropriate to a viol. A new neck, head and fittings were made by strictly copying a fully preserved example of the same master's work from the same period in another museum. This method of restoration seems justified as the authentic parts remained untouched while the obvious additions were replaced by more exact copies. The playability was restored. The second example concerns a sixteenth-century alto crumhorn having an open key consisting of a one-armed lever covered by a metal capsule. This key was thought not to be original for reasons of style (it seemed neo-gothic) and construction (a one-armed lever was thought to be impossible at so early a date), and was consequently removed after a confirming discussion with an organologist. The wood cut out to hold the key was filled with plastic wood touched up to match the surrounding colour; the former keyhole now functioned as a vent hole. Years later, a colleague restorer and recognized expert of early woodwind instruments drew my attention to a similar crumhorn in an Italian collection, showing exactly the same key and also an identical maker's mark. As no common nineteenth-century restorer can be assumed for both the Nürnberg and the Italian instrument the key in question must be original. Fortunately, my repair was fully reversible as all removed parts were carefully preserved and the executed alterations easily removable. The general mistake illustrated by this case was that we so often tend to be over-critical towards the unexpected and that we only accept as original what corresponds to previous observations. Instead we should admit our limited experience and be open to the unfamiliar. A thorough examination of the materials used in the construction of the key could also have given a warning.

d. *Disinfection of wood*

Disinfection against fungus or insects is necessary if an instrument displays signs of mould or active woodworm. Treatment can be carried out with gas (fumigation), liquids (impregnation) or sprays. Mould on the surface should be brushed away in the open air. If the instrument is kept under normal conditions (not above 55 per cent relative humidity and not warmer than 20°C) a further treatment will rarely become necessary. Fumigation is most to be recommended as it has the greatest penetrating power and can be applied in large doses. Ethylene oxide acts against both insects and fungus. When pure it is highly explosive; it is, therefore, often mixed with carbon dioxide. Its application must be arranged with a firm of specialists. Another poisonous gas is hydrogen cyanide which is used by a number of museums (disposing of special equipment) for the disinfection of wood, textiles, skins and other material; hydrogen cyanide has only insecticidal properties. The same applies to methylene bromide. The latter may darken certain lead-containing pigments and may form compounds of unpleasant odour with some organic material such as horse-hair, leather or feathers.

Carbon disulphide is another effective insecticide for all kinds of even the most delicate material. At normal temperatures it is a clear liquid which quickly evaporates and thereby readily forms explosive mixtures with air. It can be used also in improvised set-ups if the necessary precautions against naked light (including cigarette-smoking!) are taken. The object is placed in an air-tight plastic bag, and dishes of liquid carbon disulphide are placed above the object in the bag which is then carefully sealed. About 100 ml of the liquid should be used for every cubic metre of space in the bag. The liquid evaporates within a few hours. After one week the liquid is renewed and the instrument left in the bag for another week or two. The unpleasant odour after fumigation will disappear after a short time. In order to reduce the danger of fire, carbon disulphide can be mixed with carbon tetrachloride; in this case the time of exposure to the vapours must be prolonged.

In no case can fumigation provide a lasting protection as it is effective only during the treatment. It is a cure but not a prevention against future infection.

Impregnation of infected wood may be accomplished either by injection with a syringe or by application with a brush. Various products are on the market; they usually contain poisonous compounds such as DDT, chlorophenols or naphthalenates dissolved in organic solvents with the addition of liquids improving the penetration into the fibres of wood. The technical data sheets of the various brands should be carefully studied, especially in view of possible discoloration of the impregnated object.

Sprays can also be used for disinfection; they have little effect on wood-boring insects but may, however, kill their eggs or their larvae when these are near the surface. Sprays can also provide protection from moths.

Impregnation, and in some cases also spraying, provide a long-term protection against renewed attack through the deposit of poisonous matter.

Although disinfection is usually carried out before restoration in order to prevent the infection of the restorer's premises, it may in some cases (e.g. when prophylactic) seem advisable to postpone the application of liquid pesticides because of their oily components which render gluing more difficult when absorbed by the wood.

e. *Disassembling an instrument*

Disassembling an instrument is one of the most exciting procedures in the course of a restoration, greatly satisfying the restorer's curiosity. He should however resist the temptation of taking things apart which can be repaired by other perhaps less traditional means. An example from museum practice will illustrate this point:

The soundness of glued joints is often tested by tapping them with the finger; a resulting rattling noise would indicate that the joint has come unglued. This technique was recently applied to an early keyboard instrument, a harpsichord by Giovanni Battista Giusti of Lucca, 1681. A rattling noise could indeed be heard when the soundboard was tapped at some distance from the bass end of the bridge. This suggested that a bar had come partly loose. Needing confirmation, the restorer resisted the temptation of taking the soundboard out and instead took a radiograph from the side of the instrument which would show any separation of the bar from the soundboard. The result proved unsatisfactory because the heavily painted sides rendered the radiograph rather dim. Then a stereoscopic x-ray of this section of the instrument was taken from above which came out very clearly. When viewed with the aid of a Wheatstone's stereoscope (a pair of mirrors which reflect the stereo pair separately into the observer's eyes) the resulting three-dimensional image gave a clear explanation of the cause of the rattling: a wooden rod had been inserted into the bottom plank of the instrument reaching up to the soundboard and touching it in the immediate neighbourhood of a bar. It was obviously intended to press the badly glued bar against the soundboard, however, it missed the bar by about one centimetre! The rod was easily located in the bottom plank and was carefully taken out without letting it fall into the instrument. The rattling noise was now even stronger. With the aid of a dentist's small mirror and a miniature electric light bulb inserted into the hole from which the wooden rod had been taken (about 12 mm wide) the loose bar could be seen very clearly. Subsequently a thin plastic tube was inserted near the unstuck joint through which a few millilitres of water were passed in order to soften the old glue. A minute quantity of a suitable detergent helped as a wetting agent. For the actual gluing, hide glue was used, being carefully kept warm while it was poured into a syringe from which it was forced into the tube. By pressing the soundboard up and down the glue was caused to be sucked into the joint. After one day of drying time the treatment proved successful. The whole operation was observed in the mirror. Though the total amount of time spent was quite considerable the procedure was certainly much quicker than the traditional removal of the soundboard. However, the greatest advantage lay in the minimal interference with the original.

*

Here are a few practical hints about disassembly: make sure the documentation is sufficiently complete before taking an instrument apart.

A screw which has rusted in the wood can often be loosened by pressing a hot soldering iron on to its head for several minutes. (Make sure the surrounding wood does not get burnt!) The restorer can then unscrew it quite easily. Every screw must be marked so that it can later be refastened in its individual hole. Metal tubes are often not soldered together but inserted into each other. When difficult to separate they can either be carefully warmed with a flame or tapped lightly with a hammer. The faces of a planishing hammer should be polished and slightly convex.

The action of pianos can only be taken out when all the hammers are in their lowest position; if this point is not carefully observed the hammer heads will be broken off. Sometimes the restorer has to press the hammers down from above with a piece of wire. Often the dampers have to be lifted or even fully taken out before the action can be pulled out. Unless the dampers carry numbers their sequence must be marked with small adhesive labels.

If the removal of strings from a keyboard instrument cannot be avoided their gauges should first be measured as a guide for the calculation of a new set. If the wrest pins have no hole the strings are difficult to put back on, because they will slip on the pin or break when under tension.

Wrest pins taken from old keyboard instruments should be kept in their original order because each of the individually made pins has a slightly different diameter.

Glued joints in wooden constructions can be separated either wet or dry. Both operations require a skilled and experienced hand. For dry separation the restorer inserts a sharp knife with a thin blade (an old steel table-knife will do) into the joint, carefully avoided cutting into the wood on either side.

The procedure of separating a joint glued with hide glue is made easier by wetting the blade with alcohol. This tends to 'break' the joint up, probably by rapid absorption of moisture from the glue into the alcohol; the glue thus becomes more brittle and tends to break under the tension of the wedge-like knife blade. Care should be taken to avoid any possible solvent action of alcohol on varnishes near the joint.

The wet separation of a joint makes use of the swelling effect of water on hide glue and also, to a certain degree, on white glues (PVA). The immediate surrounding of the joint is padded with wet cotton wool for several hours, or overnight, and evaporation of the water is reduced by covering the wet cotton wool with aluminium foil. When subsequently separating the joint with a knife, care must be taken neither to cut into the softened wood nor to split it. The possible risk of damage to layers of paint or varnishes through the absorption of water (blooming) must be calculated before the treatment.

Casein glues, epoxy resins, polyester adhesives and many kinds of white glue (mostly polyvinylacetate emulsions) cannot be treated in the described way. Because joints glued with them require strong organic solvents, or may even be totally inseparable, their use should be restricted (as in the making of new instruments).

f. *Cleaning and repair techniques*

Unlike many other fields of museum conservation, musical-instrument restoration is confronted with an exceptionally large number of materials each requiring individual techniques. Dealing with all of them would make this chapter far too long; however, the treatment of two materials, namely wood and metal, will be briefly discussed to show the most important problems and methods.

WOOD Wood without a finish is cleaned 'dry': a vacuum cleaner can remove the worst dust and dirt, and afterwards an eraser gum of soft grade produces a dust-free, clean surface (a suitable kind of soft eraser originally intended for the cleaning of wallpapers etc. is produced by Akachemie, D–7315 Weilheim, under the trade name 'Wishab'). Wet cleaning may sometimes be necessary for the removal of disfiguring spots, for which water, alcohol, white spirit and other solvents can be used. Surfaces that are covered with some kind of polish, lacquer, varnish or paint-layer are more difficult to clean because of the more firmly adhering dirt. After thorough dry treatment a solvent has to be used in most cases. Its choice depends on the composition of the coating and has to be adjusted to its properties. No general advice can be given since even water may display an unwanted effect on certain types of varnishes. Solvents used by conservators include acetone, ethanol, isopropanole, trichlor-ethylene (trichlorethane is equally effective but less poisonous), white spirit and ammonia solution. An effective but comparatively harmless cleaning emulsion for many types of polishes and varnishes can be prepared as follows:

olive or almond oil	250 ml
turpentine oil	250 ml
vinegar	250 ml
ethanol	10 ml
mild detergent	a few drops

This emulsion has to be shaken well before use, applied moderately with a piece of cloth, and rubbed dry. It is especially recommended for all types of furniture, polished casework of keyboard instruments and the like, most violins and other instruments. Care has to be taken that open cracks are glued before cleaning as the oil content in the emulsion may make later gluing very difficult.

The cleaning of paintings and decorated soundboards should be left entirely to an experienced conservator.

In no case should restorers be allowed to consider the scraping or sandpapering of old wood as a cleaning method. This procedure is an offence to the connoisseur's eye.

*

When wood has cracked or joints have separated gluing becomes necessary. A variety of glues is at the modern restorer's disposal, the traditional hide and fish glues still being the most important ones. Their use is difficult and inconvenient only to the inexperienced; their advantage, however, is an excellent reversibility with a mild solvent (water) even after very long periods. A good-quality hide glue is transparent, of light yellow colour and of excellent adhesive power. Fish glue when heated is never as smooth as hide glue but has a better gluing effect for ivory, bone and many tropical hardwoods.

The use of modern synthetic adhesives in the repair of musical instruments should be restricted to special cases demanding an exceptionally strong joint without the necessity of eventual reversibility. A word of warning must also be said against the use of white glues (mostly polyvinylacetate emulsions) some of which seem to lose their stability or their solubility after a comparatively short period.

*

Cracks that are too wide to be glued are filled with a small strip of wood (shimming). This process is often necessary in the treatment of flat wooden boards such as soundboards, bottom planks, backs of viols or the like, and sometimes even in turned pieces of wood such as woodwind instruments. Since the gap is in almost every case a result of insufficient humidity control, the repair has to be undertaken under strict observation of climatic conditions as already discussed. Often a reduced humidity (5–10 per cent below normal) is advantageous during the repair because it helps to ensure against future cracking as a result of further possible shrinkage. The crack is carefully cleaned to remove dirt and old glue, and filed straight with a thin file (which is obtainable as thin as 0.5 mm); a shim of the same species of wood is cut, planed, filed, and made to match the direction of the grain of the original with the greatest accuracy. Only when the fibres of the original and the repair wood run parallel to each other in all three dimensions can treatment be made invisible during the subsequent retouching to match the surrounding wood.

Missing fragments should be added where possible without cutting the surface straight in order to produce a smoother gluing surface. Although the fitting of a piece of wood will prove more difficult this way the resulting joint will be much stronger and aesthetically more satisfying besides the fact that the original will have been fully preserved. The piece to be added should be carefully selected to match the grain and colour of the original, and should be fitted with fine carving gouges and if necessary with dental milling cutters.

*

The consolidation of worm-eaten wood is a problem of special difficulty to the musical-instrument restorer, because wood in instruments not only has to fulfil a static purpose but has often to vibrate too. No systematic investigation has been made into the alteration of the acoustical properties of wood after a consolidating treatment. In no case should worm-eaten wood be replaced, but technical possibilities must be found to preserve and strengthen the original material. Various procedures and products have been used, the choice of which depends on the size and shape of the piece in question, the kind of wood, its surface treatment (varnishes, paint-layers) and the extent or rate of damage. As consolidating material, synthetic resins are used to an increasing degree. These resins must be fluid enough to penetrate into the affected wood. Solutions of nitrocellulose or similar materials (e.g. hardening wood disinfectants) are often used; the shrinkage during the evaporation of the solvent restricts their application to smaller objects. Epoxy and some polyester resins avoid the disadvantage of shrinking and are therefore preferred by many conservators. The monomeric resin is mixed together with the hardener to form a clear liquid of low or medium viscosity. After injection into the worm-eaten wood these set to a solid, slightly flexible polymer substance. A possibility of discoloration must be taken into account with all kinds of consolidants; unwanted effects on varnishes, paint-layers (softening) and even wood itself (swelling) are possible with products containing organic solvents.

*

Retouching is often necessary to adjust the colour of new material to that of the old one. Though this is sometimes not difficult on pieces of furniture such as cases of keyboard instruments, soundboard shimmings etc., it is a job restricted to an experienced hand on painted decorations and varnishes on stringed instruments. Opinions about the extent to which a retouching should hide previous damage differ widely. As a reaction against over-generous renovation of erased details during the nineteenth and the beginning of the twentieth centuries, museum conservators nowadays tend to reject extensive retouching in order to preserve a clearer picture of what has been preserved of the original.

METAL   The cleaning of metals is a technical and at the same time aesthetic problem. Since the natural sciences have started to devote much research work to the chemistry and physics of the deteriorating processes of metals, a larger number of different treatments have been developed by conservators. At the same time it has become clear that a number of the traditional cleaning and repair methods still used by craftsmen are detrimental to the preservation of works of art. The treatment of metals, therefore, requires a basic understanding of corrosion and other deteriorating processes, and a more detailed knowledge of modern conservation techniques.

Out of the many questions arising from work on metal objects only two will be briefly discussed here, namely the cleaning of brass and the de-rusting of iron. Both pose technical and aesthetic problems to which solutions will differ in relation to the craftsman's personal understanding of musical instruments and of their conservation in general. In this context the predominant question is whether or not patinas have to be removed to give the object the appearance it presumably had at the time when it was new. In general, conservators tend to allow the instrument to demonstrate the course of history through which it has passed, but at the same time they would take into account possible requirements with regard to metallic gloss that were valid at the time when the instrument was still in use. Thus a bell from a church-tower must not lose its patina, but an early trumpet may be cleaned to show its golden brass colour which was certainly of importance to a largely heraldic instrument. However, any cleaning treatment should avoid trying to make an old object look new or, worse, like a replica from the nineteenth century. Thus polishing wheels, coarse-grade emery cloth, and coarse polishing powders are absolutely inappropriate to the cleaning of any old piece of metal from the aesthetic point of view. It is the original metallic surface that gives the authentic appearance to an old instrument, undisturbed by coarse scratch marks or by an extremely fine polish alien to most old objects.

*

Brass, a copper-zinc alloy, as found in European musical instruments, is rarely corroded to the extent met with in archaeological finds. Nevertheless, many instruments or parts thereof made of brass show symptoms of deterioration typical of archaeological finds. The cleaning techniques adopted for the treatment of musical instruments have, therefore, been taken over from archaeological conservators. All cleaning procedures recommended in the technical literature of conservation make use of an immersion process in order to remove tarnish and oxidization. Besides a 5–10 per cent solution of sulphuric acid, which gives a dull, dead surface, complexing agents are widely used. The most important ones are the derivates of ethylene-diamino-tetraacetic acid (EDTA) which are available under brand names like Titriplex, Etorex, Chelatoplex, Komplexone, and others. Their application is easy, once technical problems like the supply of sufficient quantities of distilled water have been overcome and the solutions have been prepared. After de-greasing and de-lacquering in a suitable solvent (toluol, trichlorethane, etc.) the object is immersed in the EDTA solution until it has become clean, then it is thoroughly rinsed, and finally dried. After the actual cleaning process the object may be polished lightly to add a little shine to it. Precipitated calcium carbonate or mild jewellery abrasives seem suitable. Before drying, the object can be immersed in a solution of benzotriazole (BTA), which acts as an inhibitor against quick retarnishing. It is advisable to give the object a protective coating of wax or lacquer (polymethacrylic resins like Acryolid B 72 have shown favourable properties; 'Incralac' is a ready mixed formula which also contains an inhibitor). As a result of the immersion the inside of a brass instrument receives a treatment equivalent to that of the outside. It is impossible and also undesirable for musical reasons to provide the inside with a protective lacquer; nevertheless, the treatment with BTA offers a certain anti-corrosive protection against saliva and condensating moisture.

Instruments cleaned in this way should receive the same amount of care which is accorded to other objects of art in museums: to protect the lacquer from flaking, avoid bumping against other hard instruments, and handle with cotton gloves to avoid finger-marks.

*

For the de-rusting of iron several processes can be applied to parts of musical instruments corroded only at the surface. Thin rust spots on polished iron or steel can be removed mechanically by softening the rust with paraffin oil for a few hours, followed by rubbing locally with a glass brush, fine emery paper or even a small piece of wood. The object is subsequently rubbed dry with a piece of cloth and treated with lubricating oil for rust protection. If oil as a preservative is unsuitable (e.g. for wrest pins), a wax mixture can be applied. After first removing the paraffin oil with trichlorethylene the object is immersed in a hot solution of waxes,[1] and subsequently rubbed to remove surplus wax. It is also possible to use locally an electrically heated spatula.

Immersion is another technically simple method; de-rusting solutions contain phosphoric acid and inhibitors reducing the attack into elementary iron. In addition, phosphoric acid provides a certain anti-rust effect after the treatment. After de-greasing and de-lacquering, the object is put into the solution from which it is removed from time to time to be treated with a hard bristle brush. After thorough rinsing it is immersed in alcohol which absorbs the water and quickens the drying. All products containing phosphoric acid will develop a grey metallic surface resembling that of lead. This is unimportant in the case of small parts like screws or wrest pins; however, in the case of keyboard instrument pedals, hinges, levers etc., the natural silverish colour is preferable (as an immersion solution thioglycolic acid has been occasionally used to remedy the discoloration).

Another method that has many merits is electrolytic reduction. However, unless careful precautions have been taken, secondary effects may lead to an unwanted deposit of metal on the object. Many conservators, therefore, prefer mechanical or purely chemical treatment to the electrochemical process.

*

The repair of metal poses a number of problems. Very often tubes of brass instruments have dents from careless handling. Their repair is executed with metal bolts of varying diameter which are inserted into the tube, the first bolt being pushed in by a second hammering against it as a result of the instrument being vigorously shaken. Thus dents are pressed out from the inside and can be carefully corrected with a planishing hammer from the outside.

*

Cracks or open joints in uncorroded metal are traditionally repaired by soldering. An alloy of a melting point lower than the metal to be repaired is made to flow into the joint. Solders with a melting temperature above 600°C are called hard solders; soft solders are mixtures of lead and tin with a temperature range between 163°C and 327°C. For both kinds of solders the object has to be heated so that the solder can flow freely. Fluxes help to avoid renewed oxidization of the metal which has previously been cleaned of all tarnish, corrosion products and other impurities. Many fluxes have a strong corrosive effect, resulting, for example, in the de-zincification of brass during the soldering process and even afterwards. In addition, the heat required in the melting of the solder can sometimes be the cause of minute new cracks hardly visible to the eye. Thus soldering should only be applied to sound objects of solid dimensions. It should be avoided with regard to fragile instruments made of extremely thin sheet-metal like early trumpets, trombones, horns, and the like. Even instruments from the nineteenth century are often in a much less healthy state of preservation than we would assume after superficial examination. A microscopical examination will reveal the deplorable state of many instruments.

1. See Plenderleith and Werner, *op cit*, p. 374.

In many cases the use of modern adhesives is therefore preferred to soldering. Epoxy resins are especially suitable. Pieces of thin sheet metal (0.2 mm or less) can serve as a support overlapping the joint, crack or small gap. Joints thus glued can be easily separated by immersing the object in boiling water or by applying very moderate heat for a few seconds.

g. *Making missing parts*

This is often necessary with musical instruments in order to restore their appearance and musical function. It has very little to do with conservation and is more the type of work done by musical-instrument makers. It requires manual skill and demands a sound knowledge of authentic instruments. This knowledge should prevent us from making unhistorical products wrong in material, shape, surface treatment and style. There is little to condemn the wish that these parts should look as original as possible for aesthetic reasons; it is, however, dishonest if this is done for the purpose of deception. In any case the restoration report should state clearly which parts are new; some restorers even have a metal stamp which they punch into every new part.

h. *Stringing, regulating, voicing, tuning*

A few general remarks will suffice here as all necessary details will be found elsewhere in this book.

Like the section on the making of missing parts this section asks for a restorer who combines a training as a musical-instrument maker with the skill of a craftsman, an educated ear, and experience in the playing of the musical instruments concerned. However, a further development of these abilities in regard to authentic instruments is absolutely necessary to restore what are assumed to be the original playing and tonal properties.

The stringing of keyboard instruments, especially that of harpsichords, has been extensively discussed in recent literature. It has become clear that Frank Hubbard's statement, 'One strings by ear and not by physics,'[1] needs correction in that a basic knowledge of acoustics and of the mechanics of vibrations is absolutely indispensable to the keyboard restorer.

Similarly the tuning or the understanding of the intonation of an instrument requires knowledge of musical intervals, scales, chords, of historical temperaments and their calculation. Without such knowledge, a 'restorer' will be tempted to 'improve' the intonation of an old woodwind instrument. He ought to know that many an instrument of this type still shows signs of historical temperaments or at least uneven tone steps. The sound of organs and stringed keyboard instruments is improved to an unexpected degree by adopting period temperaments. Most of the historical temperaments are more easily realized than the equal temperament which has only one pure interval (the octave), while for example the mean-tone temperament has also eight pure major thirds. Pure intervals or chords somehow seem to augment the tonal volume of an instrument; at the same time the uneven scales make a musical piece appear much more alive. Reference to practical instructions for the tuning of historical temperaments can be found in the bibliography.

1. Frank Hubbard, *Three Centuries of Harpsichord Making*, Cambridge, Mass., 1965, p. 5.

5. Documentation

Any treatment or proposed treatment of an instrument should have detailed accompanying documentation, which is usually compiled by the restorer into whose hands the instrument has been put. This documentation contains an organological description of the instrument; notes on the possible original state of the instrument; a description of its condition before and after treatment; a report on the steps taken during the treatment; photographs, and possibly drawings and other documents such as radiographs; and notes on how to prevent future damage to the instrument.

Extensive documentation is most important and should be carefully compiled regardless of whether the instrument has been entrusted to a commercial or museum restorer and whether it forms part of a private or public collection. Such documentation should give the best possible insight into the technical construction and the original design of an instrument; it will permit a subsequent control over the effectiveness of the restoration methods applied, and will provide data for future organological or technological research into details hitherto neglected. The owner of the instrument receives the original documentation, and a duplicate is kept by the restorer.

a. *The organological description*

Such a description should be started before the treatment and completed or corrected during or after it. Various catalogues of musical instrument collections may serve as models: a comparatively recent one is that of the Carel van Leeuwen Boomkamp Collection compiled by the owner and J. H. van der Meer.[1]

b. *The technical report*

First this contains a description of the condition of the instrument when received at the restoration laboratory; it is written as far as possible without disassembling the instrument. The general state of the object in respect of dirt, woodworm, mechanical soundness, corrosion, missing parts, playing condition etc., is described, and followed by the results of examination of the various parts of which the instrument consists. Together with the organological description this section of the report allows for conclusions to be drawn on previous alterations and on the possible original state of the instrument, taking into account other instruments of the same type, period or maker.

The aim of restoration and, most important, the means planned for its execution, are also set out. The actual restoration is then described in detail stating the techniques applied and the materials used (brands and if possible ingredients of glues, fluxes, lacquers, varnishes, waxes, cleaners, etc., their makers, concentration of solutions, conditions under which materials were used, etc.). The condition after the restoration is then documented: the report should set out the extent to which the damages have been repaired, under what conditions the instrument may be handled in the future, whether it is playable and under what conditions (possible pitch or maximum tension of strings, possible

---

1 Published by Frits Knuf, Amsterdam, 1971.

moisture effects on metal or woodwind instruments through blowing, sensitivity of fresh varnishes, fragility of repaired fractures etc.). Finally the private owner's attention should be drawn to necessary conditions of storage, climate and so on.

The following headings could serve as a model when writing out a technical restoration report:

1. Type of instrument.
2. Maker, place, date.
3. Owner, inventory number.
4. Reasons for undertaking treatment.
5. Condition of instrument before treatment.
6. Reconstruction of original state of instrument.
7. Aims of present restoration and methods to be applied.
8. Description of execution of restoration.
9. Condition of instrument after treatment.
10. Parts removed.
11. New parts made.
12. Remarks for future preservation.
13. Treatment executed by. . . .
14. Documentation compiled by. . . .

c. *Photography*

It goes without saying that photographs are the ideal illustration for a technical conservation report. Photographs should be taken before, during, and after the treatment, thus complementing the written report. Where possible views should be taken face on to the instrument so that optical distortion is at its minimum. Single lens reflex cameras of the 35 mm or, even better, 6 × 6 cm (2¼ × 2¼ in) sizes are ideal, especially so because close-ups can be taken without any trouble. Black-and-white films of low or medium speed give good results, and enlargements should not be smaller than 13 × 18 cm (5 × 7 in) printed on monochrome glossy paper. Colour slides on daylight film can be taken in the open air on an overcast day; but since they can be looked at only with the aid of a viewer or projector, colour prints seem preferable. However, it is difficult to obtain good-quality prints from either reversal or negative film, and they should be left to the professional photographer.

Ultra-violet photographs on black-and-white film can be taken easily in a darkened room. The object is illuminated by a strong uv source; the camera is mounted with a uv barrier filter (a non-fluorescent light-to-medium yellow) – ordinary haze filters are not suitable. The exposure values measured through the filter should be used as a rough guide for a series of shots with different exposures. Enlargement on hard paper will usually improve the quality of the picture.

d. *Drawings*

These give a clear undistorted picture at a fixed scale and are therefore especially suitable for illustrating the construction of many types of musical instruments. They should be drawn to full size if possible, and should contain enough details for a reproduction of the part or instrument to be made referring only to the plan. The drawing should follow as closely as possible the national rules for the execution of technical drawings as laid down by the Bureaux of Standards and the like.

Radiographs are most useful in the preparation of drawings of hidden constructional details, revealing for example the dimensions and construction systems of wooden bars in stringed and keyboard instruments.

e. *Conclusion*

It is suggested that the primary motive for restoration and conservation should be to retain as much of the original state as is now possible with the use of recently developed techniques; and that whatever decision is taken on how far to go, a complete record should be kept of the condition in which the instrument is found, and of all subsequent stages in the treatment undertaken. Instruments are for our use and pleasure, but surviving specimens are also valuable for the information they preserve for us; and it is our responsibility to find a good working resolution for this dual aim. Our reward is the beauty of the old instruments themselves.

Plates

I Baroque seven-string bass viol by Dietrich Kessler after Richard Meares

II Inside view of the large octave bass lute by Michielle Harton, Padua 1602
(Germanisches Nationalmuseum, Nürnberg)

III Eight-course lute by Charles Ford after Harton

IV Viola by Adam Paul

V Cross-sections of a modern and a Baroque violin, illustrating the differing
construction details

VI Guitar by José Romanillos based on a design by Hermann Hauser sen.

VII Front and reverse sides of the head

VIII Harpsichord by Michael Johnson after Taskin

IX The harpsichord and its keyboard before assembly

X Plan view of a harpsichord by Giovanni Battista Giusti, Lucca 1681
(Sammlung Historischer Musikinstrumente, Germanisches Nationalmuseum, Nürnberg)

XI A radiograph of the instrument showing details of the interior

XII Technical drawing of the harpsichord by G. B. Giusti. Details taken
from radiographs, the instrument was not opened

XIII Two details of a harpsichord soundboard, one showing where bars from a
recent restoration have been removed and the other where the glue marks
left by the original barring have been made visible by the fluorescence from
ultra-violet radiation
*(Double-manual Italian harpsichord, seventeenth century. Germanisches Nationalmuseum,
Nürnberg)*

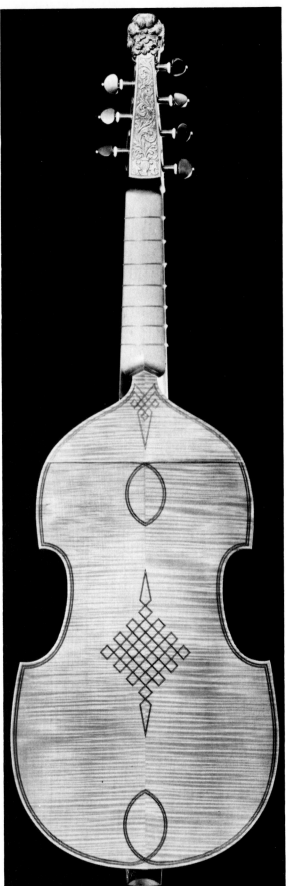

1 *Baroque seven-string bass viol by Dietrich Kessler after Richard Meares*

II *Inside view of the large octave bass lute by Michielle Harton, Padua 1602; the original soundboard and barring of the instrument;* III (below), *eight-course lute by Charles Ford after Harton*

IV *Viola by Adam Paul;* V (below), *cross-sections of (top) a modern and (bottom) a Baroque violin, illustrating the differing construction details*

VI *Guitar by José Romanillos based on a design by Hermann Hauser sen.;* VII (below), *front and reverse sides of the head*

VIII *Harpsichord by Michael Johnson after Taskin;* IX (below), *the harpsichord and its keyboard before assembly*

x (left), *Plan view of a harpsichord by Giovanni Battista Giusti, Lucca 1681;* xi (right), *radiograph of the instrument showing details of the interior*

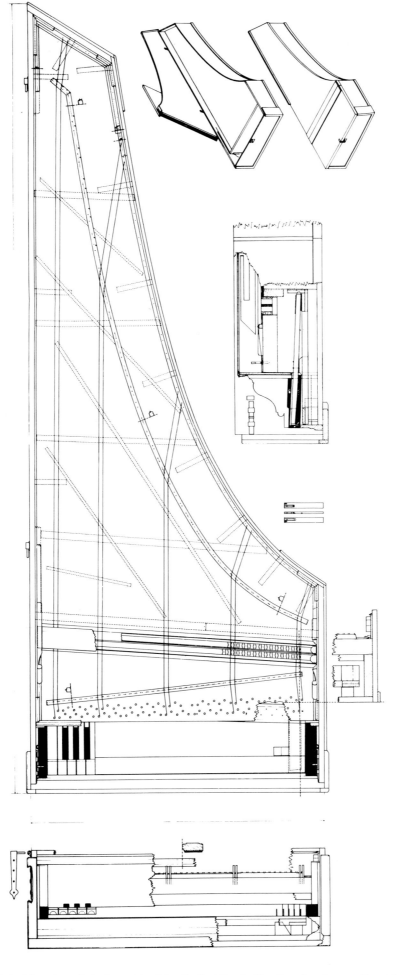

XII *Technical drawing of the harpsichord by G. B. Giusti. Details taken from radiographs, the instrument was not opened*

XIII *Two details of a harpsichord soundboard showing,* top, *where bars from a recent restoration have been removed, and,* below, *the glue marks left by the original barring, made visible by the fluorescence from ultra-violet radiation*

About the Contributors

Anthony Baines (Introduction)

is the distinguished author of a number of books on musical instruments including *European & American Musical Instruments, Woodwind Instruments and their History*, and *Brass Instruments*, all of which have become standard works. Well known as both professional musician and scholar, he is a founder member of the Galpin Society and editor of its Journal. He is Curator of the Bate Collection of historical wind instruments at Oxford.

Charles Ford (Editor)

is a professional lute maker and has taught instrument making for two years; he has also worked in an editorial capacity on several important music books including the five-volume biography of Haydn by H. C. Robbins Landon.

Dietrich Kessler (The Viol)

is a leading maker of Baroque viols with more than thirty years' experience; his instruments are used by professional players throughout the world. He is himself a professional performer on the viol.

Ian Harwood (The Lute)

is well known in the world of early music for his pioneering work on the lute in the 1950s and, more recently, in re-establishing the status of the Renaissance viol. A maker of both lutes and viols, Mr Harwood also teaches the making of early fretted string instruments at the London College of Furniture.

Adam Paul (The Violin)

was trained as a maker of violins at the Cremona School of Violin Making and now works as a professional maker in Suffolk, England.

José Romanillos (The Classical Guitar)

is a maker of guitars with many years' experience, whose instruments are played by many of the best-known guitarists. Mr Romanillos is also an authority on Antonio Torres and is currently researching the life and work of that luthier.

Michael Johnson (The Harpsichord)

worked for Broadwood and became well known for his expert piano restorations; he has since for many years been building harpsichords which have given him a distinguished reputation.

Friedemann Hellwig (Restoration and Conservation)

is conservator of the musical instrument collection of the Germanisches Nationalmuseum, Nürnberg, and is one of the best-known authorities in this field. As well as his researches into the conservation of musical instruments, he has also written many valuable papers on the historical development and construction of various musical instruments.

Bibliographies

1 The Viol

Dolmetsch, A., 'The Viol', *The Connoisseur* x, xiii, London, 1904.

Dolmetsch, N., 'Of the Sizes of Viols', *Galpin Society Journal*, xvii, 1964.

Harwood, I., 'An Introduction to Renaissance Viols', *Early Music*, Vol. 2, No. 4, London, October 1974.

Hayes, G. R., *Musical Instruments and their Music, 1500–1750: II. The Viols, and other Bowed Instruments*, London, 1930. Reprint, New York, Broude Bros Ltd, 1970, as *The Viols and Other Bowed Instruments*.

Michelman, Joseph, *Violin Varnish*, published by the author, Cincinnati, 1946.

Rousseau, J., *Traité de la viole*, Paris, 1687. Reprint Amsterdam, 1965.

Simpson, C., *The Division-Violist*, London, 1659, second ed. as *The Division-Viol*, London 1665/67; facs. of second ed. London, Faber, 1955.

2 The Lute

Abbott, Djilda, and Ephraim Segerman, 'Strings in the 16th and 17th Centuries', *Galpin Society Journal*, xxvii, 1974. 'Gut Strings', *Early Music*, Vol. 4, No. 4, 1976.

Baron, E. G., *Historisch-theoretische und praketische untersuching des Instruments der Lauten*, Nuremberg, 1727. Reprint, New York, Broude Bros Ltd, n.d.

Bermudo, J., *Declaración de instrumentos musicales*, Osuna, 1549; facs. reprint Kassell, 1957.

Burwell Lute Tutor, The, c. 1668–71, Leeds, Boethius Press, facsimile 1974.

Dolmetsch, A., 'The Lute', *The Connoisseur*, viii, ix, London, 1904.

Edwards, David, 'A geometrical construction for a lute profile', *Lute Society Journal*, xv, 1973.

Gill, D., 'The Elizabethan Lute', *Galpin Society Journal*, xii, 1959.

Harwood, I., 'A Fifteenth-century Lute Design', *Lute Society Journal*, ii, 1960. *A Brief History of the Lute*, Lute Society Booklets, Richmond, 1975.

Hellwig, F., 'Lutemaking in the late 15th and 16th Century, *Lute Society Journal*, xvi, 1974. 'Lute Construction in the Renaissance and the Baroque', *Galpin Society Journal*, xxvii, 1974. 'On the Construction of the Lute Belly', *Galpin Society Journal*, xxi, 1968.

Lowe, M., 'The Historical Development of the Lute in the 17th Century', *Galpin Society Journal*, xxix, 1976.

Mace, T., *Musick's Monument*, London, 1676. Facs. reprint, Paris, 1958. Reprint, New York, Broude Bros Ltd, n.d.

Pohlmann, E., *Laute, Theorbe, Chitarrone*, Bremen, 1968, 1975.

Poulton, D., *John Dowland*, London, Faber, and Berkeley, Univ. of California Press, 1972.

Prynne, M., 'Lute Bellies and Barring', *Lute Society Journal*, vi, 1964.

Zuth, J., *Handbuch der Laute und Gitarre*, Vienna, 1928, 1972.

3 The Violin

Alton, R., *Violin and Cello Building and Repairing*, London, W. Reeves, 1950; reprint of 1946 ed., St. Clair Shores, Michigan, Scholarly Press, 1976.

Boyden, D., *The History of Violin Playing, from Its Origins to 1761 and Its Relationship to the Violin and Violin Music*, London, Oxford University Press, and New York, Oxford University Press Inc., 1965.

Farga, F., *Violins and Violinists*, London, Barrie & Rockliff, 1950. Revised and enlarged, New York, Praeger Pubs, 1969.

Hart, G., *The Violin, Its Famous Makers and Their Imitators*, London, 1884; New York, Broude Bros Inc., n.d.; Westport, Conn., Greenwood Press, n.d.
The Violin, London, 1885. Reprint Kennebunkport, Maine, Longwood Press, 1976 as *The Violin and Its Music*.

Henley, W., *Antonio Stradivari, 1644-1737, His Life and Instruments: A complete Biography*, New York, William S. Heinman, 1961.

Heron-Allen, E., *Violin Making as It Was and Is*, London, Ward Lock, 1884 etc. Reprint Cedar Knolls, New Jersey, Wehman Bros, Inc., n.d.

Hill, W. H. and A. F., *Antonio Stradivari: His Life and Work, 1644-1737*, London, Dover Publications, and Magnolia, Mass., Peter Smith Publishers Inc., 1963.
The Violin-Makers of the Guarneri Family (1626-1762), London, 1931. Reprint, New York, AMS Press Inc., n.d.

4 *The Classical Guitar*

Baldini, U., *Nota di tecnologia costruttiva su la chitarra*, Bologna, 1957
Una Innovazione nella costruzione della chitarra, Milan, 1957.

Bellow, A., *The Illustrated History of the Guitar*, Colombo, 1970.

Bone, P. J., *The Guitar and Mandolin*, London, Schott & Co., 1914, 1954, 1972.

Ciurlo, F., 'La Chitarra nella liuteria moderna', *Il Fronimo*, 1974.

Evans, T. & M., *Guitars: Music, History, Construction & Players*, Paddington Press Ltd., New York & London, 1977.

Gill, Donald, *Gut-strung Plucked Instruments...*, Lute Society Booklets, Richmond, 1976.

Huttig, H. E. (II), 'Guitar Construction from A to Z', *Guitar Review*, 28, New York, 1965.

Jahnel, F., *Die Gitarre und ihr Bau*, Frankfurt, 1963.

McCleod, D., & R. Welford, *Classic Guitar, Design and Construction*, Leicester, 1971.

Maugin, J. C., *Manuel de luthier*, Paris, 1834.

Muñoz, R., *Technology of the Argentine Guitar*, Buenos Aires, 1952.

Overholtzer, A. E., *Classic Guitar Making*, Chico, California, 1934, 1974.

Revuelta, V. B., *La Guitara*, Madrid, 1962.

Ridge, E. V., *The Birth of a Guitar or Making a Concert Guitar*, New York, 1961.

Sharpe, A. P., *The Story of the Spanish Guitar*, London, Music Sales, 1954.

Sloane, I., *Classic Guitar Construction*, New York, E. P. Dutton & Co., 1966.

Sloane, I., *Guitar Repair*, London, Nelson, and New York, E. P. Dutton & Co., 1973.

Tyler, James, *The Early Guitar*, London, Oxford University Press, 1979.

Turnbull, H., *The Guitar: from the Renaissance to the Present Day*, London, 1974.

Usher, T., 'The Spanish Guitar in the Nineteenth and Twentieth Centuries', *Galpin Society Journal*, IX, 1956.

5 *The Harpsichord*

Boalch, D. N., *Makers of the Harpsichord and Clavichord 1440-1840*, London, Oxford University Press, 1956, 1976. Second ed., New York, Oxford University Press Inc., 1974.

Hellwig, Friedemann, 'Strings and Stringing', *Galpin Society Journal*, XXIX, 1976.

Hubbard, F., *Three Centuries of Harpsichord Making*, Cambridge, Mass., Harvard University Press, 1965, 1972, etc.

James, P., *Early Keyboard Instruments*, London, Holland Press, 1930.

Meer, J. H. van der, *Die klavierhistorische Sammlung Neupert*, Nürnberg, 1969.

Russell, R., *Early Keyboard Instruments*, Edinburgh, Edinburgh University Press, 1959.
The Harpsichord and Clavichord, London, Faber, and New York, W. W. Norton & Co. Inc., 1959, 1973, etc.

Schott, H., *Playing the Harpsichord*, London, Faber, and New York, St Martin's Press, 1971.

6 Restoration and Conservation

The number of publications relating directly to musical instruments is still very limited. However, many conservation problems met with in other kinds of works of art are also relevant to instruments. Besides a few standard works on the care of instruments, a small number of publications of a more general character has been included.

BOOKS

Berner, A., J. H. van der Meer, G. Thibault, with the collaboration of N. Bromelle, *Preservation and Restoration of Musical Instruments. Provisional Recommendations*, The International Council of Museums, London, Evelyn, 1967.

Contents: I Materials used in the making of instruments. II General recommendations on preservation. III The problem of restoration (of the basic types of European instruments and their parts). IV Bibliography (museological and organological). V Materials (synthetic) used in conservation (by N. Bromelle). VI Plates with comments (illustrations from historic treatises).

Conservation of Wooden Objects. Preprints of the contributions to the New York Conference on Conservation of Stone and Wooden Objects, 7–13 June 1970, Vol. 2, New York, The International Institute for Conservation of Historic and Artistic Works, 2nd ed. 1971.

Papers deal with wood deterioration, consolidation, wood-destroying insects, etc.

Jenkins, J. (ed.) *Ethnic Musical Instruments: Conservation and Identification*, The International Council of Museums, London, Evelyn, 1970; New York, British Book Center, 1974.

Contains a short general note on conservation.

Plenderleith, H. J., and A. E. A. Werner, *The Conservation of Antiquities and Works of Art: Treatment, Repair and Restoration*, London, Oxford University Press, 1956, 1971, 1976 (see ed. of 1971); 2nd ed., New York, Oxford University Press Inc., 1971.

This is a standard handbook. Contains most valuable information on the deterioration and preservation of all materials found in works of art together with extensive practical instructions on their treatment and restoration. This book should be indispensable to any restorer.

Ruckers Genootschap, Antwerpen (ed.), *Colloquium Restauratie-problemen van Antwerpse Klavecimbels* (Museum Vleeshuis 10 to 12 May 1970), Antwerp, 1971.
With contributions in Dutch, English and German on various aspects of Flemish harpsichords, their construction, later alterations (ravalement), general conservation rules and a report on an actual restoration of a seventeenth-century virginal.

Schwarz, Vera (ed.), *Der klangliche Aspekt beim Restaurieren von Saitenklavieren. Bericht der internationalen Tagung von Restauratoren für besaitete Tasteninstrument am Institut für Aufführungspraxis der Hochschule für Musik und darstellende Kunst in Graz unter Leitung von J. H. van der Meer* ('Aspects of sound in the restoration of stringed keyboard instruments. Report of the international symposium of restorers of stringed keyboard instruments held at the Institute for Performance Practice of the Hochschule für Musik und darstellende Kunst at Graz under the direction of J. H. van der Meer'), Graz 13–16.9.1971. Beiträge zur Aufführungspraxis 2, Graz 1973.

Papers in English and German deal with questions of methods, restoration of tonal qualities, stringing of harpsichords, regulating of hammer actions, musical temperaments of the past, historical instructions for quilling, etc.

Stolow, N., *Controlled Environment for Works of Art in Transit*, International Center for the Study of Conservation of Cultural Property, London, Butterworth, 1966.

The characteristics of hygroscopical materials like wood are discussed and methods of packing with protection against environmental damage are proposed.

Thomson, Garry (ed.), *Museum Climatology*, Contributions to the London Conference on Museum Climatology, 18–23 September 1967. London, International Institute for Conservation of Historic and Artistic Works, 1968.

Papers deal with museum design, the environmental control in museum buildings, effect of air pollution, humidity and lighting on works of art.

PERIODICALS
(see pp. 186–7 for addresses)

Art and Archaeology Technical Abstracts (*AATA*, published at the Institute of Fine Arts, New York University, for the International Institute for Conservation of Historic and Artistic Works, London, vol. 1, 1955, etc. (Formerly called *IIC Abstracts*.)

An extremely useful bilbiography on the preservation, examination and treatment of any kind of cultural heritage. About a thousand publications are listed per annum, with short summaries. Books and articles on the care of musical instruments are also included. Members of the International Institute for Conservation (IIC) receive this journal automatically. (See *Studies in Conservation*.)

The Galpin Society Journal, Vol. 1, 1948, etc.

The journal of the Galpin Society, founded in 1946 for the publication of research into the history, construction and use of musical instruments. The best-known periodical on a wide range of aspects of mostly historical and ethnographical instruments. (See, for example, F. Hellwig, 'An Example of Lute Restoration', *GSJ*, XXIII, 1970.)

Musical Instrument Conservation and Technology (*MICAT*).

A new periodical in two parts (*MICAT News* and *MICAT Journal*), dealing with the technological examination, preservation, restoration, conservation and history of materials used in musical instruments. Contains also an extensive annotated bibliography on publications in the field. Contributions mostly in English, but also in French and German.

Répertoire International de Littérature Musicale (*rilm abstracts of music literature*), vol. 1, 1967, etc.

A bibliography of publications on all aspects of music with inclusion of musical instruments. Contains especially valuable references to organological works.

Studies in Conservation. The journal of the International Institute for Conservation of Historic and Artistic Works, London, vol. 1, 1955, etc.

A periodical on a high scientific level publishing original contributions on the preservation, examination and treatment of works of art. Members of the International Institute for Conservation (IIC) receive this journal automatically.

Agricola, M., *Musica Instrumentalis Deudsch*, Wittenberg, 1529. Reprinted Leipzig, 1896, and Hildesheim, 1967.

Baines, A., *European and American Musical Instruments*, London, Batsford, 1966; New York, Viking Press, 1966.

(ed.), *Musical Instruments through the Ages*, London, Faber, 1961, 1963; New York, Walker & Co., 1975.

Berlioz, H., *Grand traité de l'instrumentation et d'orchestration modernes*, Paris, 1844; ed. of 1904 with appendix by C. M. Widor; rev. ed. R. Strauss, Leipzig, 1905, Eng. tr. Theodore Frost, New York, 1948.

Bessaraboff, N., *Ancient European Musical Instruments*, Boston, 1941. (An organological study of the musical instruments in the Leslie Lindsey Mason Collection at the Museum of Fine Arts, Boston.)

Buchner, A., *Musical Instruments through the Ages*, London, 1955.

Cocks, W. A., and J. F. Bryan, *The Northumberland Bagpipes*, Newcastle-upon-Tyne, The Northumberland Pipers' Society, 1967.

Denis, V., *De Muziekinstrumenten in de Nederlenden en in Italie naar hun Afbeelding in de 15ᵉ Eeuwsche Kunst*, Antwerp, 1944. (Translation of parts in *Galpin Society Journal*, 11, 1949.)

Diderot, Denis, and Jean d'Alembert, *Encyclopédie*, Paris, 1767, 1776; Elmsford, New York, Maxwell Scientific Intl., 1971 (Section 'Lutherie').

Donington, R., *The Instruments of Music*, London, Methuen, 1949, 1951, 1962, 1970; 3rd rev. and enl ed., New York, Barnes & Noble Inc., 1970.

Galpin, F. W., *Old English Instruments of Music*, London, Methuen, 1910, 1932, 1965; 3rd rev. ed., St Clair Shores, Mich., Scholarly Press, 1932.

A Textbook of European Musical Instruments, London, Benn, 1937; reprint of 1956 ed., Westport Conn., Greenwood Press, 1976.

Geiringer, K., *Musical Instruments*, London, Allen & Unwin, 1943; New York, Oxford University Press Inc., 1945.

Grove's Dictionary of Music and Musicians, Fifth Edn., ed. Eric Blom, London, Macmillan, and New York, St Martin's Press, 1954. (Sixth Edn., ed. Stanley Sadie, in preparation.)

Harrison, F., & J. Rimmer, *European Musical Instruments*, London, Studio Vista, 1964.

Hipkins, A. J., & W. Gibb, *Musical Instruments, Historic, Rare and Unique*, Edinburgh, 1888, etc; London, 1945. Reprint, New York, AMS Press Inc. n.d.

Kinsky, G., *History of Music in Pictures*, Leipzig, 1929; London, 1930, 1937; St Clair Shores, Mich., Scholarly Press, 1934; New York, 1951.

Kircher, A., *Musurgia universalis*, Rome, 1650.

Majer, J. F. B. C., *Museum musicum*, Halle, 1732. Reprinted Kassel, 1954.

Marcuse, S., *Musical Instruments: a Comprehensive Dictionary*, London, 1966; New York, W. W. Norton & Co. Inc., 1964, 1975.

Mersenne, M., *Harmonie universelle*, Paris, 2 parts, 1636–37. Reprint, Paris, 1963. Latin edition (*Harmonicorum Libri*, Paris, 1635) transl. Chapman, R. E., The Hague, 1957.

Montagu, J., *The World of Medieval & Renaissance Musical Instruments*, David & Charles, 1976; New York, Overlook Press.

Munrow, D., *Instruments of the Middle Ages and Renaissance*, London, Oxford University Press, 1976.

Ott, A., *Tausend Jahre Musikleben*, Munich, 1961. (With photographs of instruments in the Germanisches Nationalmuseum, Nuremberg.)

Poulton, Diana, *John Dowland*, London, Faber, and Berkeley, Univ. of California Press, 1972.

Praetorius, M., *Syntagma Musicum*, Tome 11, *De Organographia*, Wolfenbüttel, 1618. Reprints Kassel, 1929, 1964, and New York, Da Capo Press Inc., 1975.

Sachs, C., *Reallexikon der Musikinstrumente*, Berlin, 1913. Reprinted Hildesheim, 1962.

Handbuch der Musikinstrumentenkunde, Leipzig, 1930.

Bibliographies

The History of Musical Instruments, New York, 1940; London, Dent, 1952.

Virdung, S., *Musica Getuscht*, Basel, 1511. Reprints Kassel, 1931; Hilversum, Netherlands, Fritz Knuf, 1968.

Winternitz, E., *Musical Instruments and their Symbolism in Western Art*, London, Faber, 1967.

Wright, R., *Dictionnaire des instruments de musique: étude de lexicologie*, London, Bailey, 1941.

Catalogues and Guidebooks

Amsterdam, Carel van Leeuwen Boomkamp and J. H. van der Meer, *Carel van Leeuwen Boomkamp Collection of Musical Instruments*, Amsterdam, Frits Knuf, 1971. (Now in Den Haag, Gemeentemuseum.)

Ann Arbor, University of Michigan. A.A. Stanley, *Catalogue of the Stearns Collection of Musical Instruments*, Ann Arbor, 1921.

Basel, Historisches Museum. K. Nef, *Katalog No. IV: Musikinstrumente*, Basel, 1906.

Berlin, Staatliche Hochschule für Musik. C. Sachs, *Sammlung alter Musikinstrumente*, Berlin, 1922. (Collection now incorporated in Staatliches Institut für Musikforschung, Musikinstrumenten-Sammlung, Berlin.)

Boston, Museum of Fine Arts. (*See* General Bibliography, Bessaraboff.)

Brunswick, Städtische Museum. H. Schröder, *Verzeichnis der Sammlung alter Musikinstrumente*, Brunswick, 1928.

Brussels, Musée Instrumental du Conservatoire royal de Musique. F.-V. Mahillon, *Catalogue descriptif et analytique*, 5 vols, Ghent, 1893–1912; *Catalogue abregé*, Ghent, 1911. (Technical drawings available.)

Cologne, Musikhistorisches Museum von Wilhelm Heyer. G. Kinsky, *Katalog*, Vol. 11 (Stringed instruments), Cologne, 1912; *Kleiner Katalog der Sammlung alter Musikinstrumente*, Cologne, 1913. (Collection later transferred to Leipzig and now in the Karl-Marx-Universität, Leipzig.)

Copenhagen, Claudius Collection. *Carl Claudius Sammlung af Gamble Musikinstrumenter*, Copenhagen, 1931.

Copenhagen, Musikhistorisk Museum. A. Hammerich, *Beskrivende Illustreret Katalog*, Copenhagen, 1909.

Edinburgh, University of, St Cecilia's Hall, *Russell Collection of Harpsichords and Clavichords*. (Technical drawings available.)

Eisenach, Bachhaus. E. Behle, *Verzeichnis der Sammlung alter Musikinstrumente*, Leipzig, 1913; Revised, C. Sachs, Leipzig, 1918.

Florence, Museo del Reale Istituto Luigi Cherubini. L. Bargagnana, *Catalogo*, 1911.

Frankfurt-am-Main, Historisches Museum. *Sammlung alter Musikinstrumente*, P. Epstein, Frankfurt, 1927.

Ghent, Snoeck Collection. C. C. Snoeck, *Catalogue de la collection d'instruments de musique*, Ghent, 1894. (Collection later dispersed, a part to Brussels (q.v.), and a part to Berlin (q.v.).)

Halle, Saale, Händelhaus. K. Sasse, *Guidebook*, 1958.

Hague, The, Gemeente-Museum. D. J. Balfoort, *De Muziekhistorische Afdeeling* (*Verz. D. F. Scheurleer*), 1935.

Hamburg, Museum für Hamburgische Geschichte. H. Schröder, *Verzeichnis der Sammlung alter Musikinstrumente*, Hamburg, 1930.

Leipzig, Karl-Marx-Universität. (*See* Cologne.) P. Rubardt, *Führer durch das Musik-instrumenten-museum*, Leipzig, 1955.

Linz, Oberösterreichischen Landesmuseum. O. Wessely, *Die Musikinstrumenten Sammlung*, 1952.

Lisbon, V. Festival Gulbenkian De Music: *Exposicão internacional de instrumentos antigos*, Lisbon, 1961. (Instruments from the Conservatorio Nacional, Lisbon, and the Conservatoire royal de musique, Brussels.)

Lisbon, Museu Instrumental en Lisboa. M. Lambertini, *Catologo Summario*, Lisbon, 1914.

London, Music Loan Exhibition, 1904. *Illustrated Catalogue*, London, 1909.

London, Royal College of Music (Donaldson Collection). Sir George Dyson, *Catalogue of Historical Musical Instruments, Paintings, Sculptures and Drawings*, London, 1952. (Technical drawings available.)

Bibliographies

London, Galpin Society: British Musical Instruments, 7–30 August 1951. *Catalogue*, 1951.

London, Victoria and Albert Museum. C. Engel, *Descriptive Catalogue of the Musical Instruments in the South Kensington Museum*, London, 1874; A. Baines, *Catalogue of the Musical Instruments*, II, 1968, 1978. *Musical Instruments as Works of Art*, 1968.

Milan, Museo Civico di Antichi Strumenti Musicali. N. Gallini, *Catologo*, Milan, 1958, 1963.

Munich, Bayerisches Nationalmuseum. K. A. Bierdimpfl, *Catalogue*, 1883.

Munich, Ausstellung alte Musik, 1951. A. Ott, *Katalog*, Munich, 1951. (Instruments from the Bayer, Nationalmuseum, Städtisches Instrumentensammlung, and elsewhere.)

New York, Metropolitan Museum of Art. *Catalogue of the Crosby Brown Collection of Musical Instruments of all Nations*, Handbook No. 13, i. *Europe*. New York, 1902, 1904. (Technical drawings available.)

Nürnberg, Germanisches Nationalmuseum. J. H. van der Meer, *Wegweiser durch die Sammlung historisches Musikinstrumente*, 1976. (Technical drawings and radiographs available.) 19—. (Technical drawings available.)

Oxford, Ashmolean Museum. D. D. Boyden, *Catalogue of the Hill Collection of Musical Instruments in the Ashmolean Museum, Oxford*, London, 1969.

Paris, Musée National de Musique. G. Chouquet, *Catalogue descriptif et raisonné*, Paris, 1884. Supplements by L. Pillaut, 1894, 1899, 1903.

Prague, National Museum, Exhibition of Musical Instruments, 1950. A. Buchner, *Catalogue*, Prague, 1952.

Salzburg, Museum Carolino Augusteum. K. Geiringer, *Alte Musikinstrumente*, Leipzig, 1932.

Stockholm, Musikhistorisk Museet. J. Svanberg, *Catalogue*, Stockholm, 1902.

Vienna, Kunsthistorisches Museum. (*See* Addenda.)

Vienna, Gesellschaft der Musikfreunde, Sammlung der K. K. Gesellschaft der Musikfreunde in Wien. E. Mandyczewski, *Catalogue*, Vienna, 1912. (Collection on loan to Kunsthistorisches Museum, Vienna.)

Washington, Smithsonian Institution. *Handbook of the Collection of Musical Instruments in the United States National Museum*, Bulletin 136, Washington, 1927.

Yale, University. W. Skinner, *The Belle Skinner Collection of Old Musical Instruments, Holyoke, Massachusetts*, Holyoke, 1933. (Collection on loan to Yale University Collection of Musical Instruments.) S. Marcuse, *Musical Instruments at Yale*, New Haven, Connecticut, 1960.

York, Castle Museum. G. B. Wood, *Musical Instruments in York Castle Museum*, York, n.d.

Addenda

Berlin, Musikinstrumenten-Museum. Staatliches Institut für Musikforschung, Stiftung Preußischer Kulturbesitz. J. Otto and O. Adelmann, *Katalog der Streichinstrumente*, Berlin, 1975. D. Krickeberg and W. Rauch, *Katalog der Blechblasinstrumente*, Berlin, 1976.

Cologne, Musikhistorisches Museum von Wilhelm Heyer. G. Kinsky, *Katalog*, I. *Besaitete Tasteninstrumente . . .*, Cologne, 1910.

Eisenach, Bachhaus. Catalogue: H. Heyde, *Historische Musikinstrumente im Bachhaus Eisenach*, Eisenach, 1976.

Florence, Museo del Conservatorio 'Luigi Cherubini'. V. Gai, *Gli Strumenti Musicali della Corte Medicea e il Museo del Conservatorio 'Luigi Cherubini' di Firenze*, Florence, 1969.

Hague, The, Gemeentemuseum. L. J. Plenckers, *Catalogus*, I, *Hoornen trompetachtige blaasinstrumenten*, Amsterdam, 1970.

Halle (Saale), Händel-Haus. K. Sasse, *Katalog zu den Sammlungen des Händel-Hauses in Halle*, V, *Musikinstrumentensammlung, Besaitete Tasteninstrumente*, Halle, 1966. – VI, *Streich- und Zupfinstrumente*, Halle, 1972.

London, Victoria and Albert Museum.
R. Russell, *Catalogue of the Musical Instruments*, II, *Keyboard Instruments*, London, 1968.

Newhaven, Connecticut, Yale University, Yale Collection of Musical Instruments. *Checklist*. Yale, 1968.

New York, Metropolitan Museum of Art. *A Checklist of Western European Flageolets, Recorders, and Tabor Pipes*, New York, 1968.

A Checklist of Western European Fifes, Piccolos, and Transverse Flutes, New York, 1977.

A Checklist of Bagpipes, New York, 1977.

Prague, National Museum. (E. Hradrecky), *Hudební Nástroje v Národním Muzeu. Katalog Stálé Exposice Hudebních Nástroju na Velkopřevorském Náměstí*, Prague, 1970.

Salzburg, Museum Carolino Augusteum.
K. Birsak, *Die Holzblasinstrumente im Salzburger Museum Carolino Augusteum*, Salzburg, 1973. – *Die Blechblasinstrumente im Salzburger Museum Carolino Augusteum*, in: Jahresschrift (of the museum) 22, 1976, Salzburg, 1977, pp. 7–32.

Vienna, Kunsthistorisches Museum. (V. Luithlen), *Katalog der Sammlung alter Musikinstrumente*, I, *Saitenklaviere*, Vienna, 1966.

Schlosser, J., *Die Sammlung alter Musikinstrumente* (Kunsthistorisches Museum in Wien). Vienna, 1920. Reprint Hildesheim, Germany, 1967.

Washington, D.C., Smithsonian Institution. *A Checklist of Keyboard Instruments at the Smithsonian Institution*, Washington, D.C., 1967.

American Musical Instrument Society
  Membership Office
  V.S.D. Box 194
  Vermillion, South Dakota 57069
  USA

Guild of American Luthiers
  8222 South Park Avenue
  Tacoma, Washington 98408
  USA

American Society of Ancient Instruments
  7445 Devon Street
  Philadelphia, Pennsylvania 19119
  USA

Catgut Acoustical Society
  112 Essex Avenue
  Montclair, New Jersey 07042
  USA

Crafts Advisory Council (monthly
magazine)
  12 Waterloo Place
  London SW1
  England

Council for Small Industries in Rural Areas
  35 Camp Road
  Wimbledon Common
  London SW19
  England

Early Music Centre
  62 Princedale Road
  London W11
  England

Early Music (quarterly magazine)
  Oxford University Press
  Ely House
  37 Dover Street
  London W1
  England

Fellowship of Makers and Restorers of
Historic Instruments (quarterly bulletin)
  7 Pickwick Road
  Dulwich Village
  London SE21
  England

Galpin Society (annual journal)
  Rose Cottage
  Bois Lane
  Chesham Bois
  Amersham
  Buckinghamshire
  England

Guitar (monthly magazine)
  8 Horse and Dolphin Yard
  Macclesfield Street
  London W1
  England

International Association of Musical
Instrument Collections (newsletter)
  c/o Musikhistoriska Museet
  Scottsbacken 6
  S-III 30 Stockholm
  Sweden

International Institute for Conservation of
Historic and Artistic Works
  608 Grand Buildings
  Trafalgar Square
  London WC2
  England
  (publishers of *Art and Archaeology Technical
  Abstracts* (*AATA*), formerly called *IIC
  Abstracts*, and *Studies in Conservation*)

Journal of the Acoustical Society of America
Published by the American Institute of
Physics
  335 East 45th Street
  New York, New York 10017
  USA

London College of Furniture
  (Musical Instrument Dept)
  Commercial Road
  London E1
  England

Societies

Lute Society (annual journal)
  71 Priory Road
  Kew Gardens
  Richmond
  Surrey
  England

Lute Society of America (journal)
  1930 Cameron Court
  Concord, California 94518
  USA

Musical Instrument Conservation and Technology
(*MICAT*)
  Editor, Mr Cary Karp
  Musikhistoriska Museet
  Scottsbacken 6
  S-111 30 Stockholm
  Sweden
  (published in two parts: *MICAT News* and
  MICAT Journal)

Répertoire International de Littérature
Musicale (rilm abstracts)
  Bärenreiter Verlag
  Heinrich-Schütz-Allee 31-37
  D-3500 Kassel-Wilhelmshöhe
  Germany

and
International RILM Center
  The City University of New York
  33 West 42nd Street
  New York, New York 10036
  USA

Society of the Classic Guitar (*Guitar Review*)
  409 East 50th Street
  New York, New York 10022
  USA

The Strad (monthly magazine)
  Novello & Co. Ltd
  1-3 Upper James Street
  London w1
  England

Index

Compiled by the Editor

Principal references in the text
appear in bold type;
references to plate illustrations
appear in roman numerals

Aguado, Dionisio *(1784–1849)*, 101
arcade cutter, 146, 147 (fig.)
arcades, 146f
arching: *Guitar,* 111; *Viol,* 27f; *Violin,* back, 79,
   82 (fig.); belly, 79, 82 (fig.)
Arnault, Henri, of Zwolle *(fl.c.1450)*, 37
ash *(Fraxinus excelsior)*, 141
axle pin, 149, 150ff

back: *Guitar,* **109–12,** 110 (fig.); barring, 111;
   inlay for, 111f; reinforcement strip, 111;
   selecting the wood, 109; thicknessing, 111:
   Viol, 20, **23–6,** 158; back-to-ribs assembly
   method, 26; barring, 24f; bent-angle, 24;
   joining method, 23; reinforcement strip, 26;
   selecting the wood, 23; swelling & shrinkage
   precautions, 25: *Violin,* **83,** 84 (fig.)
bars: *Guitar,* 104 (fig.), 105f, **106–7,** 110 (fig.),
   111, 114: *Harpsichord,* **142f:** *Lute,* 52 (fig.), 53,
   54, 55 (fig.): *Viol,* bass-bar, 29f; break-bar,
   25; transverse, 21 (fig.), 24f: *Violin,* bass-bar,
   81–3, 94–5 (figs.), 96f., 99
belly *(see also* soundboard): *Viol,* 20, 25, **26–31;**
   archings, 27f; bass-bar, 29f; belly-to-ribs
   assembly method, 30; joining method, 26f;
   ornamentation *(see also* purfling), 28, 30f;
   selecting the wood, 26; soundholes, 29;
   thicknessing & hollowing-out, 28f, 28 (fig.):
   Violin, **78–83,** 80 & 82 (figs.); archings, 79,
   82 (fig.); bass-bar, 81–3; border, marking out,
   79; joining method, 78; purfling, 85ff;
   selecting the wood, 78; soundholes, 79f;
   thicknessing, 84 (fig.)
bending-iron, 15f, 16 (fig.), 43n, 102
bending wood, process for, **22, 44,** 76f, 109

bichromate, potassium *see* stain
blocks: *Guitar,* 110 (fig.), 112f; *Lute,* front, 43f,
   43 (fig.); *Viol,* 20, 25, 26; *Violin* 74 (fig.), 76,
   77f, 83, 85
bone, 123, 146; gluing, 168
boxwood *(Buxus sempervirens)*, **18,** 57, 59, 63
brass, cleaning of, 170
bridge, 156: *Guitar,* 114, 119, 124 (fig.), **125f;**
   cordal block, 125; gluing, 125; selecting the
   wood, 125: *Harpsichord,* **140–2;** bass & treble
   hook, jointing, 141; bridge pins, 141; gluing,
   141; marking out, 141; selecting the wood,
   141; shaping & taper, 141: *Lute,* 38, **57–60,**
   58 (fig.); cramping method, 60; drilling string
   holes, 59; gluing, 59; selecting the wood, 59;
   string height, 57, 59: *Viol,* 29, 36: *Violin,* 57,
   81, 94–5 (figs.), 98f.
brushes, varnish, 6of

callipers, thicknessing, 17, 17 (fig.)
capping strip, 46–7, 47 (fig.)
carbon tetrachloride (CCl₄), 45, 55, 59
casting, metal, 144
cedar: Honduras *(Cedrela mexicana)*, 107, 111,
   123; western red *(Thuja plicata)*, 51, 102, 139
cherrywood *(Prunus avium)*, 18
chin rest, *Violin,* 95
circle cutter, 53, 103, 142, 142 (fig.)
Clarke, Jane, 131
conservation *see* restoration
corrosion of metals *see* restoration
Couperin, François *(1668–1733)*, 19
cramps, **16,** 17 (fig.), 32, 46, 57, 60, 114, 115,
   125; cramping jig *(see also* go-bar), 106 (fig.),
   111, 127f, 128 (fig.)

Dolmetsch family, 11

Dowland, John *(1563–1626)*, 64

ebony *(Diospyros ebenum)*, **18**, 32, 56, 63, 87, 97, 101, 117, 121, 146

end-clasp *see* capping-strip

eye-twisting tool, 144, 145 (fig.)

fan struts *(see also* bars), *Guitar*, 105, **106–7**

filler *(see also* varnish), 126

fingerboard: *Guitar*, **117–20**, 125: *Lute*, 56f: *Viol*, 31ff: *Violin*, 88f, **89**, 93, 94–5 (fig.), 98f; Baroque, 95 (fig.), 98f

former *see* rib-former & mould

frame *see* harpsichord

french polish, 61; method, 126f

fret, spacing, 64, 117, **119**; tying, 65, 65 (fig.)

frets: *Guitar*, 117–20; *Lute*, 64–6; *Viol*, 36

fungus, growth in wood, 156, 160; treatment, 164f

G-cramp *see* cramps

Giusta, Giovanni Battista *(fl.1680)*, 165, X, XI, XIII

glue: animal (hide, Scotch, etc.), **18f**, 45n, 46, 54, 55f, 59, 102f, 112, 114, 135, 140, 167; preparation, 19: Contact cement ('impact' adhesive, etc.), 45: Epoxy, 59, restricted use of, 167: Fish, 168: PVA (Polyvinylacetate), 41, 48, 50, 55, 57, 59, 102, 128, 140, 167; cautionary remarks, 48, 59, 168: Synthetic resin ('Cascamite', etc.), 126, 135, 137, 140

go-bar, 125, 141, 143

GUITAR ('classical'), **101–29**, 158, 159, VI, VII: assembly, 112–15, 113 (fig.); back, 109–12, 110 (fig.); bars & struts, 106–7; bridge, 124 (fig.), 125f; cleaning & polishing, 126f; fingerboard, 117–20; fretting, 119f; head, 115–17, 116 (fig.), 118 (fig.); heel, shaping, 108 (fig.), 120; inlays & purflings, 120–2; neck, 107–9, 108 (fig.), 122f; nut & saddle, 123; rosette-designing & making, 127–9, 128 (fig.); soundboard, 103–6, 104 (fig.); stringing & tuning, 129

hammer, planishing, 166

HARPSICHORD, **131–53**, 159, 163, 165f, 172, VIII, IX, X, XI, XII, XIII: action, setting up, 152; barring, 142f; bent-side former, 133f, 134 (fig.); bottom boards, 138f; bridges, 140–2; casework, 134–7; drawing a plan, 131–3; frame & linings, 137f; jacks, 149–52, 151 (fig.); keyboards, 136 (fig.), 146–9, 148 (fig.); rose, 142ff; soundboard, 139f; stringing, 144f; voicing, 152f

Harton, Michielle *(fl.1600)*, 11

Harwood, Ian, 11

Hauser, Hermann, sen. *(1882–1952)*, 101, VI, VII

hawthorn *(Crataegus oxyacanthoides)*, 120

head: *Guitar*, **115–17**, 116 (fig.), 118 (fig.); angle of, 115; head-to-neck joint, 115, 116 (fig.): *Viol*, 31f

Hernandez, Santos *(1873–?)*, 101

Heron-Allen, E., 11

hog-bristle springs, 149, 150

holly *(Ilex aquifolium)*, 120, 149

hook-bar *see* tailpin

Hubbard, Frank, 131, 172

humidifiers, 161

humidity, 36, 156, 157f, 160f; during repair work, 168

hygrometer, 160f

infra-red (IR), use of, 162

inlay *(see also* purfling), 18, 31, 111f, 120f

intonation, understanding, 172

ivory, 101, 123, 125, 146, 158; gluing, 168

joints: butt-, 31, 49; dovetail, 32; rebate, 50 (fig.); scarf, 115; separating glued, 166f; splice, 115f, 116 (fig.)

Karp, Gregory *(fl.1690)*, 164

Kessler, Dietrich, 11

knife, violin-maker's, 16, 29, 77, 81

Lacote, René François *(fl.1820)*, 101

lacquer *see* varnish

light, destructive effect on various materials, 156, 161

limewood *(Tilia platyphyllos)*, 18, 75, 134f, 142, 146

linings: *Guitar*, 113; *Harpsichord*, 137f; *Viol*, 22, 25; *Violin*, 77f, 85

LUTE, **37–67**, 158, 159, 163, II, III: alignment & assembly, 55f; barring, 52 (fig.), 54, 55 (fig.); body, 43f; bridge, 57–60, 58 (fig.); capping-strip, 46f, 47 (fig.); design, 37–41, 39 (fig.); fingerboard & points, 56f, 57n, 57 (fig.); finishing, 60–2; frets, 64f, 65 (fig.); front-block, 43f, 43 (fig.); mould, 42f, 42 (fig.); neck, 47f; nut, 63f; pegbox-to-neck joint, 49f, 50 (fig.); pegs, 62f; rib-former, 40 (fig.), 41f; ribs, 44–6; rose, 52f, 53 (fig.); stringing, 66f; tuning, 37

machine heads, *Guitar*, 117

magnifying glasses, 162

Index

mahogany, Honduras *(Swietenia macrophylla)*, 101, 107, 111, 123
maple *(Acer campestra)* (*see also* sycamore), 57, 75, 76, 97, 101
Marais, Marin *(1656–1728)*, 19
Meares, Richard *(d. c.1722)*, 19, 1
microscope, 162
mould: *Guitar*, 109; *Harpsichord*, bentside former, 133f, 134 (fig.); *Lute*, 42f, 42 (fig.); *Viol*, 19f, 20 (fig.), 26; *Viol*, 75f

neck: *Guitar*, **107-8**, 108 (fig.), 115, 120, 122f: *Lute*, 38, **47-8**: *Viol*, **31f**; neck-to-body joint, 31f; shaping, 32: *Violin*, 73, **89**, 91f, 98
Norman, Barak *(d. 1746)*, 26, 27, 32
nut, 38, 63f, 73, 88f, 89, 117, 123, 132

oak *(Quercus robur)*, 135, 146
ornament *see* inlay & purfling

Panormo, George Lewis *(1774–1842)*, 101
pearwood *(Pyrus communis)*, 18, 57, 59, 85, 141, 149
pegbox: *Lute*, 47, **48-50**, 49 (fig.); *Viol*, 31; *Violin*, 71, **88f**
pegcutter, 17, 17 (fig.), 35, 63, 93
pegs, how to make, 63; *Lute*, 62f; *Viol*, 35; *Violin*, 73, 89, 93
permanganate, potassium *see* stain
photography, of musical instruments, 174
piano, 159, removing action, 166
pitch, 129, 145, 173
plane, violin-maker's, 16
plectra holes, tool for punching, 149, 149 (fig.)
plumwood *(Prunus domestica)*, 18, 63
points, *Lute*, 57, 57 (fig.)
pollution, air-, destructive effect of, 157
poplar *(Populus tremula)*, 18, 34, 142f
priming *see* varnish
pumice powder, 34, 126, 134
purfling (*see also* inlay): *Guitar*, **120-2**; *Viol*, 18, **23f**, 28, 30; *Violin*, 79, **85-7**
purfling tool, 16, 16 (fig.), 30, 86

quill plectrum, 149ff

radiograph (*see also* x-ray), 175
reamer, peg-, **17**, 17 (fig.), 35, 49, **63**, 88, 89, 93
reinforcement strip(s), *Guitar*, 110 (fig.), 111; *Lute*, 46; *Viol*, 24, 25f
RESTORATION & CONSERVATION, of musical instruments, **155-75**: alterations to instruments, 159, 164; choosing a restorer, 161; cleaning & repair techniques, 167; climate, 159f; colour-retouching of new material, 169; cracks, repair of (wood), 168f, (metal), 171f; deterioration through playing, 159; disassembling an instrument, 165f; documentation, 173-5, importance of, 173; environmental factors, 156; examination before treatment, 162f; handling, transport, storage, 159; light, effect of, 161; making missing parts, 172; metal cleaning (brass & iron), 169-71; metal instruments, repairing dents in, 171; organological description, 173; photography, 174; protection from damage, 159-62; restoration, conservation, 162-72, general principles, 162; solder & its application, 171; stringing, regulating, voicing, tuning, 172; technical reports, 173f; treatment, 155-9, aims of, 163f, examples, of, 164, 182, motivation for, 155-9; wood, biological attack on, 156, disinfection of, 164f, warping of, 157f, 157 (fig.), 158 (fig.), worm-eaten wood (treatment), 169

saddle (*see also* bridge), 87, 123
saffron *see* stain
sash cramps *see* cramps
satinwood, East Indian *(Chloroxylon swietenia)*, 121
scraper, cabinet-maker's, 16, 46, 102, 147
scroll: *Viol* (*see also* head), 31; *Violin*, 71f, 79, **88f**
soundboard (*see also* belly), 156, 158: *Guitar*, 101, **103-6**, 104 (fig.); *Harpsichord*, **139f**; *Lute*, **50-2**, 52 (fig.)
soundhole: *Guitar*, 103, 107; *Harpsichord*, 142f; *Lute*, see rose; *Viol*, 29, 35; *Violin*, 71, 79-81
soundhole cutter, 102, 142 (fig.)
soundpost: *Viol*, 17, 25, **35**; *Violin*, **93-6**, 97
soundpost bar, *Viol*, 24
soundpost setter, 17, 17 (fig.), 35
splice-joint *see* joints
spruce *(Picea excelsa)*, 18, 51, 75, 78, 101f, 103, 139, 142
stain, use of, 33, 60, 126; bichromate, potassium, 33; gamboge, *see* varnish; permanganate, potassium, 33; powder colour, 35; saffron, 33; spirit stain, 60, 126; tea, 33; watercolour, 33
strings (*see also* frets), 64, 66f, 67n, 129, 172: gauges, 66, 129, 144f, 172; height (action), 57-9, 115, 123; length (scale), 38, 107, 117; tension, 66, 129, 159, 173
struts *see* fan struts & bars
sycamore *(Acer pseudoplantanus)* (*see also* maple), 18, 23, 31, 32, 36, 47, 60, 63, 141, 146, 149; veneer, 85

191

tailpiece: *Viol*, 31; *Violin*, 87, 94–5 (figs.), 96f

tailpin, 32

Tarrega, Francisco *(1852–1909)*, 101

Taskin, Pascal *(1723–93)*, 144, VIII

tea *see* stain

tempera *see* varnish

temperaments, 119n, 172

temperature suitable for musical instruments, 160

templates: *Guitar*, 105, 119, 125; *Harpsichord*, 132f, 141; *Lute*, 41, 43; *Viol*, 19; *Violin*, 69

theorbo, 163

Torres, Antonio *(1817–1892)*, 101

tripoli powder, 34

Tunbridge ware, 128

tuning, 172: *Guitar*, 129; *Harpsichord*, 144f, 153n; *Lute*, 37, 66f; *Viol*, 36; *Violin*, 96f

turning *see* peg

ultra-violet (UV), use of, 34, 162f

varnish, application, 27, 31, **33–4**, **60–2**, **92–3**; cleaning, 167; colour (*see also* stain), 34, 60, 62, 126; examination of old varnish, lacquer, 163; french polish, 61, method, 126f; oil-based, 34, 127; polyurethane lacquer, 61f, 127; solvents, 167f; spirit-based, 61, 127; tempera, 33, 61. Sub-varnish (fillers, primers, etc.), 33, 60, 108; coloured filler, 126; egg white, 108, 126; gamboge, 33; gelatine, 33; glue size, 33; linseed oil, 33, 127; propolis, 33; tempera, 33, 61; turpentine, 33

veneer, 85, 111

VIOL *(Baroque)*, **15–36**, 21 (fig.), 164, I: *(Renaissance)*, 19n; assembly, 30; back, 23–6; bars, 24f, 30; belly, 26–31, 28 (fig.); fingerboard, 31; fitting-up, 34ff; head & neck, 31f; mould, 19f, 20 (fig.); purfling, 23f, 28, 30f; ribs, 20–3; tailpin, 32; varnishing, 33f

viola, 159, IV

viola d'amore, 159

VIOLIN *(Baroque)*, 69, 95 (fig.), **98–9**, 159, 160, v: *(Modern)*, **69–97**, 70 (fig.), 94 (fig.), v; back, 80 & 82 (figs.), 83; bass-bar, 81–3, 84 (fig.); belly, 78f, 80 (fig.); blocks, 74 (fig.), 76; bridge, 93, 94 & 95 (figs.); fingerboard, 89, 90 (fig.), 94 & 95 (figs.); finishing, 87f, 92; form or mould, 74 (fig.), 75f; linings, 77f; models, 69–73; neck-to-body joint, 90 (fig.), 91f; pegs, 93; purfling, 85–7; ribs, 76f; scroll, 70 (fig.), 88f; setting-up, 93–7 soundholes, 79f; varnishing, 92f; wood selection, 73–5

watercolour *see* stain

willow *(Salix alba)*, 18

wind instruments, 11, 13, 158, 159, 160

wood, cleaning of, 59, 125, 126, 167; moisture content of, 25; warping, 157f, 157 (fig.), 158 (fig.)

woodworm, 156, treatment of, 164f

x-ray, 131; apparatus, 162–3